# 102 Ways to Apply Career Training in Family History/Genealogy

# 102 Ways to Apply Career Training in Family History/Genealogy

✦

## How to Find a Job, Internship, or Create Your Own Business

*Anne Hart*

ASJA Press
New York Lincoln Shanghai

**102 Ways to Apply Career Training in Family History/Genealogy**
**How to Find a Job, Internship, or Create Your Own Business**

Copyright © 2006 by Anne Hart

ASJA Press
an imprint of iUniverse, Inc.

iUniverse books may be ordered through booksellers or by contacting:

iUniverse
2021 Pine Lake Road, Suite 100
Lincoln, NE 68512
www.iuniverse.com
1-800-Authors (1-800-288-4677)

ISBN-13: 978-0-595-41316-4
ISBN-10: 0-595-41316-1

Printed in the United States of America

# Contents

# 1

## *The Future of Family History Research*

With the *future* marriage of genealogy to smart cards, online databases, or similar authentication technology for family history, population registration (census), and library research, it may be easier to research family lines, not only by DNA matches through DNA testing for deep ancestry, but also with smart, electronic cards designed for electronic identity. It's also a way to track military records as another way to trace family history.

To look to the future, you begin by scanning the past—electronically and ethnographically. You might consider working for the government in the various state libraries, working for corporations, or opening your own business researching topics or collecting antiques and old paper records related to family and social history or genealogy.

### 102 Ways to Apply Career Training in Family History/Genealogy

1. American Studies Participant/Observer/Reporter

2. Adoptions Researcher

3. Anthropologist/Applied

4. Antiques and Paper Collectibles Dealer in Family History/Postcards/Photos/Diaries

5. Archivist/State Employee

6. Area Studies Specialist

7. Attorney/Notary/Court Records Researcher

8. Banking historian

9.  Biographer

10. Book author/article writer/columnist

11. Book Locator

12. Book Packager

13. Braille Transcriber/Genealogy Records

14. Career Consultant or Counselor

15. Clarifying Secrets in Memoirs Writing/Intergenerational Writing/Publishing Specialist

16. Clergy

17. Collectibles Dealer

18. Computer Database Manager/Researcher/Designer

19. Conference and Seminar Event Planner

20. Conservator

21. Court Records Researcher/Historian

22. Diary Conservator

23. DNA-driven Genealogy Researcher

24. Documentarian

25. Estate Sales and Auction Directors

26. Ethnographer

27. Eulogy Writer

28. Family Conflicts Mediator

29. Family History Gift Basket Entrepreneur

30. Family History Internet Theater Producer

31. Family Newsletter Publisher/Designer

32. Family Recipe Publisher

33. Genealogist

58. Library of Congress Employee

59. Linguist/early handwriting specialist/Languages

60. Locator of Descendants for Restoring and Returning Historic Photos, Ephemera, and Memorabilia (found in antique shops, at estate sales, and displayed in restaurants).

61. Matchmaker

62. Medical Historian

63. Memoirs Writing Educator

64. Museum Archivist

65. Music/Musician Genealogist

66. Native American/Indigenous Peoples History/Genealogy Researcher

67. Novelist/Playwright/Memoirs Writer

68. Oral Historian

69. Paper Sales/Marketing/Manufacturing (for conservation and library or museum uses)

70. Personal Historian

71. Personalized Family History Greeting Card Design, Poems, Illustration

72. Photographer

73. Probate, Wills, and Estate Paralegal or Attorney

74. Progenealogist

75. Public Historian

76. Public Servant/Government Employee

77. Public Speaker

78. Publicist/Public Relations Director

79. Publisher

80. Rabbinical Dynasty Genealogist

81. Radio or TV Genealogy Talk Show Host

82. Real Estate Historian (world wide historical property ownership research)

83. Records Administrator

84. Reunions Planner

85. Sales/Genealogy Products/Marketing Manager

86. Satellite/Internet Connections

87. Scholarship Researcher/Ethnic, Area, or Surname Scholarships

88. Skip Tracer (locate people who moved away)

89. Social History Researcher

90. Sociologist

91. Software Designer/Family History/Genealogy

92. Specialist in Finding Women's History-Related Documents (such as maiden names)

93. Surname Group Administrator/Researcher

94. Teacher/Time Capsules and Social History

95. Time Capsules Craft

96. Transcriber

97. Translator

98. Travel Agent: Ethnic and Family Tours Specialist

99. Traveling Genealogist

100. Two-Line Tombstone Writer

101. Videographer

102. Walking Tour Guide-Extended Family and Reunion Walking Tours of Ancestors' Neighborhoods Around the World or Locally

◆     ◆     ◆

These are only a few of the possibilities of part-time businesses you can operate online or in person using what you learned in family history training courses or self-education and/or in an actual undergraduate degree in family history and genealogy. If no graduate degrees exist with the actual title of family history, then an interdisciplinary graduate degree may be used in areas of specialization such as genetics counseling, American Studies, European Area Studies, Asian Area Studies, African-American Studies, Native American Studies, Latino Studies, Hawaiian Studies, Middle East Studies or any other area of social history where you can specialize within a graduate major.

You also can obtain a graduate degree in Library Science, Journalism, Law, History in general specializing in social history, Public History, or History of Science and Medicine, depending upon the niche area of family history you want to emphasize. Genealogy and Family History as a major is an interdisciplinary program. You can also take a degree in general studies or liberal arts and emphasize family history and social history courses, languages, and

If you do major in Family History at a university such as BYU, you will greatly benefit by doing an internship. You can do research outside your country. For example, at BYU, research projects outside the USA exist in numerous European countries and in Mexico. An internship may focus on immigrant ancestor projects.

Careers and research may focus on various state libraries or historical associations. History and family studies are part of an interdisciplinary liberal arts program that emphasizes research and writing. Journalism courses help round out your ability to express in plain language the results of your reading, explorations, and interpretations.

Obtaining a degree in Family History leads to broad, interdisciplinary careers. Graduate work in library science, law, journalism, public history, or genetics counseling (with a double major in the life sciences and social work) also lead to careers in which an historical education may be used. Public history is a field where you can pursue graduate degrees, including a doctorate. A degree in family history can lead to entrepreneurship or becoming a corporate executive.

Public history as a graduate program leads to government employment or private non-profit agency employment. You'll learn analytical skills if you pursue a degree or even certification from a variety of coursework in genealogy/family history/public history.

Most jobs don't require a specific major, but rather analytical training and training in writing. If you're interested in taking courses or obtaining a degree or doing graduate work in history, family, home, social science, or area studies, focus on obtaining those analytical skills and good journalism skills for expressing in plain language for the public what you learned in your history and genealogy courses.

In addition to a degree, there are individual courses online in family history and genealogy research techniques. Some online courses are free. For example, see the personal history course at the Web site: http://www.newswriting.net/personalhistorycourse.htm. Also see the article and excerpt links and the list of my other relevant books at my Web site at http://www.newswriting.net.

Before you begin a program of study, decide which areas of the world you'd like to emphasize in your research. Another niche area of specialized history is history of the future. As odd as the term sounds, there is a history of the thousands of predictions about the future made since the invention of writing and before that, oral tradition.

Areas of genealogy could be as specialized as ethnic research or behavioral family history and medical history. For example, if you research a family reporting a dozen generations of psychics, mentalists, ESP sensitivity, or any type of special information, that is a niche of family history related to the larger field of public history.

You could work with genetic counselors documenting medical record history for persons with similar specific genetic situations, such as a long line of centenarians. For example, George Washington's drummer boy is said to have lived to the ripe old age of 103 in an age when most people didn't reach 70.

Would his descendants also have shown a genetic family history of living beyond the age of 100? Would extremely long life spans be genetic? When a genealogist and a genetics counselor meet, they have research in common in the field of medical family history studies. This is but one example of how family history research can be a niche area or part of a larger area of public history, architectural history, medical history, or area studies linking the past to the future.

Another example is studying the portraits of ancient Egyptians which show particular patterns such as one eye drawn to a corner and the opposite cheek withered which neurologists are studying as a way to detect historical instances of specialized defects in the autonomic system.

A family historian interested in medical history, art, behavior and communication can use journalism and heritage research as a bridge to communicate with scientists, physicians, and publishers.

The more you learn about family history, the more you'll discover what else you can do with training in family history combined with geographic or ethnic area studies and journalism or creative writing.

## How Many Careers or Businesses Can Make Use of Training in Family History?

Whether you actually get a degree in family history or take various courses for certification or train yourself by reading and research, working with historical documents and photos can open the door to a wide variety of related businesses or careers. One example would be becoming a dealer in rare documents. You'd purchase personal papers of people who lived many years ago. Then you'd puzzle together a life story. Dealing in rare documents is one way to use your skills in family history or genealogy research and writing.

You could open an antique paper and post card dealership and make the rounds of antique post card or paper shows in various locations. In the US there are a few dozen antique paper, post card, or document dealers. Some specialize in making time capsules. Others focus on piecing biographies or travels of times past.

## Deal in Paper Trails

In addition to genealogy records, you could deal in old photos, stock certificates, posters, legal documents such as property and notary records to homes, correspondence/letters, family bibles, diaries, old cookbooks, and crafted items of historical value. If you learn various languages, you could specialize in reading early handwriting or translations of various languages. You could organize collectible paper shows. Some dealers call collectible paper 'ephemera.' Or you could specialize in alumni records or ethnographic collectibles.

Analyzing handwriting is another niche. So are leading walking tours of neighborhoods according to genealogy records. One example might be leading a tour of extended family members on neighborhoods or old houses, cemeteries, or other property that belonged to family members in former centuries.

Time capsules and artifacts as collectibles is another niche for family history buffs. Examples would be diaries of wagon trains of the past. Dealing in antique papers is one way to put a degree or any type of training in family history to use telling a story of families as part of social history.

You could run shows twice a year, organizing other dealers. What might start out as a hobby collecting stamps, post cards, and genealogy ephemera could turn into a business or a reason to teach a class or train other collectible show organizers who want to work with photos and collectible antique papers.

Dealing in rare papers also is a sideline for genealogy-trained persons. It's a branch of antiques and suitable for show in an antique mall, library, or museum. Most shows are conducted in large meeting halls. Or space is purchased at state fairs.

Why not save a bit of history by dealing in rare papers and photos? If you specialize in old documents, your genealogy interest could branch out to dealing in old documents of a business nature. What about documents that reveal hidden facts about old gold mines or other historic business ventures? Historians will want to know the impact family history collectibles has on today's world. You could specialize in mining, ecology, environmental issues, and other ways the past made an impact on the present through the diaries of working people and the records of business transactions.

You could focus on personal touch items, sealed adoptions of the 19$^{th}$ century, or correspondence related to records of orphan trains or hospital records of a century ago. Or focus on travel descriptions written in the past by adults compared to those written by children. Contact university professors of history who are seeking documents and artifacts of the past for a special focus or emphasis such as business, medicine, travel, social issues, and personal interpretations.

Look for old documents from eras of wartime or transitions. Paper trails should be digitized and saved in a variety of ways besides preserving and conserving the original text.

# 2

## How to Produce Family Newsletters to Stay Connected

What's the best way to connect communities of relatives? It's with family story electronic and/or print newsletters that link distant and high-mobility relatives. A really good newsletter tells a *family story* with a specific theme for each issue. It's a mesmeric, one or two-page odyssey full of wit that illuminates family history news. Family story newsletters promote self-reflection.

How can your newsletter motivate your relatives to see the entire extended family in a new way? Add genealogy research.

Prepare the newsletter with a template. Use a template such as the newsletter template found in Microsoft Word, at the Microsoft template Web site at: http://www.templatecentral.com/searchResults.asp?frm=4&type=Word&Category=Newsletters. Or use Microsoft Publisher software's newsletter template.

Then save your layout to a disc and also to your computer files. Send it by email to those who have email. Up to five sheets of paper may be mailed at the one ounce postage rate. Use an envelope or fold the newsletter in half and tape the center. Never staple a document sent outside of an envelope as a metal staple breaks postage machines or rips the document.

Paper newsletters are for those without email. Upload your newsletter to a Web site. There are free Web sites available from Tripod at: http://www.tripod.com, GeoCities at: http://geocities.yahoo.com/join/, or BraveNet at: www.bravenet.com/. Or produce a family story Blog at http://www.blogger.com. The site is listed as Blogger: Free Website. Explore blogs as unique Web logs of family history. You can update them frequently—even daily. For information on video, including multimedia newsletters or family history time capsules, see my book titled, *Creating Family Newsletters & Time Capsules: How to Publish Multimedia Genealogy Periodicals or Gift Booklets* (ISBN: 0-595-39872-3).

## Showcase News of Significant Events and Turning Points

Use large print for those relatives who need it. If you have a blind relative, read the newsletter into a digital or tape recorder, and send the individual an audio cassette tape or CD.

Family publications emphasize breaking news along with insight, hindsight, and foresight. Genealogy is combined with family or ethnic history details. Share meaning as you inform family of memorable events and turning points.

## What Can You Say in One or Two Pages of News?

Produce your publication as straight news or as a one or two page *poetry* letter. There's no room for photos in a one-page family paper newsletter. You can send photos on the side. Don't try to reduce photos to insert into your newsletter. They usually print out grainy. Instead, send the photos up to a Web site where you can layout text and photos on the Web, using a template to create a multi-page newsletter. These templates and designs are available free along with a 20 mg free Web site at Tripod.com and at several other online Web hosting sites.

You can make your newsletter as many pages as you want if you save it to a CD, but mailing a CD to relatives assumes they all have computers and can open your files with compatible software. So check with the relatives first as to what they prefer to receive—paper, CD, or a Web site address to click on to read your newsletter or Web log. On line, numerous photos may be put in an album for anyone to view from anywhere. Most free Web hosting sites have templates for photo albums and directions for uploading the photos and the text.

## Laminate and Collect Family Story Newsletters

Family newsletters are collectables. Newsletters often arrive in colorful crocheted holders that may be hung above the mantelpiece like decorative pouches, Xmas stockings, or press kit folders. These light weight containers are for adding the quarterly or annual issues and updates throughout the lifetime of the family as community.

Include genealogy information or family tree charts to provide content other than breaking news. Family story newsletters usually contain announcements of reunions, anniversaries, holidays, births, weddings, graduations, celebrations of life, or news of individual family members. Focus on staying connected. For relatives without email, the printed paper newsletter may also include a disc that can be played on most DVD or CD players containing voices, music, photos, and video.

## How to Find Newsletter Topics

Create newsletter calendars. Templates range from the most simple handwritten dialogue circles and boxes on which to paste photos to multimedia software templates. Here are some ideas about which to send news or greetings.

1. **Children**: Have each child write about what they have done or are doing on an annual basis. If the child is too young, summarize in a short paragraph any updates.

2. **Parents:** Keep a separate business newsletter for updates on your business. Decide whether you want to talk about acts of kindness, promote yourself or your achievements, or ask about others. Choose a topic you want to emphasize that is universal, simple, and about values and commitment or teach a new subject to your readers with universal appeal with which they all can identify.

3. **Information:** How efficient and effective is your news information? Be informative rather than directive. Present information instead of giving them directions as commands. What are you expert at?

4. **Time Capsules of Humor:** Use uplifting, tasteful jokes, poems, art, video, writing, life story highlights, and volunteer work experiences to connect your extended family to community service which extends your family of humankind's accomplishments even further. **Create an annual time capsule** from your conception of an annual family newsletter or video newsletter. The time capsule then becomes an heirloom that can be conserved and preserved for future generations catalogued by year.

## Here are what to put into your video newsletter time capsule

1. Significant events

2. Life stories

3. Travel photos

4. Photos of events such as weddings, graduations, or grand openings

5. News of births or childbirth video clips (leave out the gore)

6. Summaries

7. Jokes

8.  Memorabilia and trivia with useful facts, such as statistics

9.  Joy of life and fun events

10. Wise sayings and original proverbs or quotes with source of origin

11. Mourning and/or celebration of life events

12. Hobbies, crafts, art, writings, poems

13. Sports enjoyed

14. Reading group: Start a family or corporate book club and discuss reading

15. Old time radio clubs, public domain video, or exchanging gifts of purchased videos from stores

16. Make your own family videos and exchange them—such as graduations and birthdays

17. Celebrations marking rites of passage, anniversaries, cruises, or other events marking dates

18. Scrap booking or quilting tips for those interested

19. Poems and skits

20. Monologues

21. Genealogy and DNA-driven genealogy reports

22. Food preferences or allergies

23. Reunions and suggesting video conference reunions for those not able to travel

24. Free courses to family members in what you are expert at doing

25. Instruction in putting video on DVDs and CDs for family newsletters or desktop publishing tips for those who want to make their own newsletters

26. Military experiences or war stories

27. Survival stories

28. Computer skill tips

29. Making natural, non-toxic cleaning or bug repellents from household kitchen baking ingredients such as cinnamon, baking soda, vinegar, or cream of tartar

30. Finding hidden markets for bargains of quality at better prices and activities

## How Much Time to Spend on Each Newsletter

If you want to email a newsletter, use a template and follow the template's guide. It will take you about two hours per issue for a two-page newsletter. Allow yourself an hour per page if you've already written the news and just need to cut and paste it from your computer file onto a newsletter template that you can email.

Other choices include writing a newsletter as a personal letter. If you use a newsletter template and print out each copy on your laser printer, it takes about six hours just to transcribe one-hour oral history tapes. If your pages increase to the business type of eight-page newsletter, allow yourself at least one full day's work. This doesn't include the time it takes to write the articles.

People like to look at other people. For short one-page newsletters, you can have newsletters with photos printed on tee shirts or mugs as gifts. Same can be said for framed plaques, trophies, and memorabilia art. Poems may be enlarged, laminated, and framed. Short skits and monologues may be put on newsletters ranging from one to eight pages in length. It's all about your budget.

## Budget

Email won't cost you if you're sending to many people, unless your email service provider charges for bulk email. Send the email one at a time to relatives or clients if you're using the relatively 'free' email you normally use to send memos. Send the email from home, not from work, unless you work for yourself at home.

Post cards would only cost about $20 or less to design, but you'd have to print them out from a computer or send photos to a film developing or digital photography processing company to put on the postcards.

It costs about $35 to write a black and white newsletter and print it out to send to a few relatives. Count on about $75 for pre-printed stationary with color print. Talk to printers who do discount or print-on-demand publishing of newsletters. Take a course in desktop publishing at a local life-long continuing education center.

Four-page newsletters cost $100 to $200 to lay out by an average printing firm. You also need to fold them for mailing with pre-printed stamps or designate places for stamps to be pasted, and envelopes. If you're doing an eight-page news-letter, it will cost you more than double because first class postage is limited to one ounce (five sheets) of standard 20 pound bond letter paper for laser computer printers.

## Photos

When you crop, size, or edit photos, you trim them on your computer to fit your print or video newsletter template. Don't waste space in your newsletter with tiny photos that can't be seen when printed. Print fewer, but larger photos, and don't make them so large that you can see the grains. It's best to use your photo digital imaging software to correct red eye or cut off an object above a head.

A photo also can be cut with a scissors and pasted on a sheet of paper, then scanned to get rid of plants growing out of a person's head or other intrusive objects. Use two photos to tell a story. Edit out of a picture too much sky and crop the photo about a quarter inch over everyone's head and below their feet. It saves space in your newsletter.

What's important with print newsletters, is selecting the weight and feel of the paper. Talk to your local printer about types of paper used in newsletters. You want to communicate also using a type of paper—color, weight, and texture. Choose bright colors or delicate lace watermarks to convey the emotional tone of the newsletter.

Collect templates. Some templates allow you to handwrite news and photo-copy the handwritten messages in templates such as squares or circles placed dec-oratively on graphic art. Some look like cartoon bubbles for writing dialogue captions.

Some circles let you write one sentence by hand in each circle. You can write six sentences on a page. Or you can reduce the font size and type a sentence in the template then cut and paste the text within the confines of a square or circle.

The templates for handwritten news usually look like a greeting card with art in the center and circles or squares for you to write one sentence inside the dia-logue boxes. It resembles a greeting card or coloring book.

Stationary supply, scrap booking stores, and craft shops sell these types of tem-plates for handwritten news. For mailing newsletters, they also can be folded into origami shapes and mailed in round or unusual shaped mailers that conform to postal regulations for mailing. One example would be tube mailers for calendars and posters or round DVD and CD mailers for video newsletters.

## Design Great Intergenerational Newsletters

What's the best way to connect the youngest to the most age-wise communities of relatives? It's with family story video podcast online newsletters that link distant and high-mobility relatives. Children and adults can work together to design and mail an annual family multimedia newsletter as a gift. A really good Web-based online video (or audio) newsletter tells a family story with a specific theme for each issue.

It's a mesmeric, one or two-page odyssey full of wit that illuminates family history news. Family story newsletters promote self-reflection.

How can your newsletter motivate your relatives to see the entire extended family in a new way? Add genealogy research.

Prepare the newsletter with a template. Use a template such as the newsletter template found in Microsoft Word, at the Microsoft template Web site at: http://www.templatecentral.com/searchResults.asp?frm=4&type=Word&Category=Newsletters. Or use Microsoft Publisher software's newsletter template.

Then save your layout to a disc and also to your computer files. Send it by email to those who have email. Up to five sheets of paper may be mailed at the one ounce postage rate. Use an envelope or fold the newsletter in half and tape the center.

Never staple a document sent outside of an envelope as a metal staple breaks postage machines or rips the document.

Paper newsletters are for those without email. Upload your newsletter to a Web site. There are free Web sites available from Tripod at: http://www.tripod.com, GeoCities at: http://geocities.yahoo.com/join/, or BraveNet at: www.bravenet.com/. Or produce a family story Blog at http://www.blogger.com. The site is listed as Blogger: Free Website. Explore blogs as unique Web logs of family history. You can update them frequently—even daily.

For information on video, including multimedia newsletters or family history time capsules, see my book titled, Creating Family Newsletters & Time Capsules: How to Publish Multimedia Genealogy Periodicals or Gift Booklets (ISBN: 0-595-39872-3).

## Showcase News of Significant Events and Turning Points

Use video, photos, art collages, and large print text for those relatives who need it. If you have a blind relative, read the newsletter into a digital or tape recorder, and send the individual an audio cassette tape or CD.

Talk about what pitfalls to avoid. Family publications emphasize breaking news along with insight, hindsight, and foresight. Genealogy is combined with family or ethnic history details. Share meaning as you inform family of memorable events and turning points.

## What Can You Say in One or Two Pages of News?

Produce your publication as straight news or as a one or two page poetry letter. There's no room for photos in a one-page family paper newsletter.

You can send photos on the side. Don't try to reduce photos to insert into your newsletter. They usually print out grainy. Instead, send the photos up to a Web site where you can layout text and photos on the Web, using a template to create a multi-page newsletter.

These templates and designs are available free along with a 20 mg free Web site at Tripod.com and at several other online Web hosting sites.

Make your video podcast or print-text newsletter as many pages as you want if you save it to a CD, but mailing a CD to relatives assumes they all have computers and can open your files with compatible software. So check with the relatives first as to what they prefer to receive—paper, CD, or a Web site address to click on to read your newsletter or Web log.

On line, numerous photos may be put in an album for anyone to view from anywhere. Most free Web hosting sites have templates for photo albums and directions for uploading the photos and the text.

## Collect Family Newsletters and Put Them in a Loose Leaf Binder

Laminate and Collect Family Story Newsletters. Family newsletters are collectables and make wonderful gifts to put inside time capsules or prayer boxes. Or photocopy the pages and put the newsletters together in a binder as a gift. Include collectible information such as recipes or family history, medical history, or DNA-driven genealogy reports.

Newsletters often arrive in colorful crocheted holders that may be hung above the mantelpiece like decorative pouches, Xmas stockings, or press kit folders. These light weight containers are for adding the quarterly or annual issues and updates throughout the lifetime of the family as community.

Include genealogy information or family tree charts to provide content other than breaking news. Family story newsletters usually contain announcements of reunions, anniversaries, holidays, births, weddings, graduations, celebrations of life, or news of individual family members.

Focus on staying connected. For relatives without email, the printed paper newsletter may also include a disc that can be played on most DVD or CD players containing voices, music, photos, and video.

## How to Find Newsletter Topics

Create newsletter calendars. Templates range from the most simple handwritten dialogue circles and boxes on which to paste photos to multimedia software templates. Here are some ideas about which to send news or greetings.

1.  Children: Have each child write about what he or she is doing on an annual basis. If the child is too young, summarize in a short paragraph any updates. Describe or photograph any item that the child has created in crafts, drawings, or words such as a poem to add to a time capsule during the year.

2.  Parents: Keep a separate business newsletter for updates on your business. Decide whether you want to talk about acts of kindness, charity, or promote yourself and your achievements, or ask about others' lives or give simple awards for creativity or service from other family members or friends. Choose a topic you want to emphasize that is universal, simple, and about values and commitment or teach a new subject to your readers with universal appeal with which they all can identify.

3.  Information: How efficient and effective is your news information? Be informative rather than directive. Present information instead of giving them directions as commands. What are you expert at?

4.  Time Capsules of Humor: Use uplifting, tasteful jokes, poems, art, video, writing, life story highlights, and volunteer work experiences to connect your extended family to community service which extends your family of humankind's accomplishments even further.

5.  Create an annual time capsule from your conception of an annual family newsletter or video newsletter. The time capsule then becomes an heirloom that can be conserved and preserved for future generations catalogued by year. Have young people interview older relatives and summarize life story highlights as skits to help older adults stimulate their memories.

# 3

## *Planning Old Maids' Parties as a Business*

Old maids' tea parties are back. The 25<sup>th</sup> birthday old maid's party became a vehicle for using genealogy pedigree charts to perpetuate arranged marriages among free-spirited female college graduates long before its peak in the roaring twenties. In Connecticut Yankee tradition, on a single woman's 25<sup>th</sup> birthday, her female friends frequently showered her with an old maid's etiquette, genealogy, and social history party.

In an era of suffragettes, the newfangled women's vote, and first-generation female college graduates, an old maid's party laced the hermetic corset on Charleston-dancing flappers. The old maid's party used genealogy 'fortune' cookies to introduce suitable beau surnames, usually four years after college graduation, when the "old maid" began to move towards independence.

By the early 1930s, when work became scarce, the old maids' parties reverted to their 1900 turn-of-the-century fame. Family tradition rules of control battled the new century's voices for women's independence. Fears of scarcity and poverty depicted women's fates as future bag ladies in silent films. The old maid's tea party fad also reasserted itself around 1900 with turn-of-the-century fervor.

In the silent film titled, *"The Old Maid's Tea Party* (1902)**,"** four old maids are seated at a table drinking tea and gossiping. According to the filmography summary written by Edison Catalog and posted on the Web at: http://us.imdb.com/title/tt0379415/, "One of the guests evidently thinks it is the last good meal she is ever to indulge in." The guest stows away cookies and other good things in the bosom of her clothing. "The hostess discovers the theft, and war is declared. The offending party is quickly dispatched. This picture is especially posed with a view to bringing out facial expressions that are very fine."

Connection became important. In contrast to the reality-based fear of old maids becoming impoverished bag ladies, the traditional old maid's party belonged to Ivy League college graduates trying to keep family connections firm by matchmaking. Higher education connected alumni communities that encouraged 50-year female friendships through correspondence and conferences.

The idea continued to be instilled in women that if they had no family of their own when old, there would still be a supportive network of classmates who went through college with them. These would serve as close, extended families of friends and mentors.

In real life, a 'certified' tea consultant arrived at the old maid's party to present the art of tea. With each major category of tea and tableware presented, the party-goers learned about the history of tea, exchanged genealogy parchments, and received gifts that included hope chests, blank diaries for journaling, and button-hook shoe coin banks.

This turning point ritual, a celebration of life, marked a significant event and biographical highlight with chamomile, collectibles, and compassion. As serendipity showers, olds maids' parties highlighted the sheltered lives of upper middle class graduates of Ivy League women's colleges.

On the other hand, should the old maid find a suitable match from one of her sorority sister's nephews or brothers, the etiquette, entertainment, or genealogy training would be useful for a corporate wife. Like an astrologer forecasting a birth chart of the houses of planets, a genealogist called to the party for entertainment would 'cast' a pedigree chart or family house crest.

These gals that would become Rosie the Riveter by the 1940s lived primarily in small towns along the Eastern seaboard from Virginia to Maine. For those who attended some women's colleges from 1921–1931, the old maid's 'diary' ceremony on a 25th birthday blended memoirs, narratives, and chronicles.

## Genealogy as Social History

An aunt-in-law of mine, celebrating her 98th birthday this August, is a class of 1931 Smith College graduate landscape architecture major. At age 25, she threw an old maid's party for herself, inviting her college friends. The old maid's party served as a ritual among single female college graduates of the economic depression years 1929–1935. Soon after her old maid's party she met and married her husband.

In October, 1926, my mom, Sally Tucker of upstate New York and Pennsylvania had her chamomile-turmeric-coriander tea party. Sage tea served also as a hair rinse. Ginger tea or friendship bread parties served to calm queasy stomachs from the floating old maids' parties if the family owned a boat. Another ritual of the infusion ceremony involved drinking jasmine tea and playing the card game of "Old Maid."

## Pedigree Chart Card Party

You play Old Maid using a pack of cards from which one queen has been removed. Players match cards. The player holding the unmatched queen at the end of the game is the loser or "old maid." Genealogy cards with family surnames and trivia or history sometimes took the form of a deck of cards, crafted by the "old maid" for the party.

The old maid trembled at the thought of being left holding the unmatched queen card at the end of the game. So often a genealogical card of family history found its place in the deck, and the unmatched queen card got lost. The symbolic word was 'unmatched,' and the purpose of the old maid party was to gather female friends for the purpose of *matching* the woman on her 25th birthday to an suitable single brother or cousin. That's why the genealogy parchments or a deck of family history 'cards' made the rounds for each friend to put a check next to the suitable bachelor's name on the pedigree chart or deck-sized card.

A quick glance at the genealogy sheet showed whether the name checked came from well-connected families. For the middle-class college graduates, a checked name meant a potential good provider or rising star—patient father material, memorable surname, and slow to anger.

Favorite surnames were bland and sounded like male first names. Old maids looked at the name first, whether it sounded like a famous book author's name…. Poe, Wolf, Crane, Brooks, Hart, Twain, or anything sounding one syllable. Tradition taught that one-syllable surnames traveled far up the corporate career ladder because people remembered 'lucky' one-syllable words.

You could determine quickly whether you were related to the young fellow's great grandfather or see if he's a descendant of someone you'd recognize or want to learn more about if you played with a deck of genealogy cards designed for a party.

An old maid's festivity emphasized genealogy questions, attitude, and personality preferences—even head size in relation to easy potential child birth if the gentleman to be introduced had a flattened occiput and narrow forehead. "Eat prunes, and forget the head shape," a dithering voice inevitably would interrupt the laughter. "Look at blood type," came the cry in the late 1930s.

Friends invited to these parties usually graduated from the same women's college classes during an era when not many women attended college. The friends acted as matchmakers clustering around a lavish, elegant grand tea party where suitable bachelors checked off the pedigree chart or card list in a desperate last attempt to connect families.

Since the early 1800s a single woman's 25th birthday marked the old maid ball in upper middle class homes with mini ballrooms that imitated the upper class's larger halls. Genealogy games played a major part in old maids' parties that historically date back to the 1800s.

## Today's Old Maids' Parties

Today, the renewed old maids' tea parties usually are set in the summer around backyard swimming pools. The Old Maid Party is a world apart from 21st century 'bachelorette' girls' night out Las Vegas-style parties. The old maid's garden party traditionally featured classical music, tea, and genealogy readings or a water paddle steam boat up the river.

Wealthy girls with family yachts sailed to secret coves with their female college friends to discuss each woman's future and family connection potential. Winter 25th birthdays gathered around the fire place for high tea, relationship chats, and seasonal décor. Independence, current issues of being a woman, and finding security within family took precedence as the major lifestyles topics focused on shift and drift.

It's no longer a rite of passage belonging to the upper middle class. The old time party rivaled an Irish wake or a Unitarian celebration-of-life party. The old maid conviviality revived in current time takes place around coed apartment complex swimming pools.

A century ago, old maids' parties flaunted extravagance and used genealogy 'readings' or 'charts' and decks of hand crafted cards that served as scrap books and pedigree presentations at individual tables. Sometimes the parties were held in the presidential suites of hotels such as the Del Coronado in San Diego. The style preserved the American equivalent of Edwardian food, flavor, and décor until the 1929 economic downturn. Ambiance ruled document and photo preservation techniques.

## Family History Memorabilia Dominated the Lavish Old Maid Party

During the 1840–1940 golden eras of lavish old maids' tea parties, the most creative memorabilia of these events appear now in some antique stores. When the 19th century hope chests are opened, inside are wonderfully conserved genealogy reports on parchment and translucent tea party china, family Bibles permeated with names, birth dates, and three-line poems, similar to Haiku, summarizing a person's attitude, purpose, or goal.

The old maid's party planners baked a form of flaky-crust fortune cookies where poems were three liners on parchment baked into a cookie that resembled dried fruit-filled Cornish pasties. The strips of paper popular in the mid-1920s with the three-line poems consisted usually of 11 syllables. The poem began with a three-syllable word followed by a five word line containing all one-syllable words. The last line would be one three-syllable word. For example, found in Sally Tucker's 1926 memorabilia from her Old Maid party are the three liners that read:

"Chocolate.

Joy but waits its turn,

Bittersweet."

Not only fortune-type cookies, scones, or pasties were baked with poems on parchment, but sometimes genealogy links of family history names or trivia found their way into the baked goods. When the old maid divided the cookie at high tea, the parchment was pulled out and read before the group.

Often it contained family history member's names of suitable cousins, nephews, or brothers that the "old maid" would drop into a button-hook shoe to savor later if she requested a formal introduction from the lady who brought the box of treats for the party.

Memorabilia and decks of the card game called "Old Maid" also included prized collectibles. Merrymakers gave genealogy time capsules wrapped in "remember to light a candle for me" cards to prized nieces on the fourth year after college graduation from numerous Ivy League women's colleges.

During the era of 1920–1935, revelers turned the ritual of 25th birthday old maids' tea, sympathy, and family history card parties into housewarming celebrations featuring gifts of translucent china, button-hook shoe coin banks, and filled hope chests for career-track ladies living alone in the big city (usually in their first apartments). Genealogists may team with social historians as collectors of old maids' party memorabilia. Items also included restored family photos, grandma's diaries, and genealogy documents, family Bibles, and keepsake albums.

By the World War II era, the idea of throwing an old maid's party on your 35th birthday, instead of your 25th, fell in step with Rosie the Riveter. You competed for marriage with war widows who frequently had small children.

In the 1939 film, "The Old Maid," Bette Davis vies with Miriam Hopkins for the affection of George Brent in the film version of Edith Wharton's 1935 play.

## Turning Points and Life Story Highlights

These showers transformed lavish coming of age rites into significant turning points by dissecting or disproving the "crusty, conservative" character of the old maid. Often the hostess at the party began to entertain by reading passages from the novel titled, *"The Old Maid,"* by Edith Wharton, born into the 1862 upper stratum of New York society.

Traditionally, the old maid's psyche was never spelled out directly. You become an old maid gradually, just like you raise a family in baby steps. And it is a coming of age and rites of passage party that the old maid presented. She became a debutante matron at her 25th birthday "last flowering" like an aging bamboo, as was thought at the turn of the current century.

In the past, women were 'destined' to become old maids, often as foretold to them by astrologers at their 25th birthday old maid's parties marking the quarter century when the average life span for women was 47 years. But you are an old maid only in the eyes of the beholders.

The true purpose of the old maid "corset unlacing" party focused on giving the old maid a *second* chance. The party centered on the flowering, rebirth, and renewal of the old maid's commitment, conservatism, and simplicity—her universal values, charm, wit, irony, and virtues. History dictates that every city and satire has its ruling families and their lifestyles. And very family has its ruling history connecting each descendant.

Décor featured a centerpiece at the old maid's party—the old maid flower, a zinnia. It had bright pink petals. Cayenne and jasmine symbolized the traditional "old maid" herbs. In fact, a dictionary definition of an old maid, besides being a spinster or elderly unmarried woman also is defined as "a person who is primly fastidious."

## What Did Friends Discuss at Old Maids' Parties?

The traditional old maid's party featured a rose garden table under topiary branches with low-hanging boughs. Petals lined the tea-cup saucers to symbolize fleeting 'loveliness.' The women drank spiced tea and discussed their plans, the weather, and the war. The more lavish the party, the more the women emphasized the utter simplicity of family commitment—keeping the relatives together, helping to put bread on the table, and universal values. The subject always centered on the reality of being an old maid.

The questions—do you get a second chance? Or have you lost your bloom? Will anyone want you now? Must you choose between visionary change and traditional family?

The whole idea of a waxing rose garden setting for an old maid's fête held, preferably in the spring, is to share the recycling of nature over tea and basil cucumber nonfat cream cheese and chives finger sandwiches. Remember to remove the crusts.

Currently, the old maid's party is back. Read references to "The Old Maids Tea Party" in such books as, *A Little Maid of Old Connecticut (The Little Maid Series)* by Alice Turner Curtis and Wuanita Smith (Feb 1997) or *A Little Maid of Old New York (Little Maid Historical Series)* by Alice Turner Curtis and Elizabeth Pilsbry (Feb 1996).

To bring back your own old maid's party, refer to different creative genealogy techniques in my book titled, ***How to Start Personal Histories and Genealogy Journalism Businesses:*** *Genealogy Course Template, Syllabus, Writing & Marketing Guide*. ISBN: 0-595-38698-9. Published, Feb-2006, ASJA Press. Or make your own deck of genealogy cards. Different ideas are found in my latest book titled, ***Creating Family Newsletters & Time Capsules: How to Publish Multimedia Genealogy Periodicals or Gift Booklets.*** **ISBN:** 0-595-39872-3. See the Web site at http://www.newswriting.net.

# 4

# *What Can You Do With a Degree in Family History?*

## Letter from a BYU Faculty Member

Amy Harris
BYU History Department
2150 JFSB
Provo, UT 84602

As a graduate of BYU's family history/genealogy program and as its newest faculty member I am excited and encouraged by the growth of academic training in genealogy. Several schools have begun to offer courses and certificates in genealogy increasing the number of professionally trained genealogists.

While no classroom instruction can provide all the experience that hands-on research can, it streamlines and focuses genealogical training and provides invaluable guidance in choosing genealogical careers.

Academic training in genealogy, especially if it has a strong background in historical methods and historical knowledge, can only help further the work of family history and genealogical research.

◆　　　◆　　　◆

## Genealogy Education—Earning a Degree in Family History or Taking Free Courses Online? Why You Need a Platform

If your own university doesn't offer a major in family history, you can specialize in family history within a department at the undergraduate level or in graduate school within majors such as American Studies, History, Area Studies, (East Asian, India Studies, African, Latin American, European, Middle Eastern, Armenian, Hellenic, Jewish, Hawaiian-Pacific Islander Studies, Native American,

Indigenous Peoples' Studies, Scandinavian, Languages and Literature, Ethnic Journalism, or any other ethnic or ethnographic studies designation.) Several colleges do offer degrees in family history, such as Brigham Young University (BYU) and Heritage Genealogy College.

You have professors teaching family economics at universities as well as family history. Have you ever considered teaching family history or starting small groups where you teach and discuss genealogy research as well as social history surrounding family history issues?

Besides working as a librarian or video documentarian, archivist, photo and document conservator or restorer, time capsule manufacturer, genealogical software designer, museum adjunct, magazine publisher, newsletter designer, oral or personal historian, researcher, transcriber, what else can you do with certification in family history?

One of the emerging areas in genealogy education is organizing workshops for teachers, couples, and parents on how to help your children love your family history. To make a career of family history and genealogy research, you need to build a platform.

Your platform is what you stand on—your reputation and visibility as a genealogist or family historian. With a genealogy platform, you're already out where potential clients, students, or employers will see you. Next, you need a specialization—such as working with old maps, probate records, or paleography (old handwriting). You'll be working with family records, vital records, and military records.

Genealogy courses as given in college or through independent study include immigrant origins for a particular area, handwriting for different parts of the world, genealogical organizations, and periodicals.

You'll learn about the Internet, regional genealogy—US and one or more other nations, research in another country—either online or through travel or contacting librarians and genealogists abroad by mail or email, US sources, surname changes, jurisdictions, gazetteers, maps, calendars, feast days, different religions, church records, finding women's maiden names in wills and on death certificates or tombstone rubbings, censuses, ethnic group research, and reading Gothic script.

Courses will cover city directories, probate and court records such as marriages and divorces, orphan trains, military records, pension applications, medical, hospital, and sanitarium or prison records, family Bible birth records, name changes at Ellis Island, ships' passenger lists, conversions, and adoption records—for a particular region of your choice.

You might be searching in an online database for an application your client's ancestor filled out for a Civil War military pension. Or you might learn how to create, organize, and manage these online genealogy databases yourself. Time may be spent indexing or creating an index that volunteers will work on for years doing data entry or research, deciphering old handwriting.

## Audience

You have an intended audience—consumers of genealogy, personal/oral, or family history. Coursework and internships in family history help you find vehicles of communication for your problem-solving research. How you communicate depends upon your personality preferences. Are you drained by face-to-face contact with people and travel? Or are you energized by public speaking and teaching? Would you rather do one-to-one client consulting? Or write columns and books for genealogy publications?

Genealogical ethnography emphasizes problem-solving skills. Additional branches of family history include genealogy-related gerontology and intergenerational writing. That's where young people interview older relatives, transcribe recordings, and write their life stories as plays, skits, vignettes, or monologues. See the books, *How to Write Plays, Monologues, or Skits from Life Stories, Social Issues, or Current Events: For All Ages:* ISBN: 0-595-31866-5; or *Writing 7-Minute Inspirational Life Experience Vignettes : Create and Link 1,500-Word True Stories:* ISBN: 0-595-32237-9.

An excellent course on DNA-driven genealogy can be designed using as a guideline or text the book titled: *Predictive Medicine for Rookies: Consumer Watchdogs, Reviews, & Genetics Testing Firms Online.* 2005. ISBN: 0-595-35146-8. Or the book titled, *How to Interpret Family History and Ancestry DNA Test Results for Beginners:* The Geography and History of Your Relatives. 2004. ISBN: 0-595-31684-0.

Another field for coursework is military oral history. Volunteer interviewers help veterans and military pensioners preserve their life stories digitally. Interviews are transcribed into text transcripts by volunteers. Transcribers work with a variety of veterans' military history projects, such as the Veteran's History Project on the Web at: http://www.loc.gov/vets/stories/ex-war-home-release3.html. Non-volunteer transcribers create text documents from oral history tapes, usually for university libraries.

## What Courses Are Available Online?

The International Internet Genealogical Society University at: http://www.iigs.org/university/index.htm.en offers courses in 11 languages and a self-paced online course in US land and property research at: http://users.arn.net/~billco/uslpr.htm. Samford University Library, Birmingham, AL at: http://www.samford.edu/schools/ighr/courses/ offers genealogy courses including research in government and law libraries through its Institute of Genealogy and Historical Research.

## Old Maps and Relatives' Descriptions

How do you find your ancestor's unrecorded home town in another country? Arrival records in the USA dated before 1906 usually don't contain the home town name. Overseas, houses may not have numbers or street addresses, only surnames. Here's where a course on locating, translating, and working with old maps comes in handy. Research house maps.

For example, to trace houses with no numbers and streets with no names, you need a map of how a city or village looked in particular year. Then you can trace the house by the way a relative who remembers his grandparents' descriptions of the house. A house may be described by size or shape in relation to similar houses on a particular street. Old map genealogy research can form the basis of an internship.

Old house map study is used when tracing Sephardic surnames to houses in Aleppo or Damascus in the 19th century using the architecture of the house or the names of next-door neighbors in the old country. See the Farhi "Flowers of the Orient" genealogy Web site at: http://www.farhi.org/Documents/Farhi_Houses.htm.

The Farhi genealogy site titled, "Flowers of the Orient" contains a map of the old walled city of Damascus. The map you can see shows, "three Farhi houses (119, 120 & 277), the Liniado (268) and the Lisbona (4941)." From this city plan, one can see that the Muallim Farhi house was the largest.

The Damascus house map on the "Flowers of the Orient" genealogy Web site is from a document written in German titled, "*Damaskus die Stadt intra muros*" in *Damsaener Mittelurgen 2* (1985) by Dorothée Sack. Ironically, old house maps help find ancestral homes. And books about these homes may be in different languages.

## Courses Given By Professional Associations

Professional associations usually offer online or regional chapter courses such as those offered online by the National Genealogical Society at: http://www. ngsgenealogy.org/Courses/Course.cfm. Or check out the educational sites on the Web of the Association of Professional Genealogists at: http://apgen.org/articles/ ready.html#education.

    The National Institute on Genealogical Research in Lanham, MD at: http:// www.rootsweb.com/~natgenin/. The National Institute on Genealogical Research has been a leader in the field of genealogical education for more than fifty years. The institute was founded in 1950 under the sponsorship of The American University, The American Society of Genealogists, the National Archives, and the Maryland Hall of Records. If you're searching records in the Washington, DC area, you can pursue these educational resources to build your platform and specialization. The Web site for The Institute for Genealogy and History for Latin America is at: http://www.infowest.com/personal/l/lplatt/ platt.html.

## Internships

The best way to start a career in genealogy or family history is by volunteering for an internship within a university's family history or ethnography center. Brigham Young University (BYU)'s Center for Family History and Genealogy is working on developing three databases: German Immigrants, Spanish Immigrants, and English Immigrants.

    Volunteers are wanted, especially those who can translate BYU's Center for Family History Web site into a variety of languages beginning with Spanish, Portuguese, French, and German. There also are internships for students studying for a degree or certificate in family history at BYU. For more information, see http://immigrants.byu.edu.

    The American Historical Association listed on the Web at: http://www. historians.org/pubs/Free/careers/Index.htm lists a wide variety of careers for history majors with an undergraduate degree, including historic preservation and cultural resources management. Teaching family history also is an option, which can be done in colleges or at adult education classes.

    Harvard University's American studies program, grants PhDs, allowing students to live for a year among an ethnic community in the USA, researching, recording, and writing about a group of people as a study in ethnography. For this and other universities' PhD programs where family history plays a part, you'd spend a year living in a community, participating in its rhythms and exploring what can be learned from the families, their ancestors, and present-day descendants.

As a genealogical ethnographer, or documentarian, you'd explore why something might be as it is, such as a sense of self or confidence in individual members. You might teach a community how to preserve old photos or documents and diaries.

## Organize and Verify with Computer Genealogy Software

Your primary job as a genealogist is to organize and verify information. At Heritage Genealogy College, Salt Lake City, you can check out the college's four-year bachelor's degree program in genealogy at: http://genealogy.edu/moodle/. One of the courses at this college is titled "Ethics and Fraud in Genealogy." Another is "Genealogical Vocabulary." Case studies are emphasized in the college's genealogical problem solving course.

A bachelor's degree in Genealogical Research at Heritage Genealogy College requires 127 hours of successfully completed mostly genealogy and a few related history, sociology, foreign language, and writing courses (and a course on using the computer with genealogical software). Each semester's courses of 15 or 16 semester hours are noted online at the college's Web site.

You'd study sources, methodology, and case studies for various regions of the USA. In past times, a graduate degree in journalism or history was enough to land you a decent teaching job, hopefully with tenure. But in today's competitive career markets, what you can do with an undergraduate degree in family history is build your platform. You could go on to law school, but what if you want a job right out of college?

Specialize in problem-solving. Heritage Genealogy College offers a course consisting of case studies in problem solving plus an internship in missing heirs, title and traditional genealogical research, or an internship in genetic genealogical research and case studies (as in DNA-driven genealogy).

Heritage Genealogy College provides training in verifying genealogical and historical research, land title searches, legal "missing heirs" research, medical genetic genealogical research coordination, genealogical writing, paleography and history.

You could take Heritage Genealogy College's course titled, "Healthy Lifestyles Research through Historical Documentation," or "Writing Family Histories." In addition to history and genealogical vocabulary courses, you'd take a foreign language course. Choose from Danish, (with Dutch, Swedish, and Norwegian equivalents), French, German, Italian, Portuguese or Spanish. There would be courses in genealogical writing, paleography, US history to 1865, and American Civilization. What you'd want to target are the internships because they are a stepping stone to the real world of family history research.

You'd take a course on how to use computer software for genealogy research and verification called "Genealogical Computer." A software program called Learning Personal Ancestral File (PAF) is used along with software called CLOOZ, which is an electronic genealogical "filing cabinet" as the Web site describes. CLOOZ organizes genealogical research and records.

## Learning to Verify Ancestral Records

The purpose of taking courses in genealogy/family history is to learn how to verify ancestral records. If you didn't want a four-year degree, there are certificate programs and individual courses. Some BYU independent study family history courses are free on the Web. See the genealogy courses offered online through BYU's Independent Study Web site at: http://ce.byu.edu/is/site/courses/.

Check out BYU's PAF software tutorial online at: http://paftutorial.byu.edu/.

Getting a four-year degree or certificate in genealogy or family history also can lead to careers performing title searches for property ownership, searching notary court records, marriages, medical records, genetics interpretations, and missing heir searches. Take a field trip to the Family History Library, Salt Lake City, UT to see how records are searched. Note the difference between paid and volunteer genealogy research.

## Courses

The Center for Family History & Genealogy at Brigham Young University (BYU), Provo, Utah, offers a four-year Bachelors degree and a certificate in genealogy and family history. There also is a BYU non-credit free course on the Web in genealogy listed under Independent Study—Distance Education at: http://ce.byu.edu/is/site/courses/freecourses.cfm.

At BYU, the undergraduate courses in family history and genealogy have numerous resources such as the Family History Center, Utah Valley Regional, the Family History Reference division, the Family History Training Center, and numerous family history computer laboratories. There also is a division for family history reference and religion, a senior missionary and family history training division as a resource, and the Utah Valley Regional Family History Center.

BYU's family history major for a bachelor's degree requires 45 units of family history courses plus other history courses for the degree, foreign language courses, and courses in writing and understanding the early handwriting, foreign handwriting and documents, writing family histories, and family and law in American history. The course requirements are listed at: http://familyhistory.byu.edu/majors.asp. The family history minor requires 24 hours of coursework. The certificate requires 18 hours of family history courses.

What you learn includes how to research personal ancestral files. You can view these files free online at: http://www.FamilySearch.org. The Web site belongs to the Family History Library, Salt Lake City. At the FamilySearch.org site you can research an ancestral file, look at a pedigree resource file, searching online and/or in person the Family History Library Catalog at the main Family History Library in Salt Lake City.

In "Introduction to Family History: Online Lessons," the beginning course at BYU, you'll learn how to research the International Genealogical Index and the Ordinance Index. An ordinance is an important ritual in Mormonism, a significant event in Christianity, or in secular terms, a law or internal regulation made by a colony or city council. It also refers to "that which is decreed by fate or a deity."

The Ordinance Index contains millions of records extracted from vital records or submitted by LDS Church members. It is *identical* to the International Genealogy Index except for the inclusion of LDS temple ordinance dates. You can learn more at: http://familyhistory.byu.edu/labs/ordinance%20index.asp. The Ordinance Index is arranged by region and event. The Ordinance Index lets you can do three types of searches: individual, marriage and parent.

The Ordinance Index also groups similar given names and similar surnames under standardizes spellings and shows Mormon Temple ordinance dates as well as provides Family History Library call numbers for sources. A beginning genealogy course in a degree program, such as the BYU curriculum also includes instruction in how to research the US Social Security Death Index, Vital Record Indexes. You receive research guidance and learn to use software such as Temple Ready for Windows. BYU also gives a course titled, "Professional Paths & Credentials in Family History."

Several free genealogy courses are on the Web. On the About Parenting site, there's a genealogy course at: http://genealogy.about.com/library/lessons/blintro.htm and a free course at the "Researching Your Family Tree" at: http://www.learnwebskills.com/family/intro.html.

## In-Depth Research

Getting a four-year university degree in family history and genealogy prepares you for a career as a researcher, teacher, or genealogy journalist. Since genealogy and family history careers are not licensed, you can train yourself with the numerous free courses online. But you need more than a beginning course for in-depth research. A free 6 week personal history course is online at http://www.newswriting.net/personalhistorycourse.htm.

If you can't afford to study for a four-year degree, or you already have one in another major, you might be interested in BYU's free Web-based courses under their Independent Studies—Distance Education division online at: http://ce.byu.edu/is/site/courses/freecourses.cfm. Whether you want a degree in family history or need to learn how to search for missing heirs, a free, online course is a good place to explore family history research.

What you can do with a degree or certification in family history is start a scholarly journal of genealogy for a specific ethnic group that doesn't already have a quality journal. Or you might establish an Institute for the Study of Genealogy or Family History for a particular area of the world.

One example is the Institute of Genealogy and History for Latin America. Their address is Institute of Genealogy and History for Latin America 2191 S. 2200 E., Mt. Springs, Utah 84757. See their catalog. Their Web site is at: http://www.genealogy.com/00000140.html. According to that Web site, The Institute of Genealogy and History for Latin America publishes books containing background information needed by family history researchers with an interest in Latin American countries, the colonial Hispanic United States, and Spain. Many of the books are available in both English and Spanish. Projects are mentioned on their Web site.

The Institute of Genealogy and History for Latin America also is working on a Surname History Project. The main purpose of this project is to compile histories of common Hispanic surnames. The Institute also has a Web site which includes the former information of the Institute of Genealogy & History of L. A., Irish, Early LDS, Linked, Documented Database, and many family and other sections: See the Web site at: http://www.kolobfamilyresearch.com

# 5

Here's how to open your own genealogy, family history journalism, or personal history business. This includes a genealogy course template and instruction on how to start and operate a home-based business working with personal and oral histories, genealogy, family history, and life story writing. You also learn how to interview people, what questions to ask, and how to put together a business and/ or a course or book on any aspect of genealogy around the world, journalism, writing, personal history, and life story writing.

Start your own course using the genealogy course template to inspire you to develop your own specialties and niche areas. Work with almost any ethnic group, and create businesses ranging from DNA-driven genealogy reporting services to family history, memoirs writing, or personal history videography services.

Use *social history* to find information such as female ancestors' maiden names that had not been recorded using hidden and niche areas of information, including ethnic, religious, and institutional sources such as widows' military pension applications. You'll learn how to write social history by using genealogy journalism resources, find hidden records, and market your own course or write your book or report in many different areas of personal history and genealogy journalism. Female ancestors' information also may be found in midwives' records, journals, or diaries and in later times, in prenatal records books.

Start your own business or set up a course and teach or train others to be genealogists or personal and oral historians. Write for historical, folkloric, or genealogy publications, specializing in writing eulogies for people or pets. Interview friends or family, and write obituaries for publications that have no staff obituary writer on board all the time. Assemble family history time capsules, keepsakes, or courseware and software. Record family history how-to lectures on audio CDs or video DVDs.

Teach life story journalism. Or write life stories as plays and skits. Do research for clients, libraries, and institutions. Learn what is appropriate to charge clients for personal history, genealogy research, or life story recording and writing services.

Make family tree charts with software or craft them in scrap books. Learn how to be an independent documentarian. Produce video and audio recordings such as DVDs for your clients or family. Develop genealogy and personal history classes anywhere. You'll make history. To start, first you need to create a course syllabus-either to teach beginners genealogy or to train professionals in other fields to use personal history techniques to find hidden information, or organize information for the reports you generate for your clients or family. Start your own business, club, franchise, or course.

One of the best ways to publicize and market your genealogy course and/or family history instructional book is to write a syllabus. Teach an online or in-person course related to the topic of your book. Require students to purchase the book. Teach the contents of the book in a how-to course. What's your hobby or field of expertise? My usual full-time working day emphasizes genealogy journalism and personal history research. My hobby combines visual anthropology and producing, viewing, and reviewing documentaries.

If your field relates to personal history or genealogy, here's how to write a syllabus to teach online (or in person) a genealogy course. You can train or teach at a variety of levels.

Starting your own classes and reserving a conference room in a library, church social hall, or community center don't require degrees or credentials, only expertise. Nothing lets you learn a subject better than if you have to teach it to beginners. If you don't like teaching face-to-face or training employees in a work setting, teach online from your Web site. Or apply to teach a course in something you can do well at online educational sites such as blackboard.com. Read online education publications such as the Virtual U Gazette. Check out GetEducated.com at: http://www.geteducated.com/vug/index.asp.

You learn more from your students' feedback than you ever learned from books in a variety of areas related to writing and publishing. The first step is to write a great syllabus that convinces others to hire you to teach a subject related to the information in your book. This technique works well with nonfiction, how-to or self-help books.

If your book is a novel, your course syllabus might emphasize plotting the novel or marketing and promotion. To sell your book in this type of class, you'd use each chapter to teach how to write "tag lines," emotions and behaviors in a novel, or portions of your novel as tools for fiction writers in the genre of your book—such as plotting the mystery or romance novel.

You'd use passages to teach consistency and transitions that move the plot forward and show how the characters grow and change or the romantic tension. A similar technique of "teaching the process" would be used if you wrote plays, poetry, or cinematic scripts. A syllabus helps you get hired and/or to recruit students so you can sell your book and teach a class or train a group of people either online or in person.

You can adapt this syllabus plan and format to the subject of your book in nearly any field. Instead of 'genealogy,' just substitute the concept and framework of your own book. Here's how to write a syllabus.

A short course may be taught online or arranged in any room available from a church basement to a library conference room. A seminar can last a few hours. A lengthy course can be planned for an entire semester at any level in adult education, for college extended studies programs, or at community centers. You need experience in your area of expertise, and a published book helps your credibility. If you're teaching a course in a community college or university for college credit you'd need a graduate degree. For public school you'd also need a teaching credential unless your expertise level is the equivalent. Teaching vocational education and using your book as instructional text is more flexible. You can teach in the extended studies (not for credit) department of universities and community colleges based on experience. Credentials in your field of work are helpful to get you hired, but without them, start your own course online or from an available room.

You can share a rented room to teach the course with other trainers or teachers. Least expensive is to teach at your Web site and sell your book online to students. At the end of the course, give them a certificate in the subject you've taught related to your book. Require students to buy your book, and use it throughout the course.

One of the easiest ways to get hired to teach a course is to offer one in genealogy and/or personal history, if you have done your research on how genealogists find their information. Since you have written a book, can you now call yourself an expert?

If genealogy, personal history, oral history, social history, anthropology, sociology, psychology, creative writing, early handwriting, or journalism interests you, a beginner's course in genealogy attracts people interested in where their ancestors came from and how they lived, ate, and played. Classes often fill up quickly.

People like to take courses where they can learn about themselves and their families' life styles. Genealogy courses work well online, at social, ethnic, and religious clubs, and at senior centers. So here's how to begin writing a syllabus for a genealogy course.

Your first genealogy course syllabus expands the four keys of genealogy research: identity, name, date information was recorded, locality, and kinship. How you organize, edit, and write a genealogy course syllabus often determines whether you'll be hired to teach a course in genealogy for beginners.

If you're a genealogist or want to promote your genealogy-oriented book or journalistic skills, teach a course in genealogy. Genealogy courses rely on verifiable details. Accidental or intentional alterations by scribes can dramatically affect information. Courses that go on year after year are evaluated by students as excellent.

Genealogists are concerned about accurate reproduction of texts or entry of information. For generations, most public family history entries were hand copied by government record clerks, clergy, and scribes deeply influenced by cultural, political, and theological disputes of their day.

Your syllabus can help students look for mistakes and intentional changes in surviving records. Can the original names be reconstructed? Genealogy course content also includes the social history of where and why these changes were made and how family historians go about reconstructing what might be the original names, relationships, and records as closely as possible.

Use your syllabus as a tool to outline your course. Students want an easy-to-follow syllabus. The *American Heritage Dictionary* defines the word 'syllabus' as an outline of a course of study. It's a table of contents with a schedule of topics, not a book proposal.

Your syllabus also needs to cover how to find records of hard-to-trace people, such as clergy. How would you direct students who want to trace nuns, priests, ministers, or rabbis?

Genealogy courses given in churches' social halls sometimes attract those who want to trace difficult-to-find genealogy records of clergy. Old books make excellent genealogy sources. Other primary sources to trace clergy or religious educators include College Alumni Records, The Clergy Lists, Crockford's Directories, Fasti Ecclesiae, Anglicanae, Parish Registers, Bishop's Records, Censuses, and County Directories.

## What you need to organize before teaching courses in genealogy journalism

1.   How to design and write family history newsletters—or teach others to do the same.

2. How much time to spend letting each student talk about the work they have done during the week—depending upon how many students you have in class.

3. How to organize family history files.

4. How to break topics into memoirs or biographies (family or clients).

5. How to keep organized and accessible research files

6. How to write inquiries and queries by email and letter.

7. How to abstract and transcribe basics.

8. How to write client or family research reports and summaries.

9. How to write personal use research reports and summaries

10. How to make time capsules.

11. How to put historical context into essays, numbering formats and citation formats.

12. How to compile and send family newsletters.

13. How to prepare to write a family history or genealogy-related book.

14. How to publish and promote a family history or genealogy book.

15. How to incorporate research

## GENEALOGY COURSE SYLLABUS TEMPLATE

A genealogy course syllabus for beginners includes answers to one of the most frequently asked questions: How do you find female ancestors and solve identity problems when maiden surnames didn't appear on the death certificates? Before you try to organize and write a syllabus, first list topics you'll cover in your syllabus.

### Planning Your Syllabus

List all obvious items. Keep this list next to your blank syllabus page. Then list items often omitted from a syllabus for a beginning course in genealogy. Compare your syllabus with other genealogy course outlines that have received great student evaluations. Your clue is whether the course is repeated year after year. There are several copyrighted genealogy course outlines on the Internet to peruse. Use them only for comparison and motivation. Keep your syllabus unique to your own course. Make a list of resources to be used in your own course before you begin writing your syllabus.

## Resources List

Social History (brief)
Genealogy sources created by women:

> Diaries, journals, letters, postcards, family Bibles, heirlooms, artifacts, oral history, legislative petitions, atypical sources, published family histories, cemetery records, tombstone inscriptions or rubbings, church records, censuses, military records, hospitals, orphanages, institutions, sanitariums, passenger arrival lists, city directories, notaries' records, voter lists/registrations, pensions, widows' pension applications/civil war, orphans and guardianship records, land records, marriage records, medical records, Eugenics Record Office, (ERO), social data, midwives' journals, doctors' journals, asylums, divorce records, wills, probate, court records, school records, ethnic sources, codicils, ethnic/religious hospital records, naturalization laws.

> After you compile this list, put it aside to refer to as you write your syllabus. Begin outlining the syllabus by starting with the course information, instructor information, text or reading materials, course descriptions, course calendar or schedule, and references or bibliography.

> Each category would get a one or two-sentence description summarizing what will be covered in the course and what assignments are required of students. Keep your syllabus short—about three pages or less. The syllabus in a semester-long college level, 3-unit genealogy course meant for beginners and taught online or in person would look like this in its layout:

## Syllabus

Course Number/Title: **Genealogy and Family History 1**
    **Name of School or College**
    **Year and Month:**
    **Department:**
    **Credit Hours 3**
    **Required Text**
    **Days/Time**
    **Instructor**
    **Location**

**Prerequisite:** None

**Course Placement:** Adult Education, Extended Studies, Community College, University Undergraduate level.

## Overview

In Genealogy 1, students will learn special strategies for uncovering hard-to-find information about their ancestors. By the end of this course, students will become more versatile in using interdisciplinary skills for researching family and social history resources.

## Course Description

Genealogy 1 is an introductory course in family and personal history research *methods* that includes learning interviewing and recording skills. This survey course covers the strategies of genealogical research in North America and introduces the student to the techniques of genealogical research around the world. Students able to read other languages may work on genealogical records in other languages if they can translate their findings, projects, or assignments to the class in English.

## Research Methods

Students are introduced to a survey of all the methods used to identify individuals and their ancestors, including paper records, online searches, surname groups online, and DNA-driven genealogy resources.

## Learning Objectives for Genealogy 1

**At the end of this course, students will have learned the following skills:**

1.  Students will be able to research the following resources:
    Original records
    Family histories
    Church records
    Censuses
    Passenger Arrival Lists
    City directories
    Family history libraries and genealogy sections of public and university libraries
    Voter lists and registrations
    Military records and pensions, widows' pensions

Land records and notary records
Marriage records
Medical records
Divorce records
Ethnic women and men
    African American
    Native American
    Jewish American
    European Immigrants
    Chinese and Japanese Immigrants in California

2. Methods for determining maiden names.

3. Solving identity problems in genealogy research

4. Methods for identifying women (midwives' records)

5. Genealogy as social history

   a.   child bearing and raising in genealogy research

   b.   children born out of wedlock and genealogy research

   c.   women's work and genealogy records,

   d.   property tax records

   e.   religion and genealogy information

   f.   women's reform movements, rights, and genealogy records

   g.   merging social and family history in genealogy research

   h.   documenting your own ancestor's history

6. Unpublished Genealogy Sources

7. Published Genealogical Sources

8. How to research population schedules

9. Probate and court records

10. Slave genealogy and schedules

11. Social history research and biographies

12. Property, Inheritance, Naturalization and Divorce laws for genealogists

13. Widows' pensions and applications-Acts and Laws, survey

14. DNA-driven genealogy, methods, resources, matrilineal and patrilineal research, surname groups and genetics associations

15. Online research resources

16. Checklist for genealogy research

17. Genealogical case studies

18. Articles and Bibliography

19. National Archives and Genealogy Research

20. How to read abstracted records

21. How to find and read microfilms and microfiche records

22. Military pensions—records in the National Archives

23. Searching records of the Veterans Administration

24. Published indexes to pension files and other aids

25. Genealogy journalism methods—interviewing and recording

26. Oral history, video and audio recording—what questions to ask.

## How Students will apply the newly learned genealogy research skills:

1. Use the methods of scientific genealogical research.

2. Establish lines of descent for the person or family you select and develop a pedigree chart or family history tree of names and critical dates such as birth, marriage, and death for each ancestor on the family tree and/or pedigree chart.

3. Organize genealogy records.

4. Interview and record relatives or selected persons.

5. Research the past.

6. Use online technology to research or supplement written records and develop a pedigree chart or family tree.

**Six Assignments and Projects: Due by End of 12-Week Course. (Insert Specific Due Dates) One assignment is due every two weeks.**

1. Write a publishable 1,000-word researched family history/genealogy article and submit it to a publication.

2. Develop a list of 30 to 60 questions (chosen from a list of suggested questions to ask from the handout) to ask another person during a genealogy-oriented or life story-oriented personal or family history recorded interview.

3. Interview using critical and creative thinking skills one or more older adults and record on audio or video tape a half-hour to one-hour life story experience to submit to an oral history archive library. Obtain a signed release form from all persons interviewed to send the recording to an oral history library. Give all persons interviewed copies of the interview recorded on tape or disc, such as a CD or DVD.

4. Use written records and online resources/technology relevant to your personal interests or selected discipline. Genealogy has several areas of emphasis including archival records research, oral history, personal history, family history, video biography/life story recording, and DNA-driven genealogy/genetics for ancestry.

5. Understand opportunities, skills, and requirements for genealogy journalism and publishing concentrations.

6. Research the diversity of cultures in North America and other countries as related to how genealogy records have been maintained.

7. Find several new or hidden ways to find genealogy information on females whose maiden names (surnames) were not recorded in the usual records such as censuses and city directories. How would you find birth certificates of women?

**Course Competencies:**

1. Learn how to perform scientific genealogical research.

2. Fill out and expand a pedigree chart and family tree—first by hand and then using technology or genealogy software.

3. Collect sources and resource information and organize the sources using records, legacies, diaries, letters, or journals.

4.  Understand the value of journaling and archiving journals, letters, and diaries.

5.  Read an article on how to restore old diaries and photos.

6.  Write and record as audio or video a life story to keep for future generations or to put in a time capsule. One copy would be text for reading and another recorded in any format, including text and photos, audio or video. Be aware technology changes, and a text copy on acid-free paper is required just in case the recorded format can no longer play.

7.  Learn how to correspond with relatives or friends and what questions to ask when asking for genealogical information.

8.  Fill out family group sheets for recorded information to be transcribed or kept in text form.

9.  Read an article on genealogical identification, orphan trains, and family skeletons or hidden facts on everything from how a person's race or religion was listed to name changes. Understand how some pre-1948 housing laws and codes excluded certain groups from buying property in various areas and how some records were changed so people could buy homes. Research articles on this subject as related to genealogy records.

10. Understand the four keys of genealogy as research tools: identity, name, date information was recorded, locality, and kinship.

11. Research the American and/or Canadian trains when children were sent from the East to the West. These trains are separate from the orphan trains. Records with the children's names are in various archives. Find out where to find the records.

12. Learn organization, documentation, filing techniques.

13. Analyze, interpret, and present genealogy-related findings.

14. Keep a research notebook that cites each source of documentation.

15. Look at working files that organize genealogical documents.

16. Listen to a recording of oral history. Read an article on restoring or preserving keepsakes, heirlooms, photos, and scrap books that document family traditions.

17. Use oral history as a research method. Learn to record oral history in audio and/or in video using a camcorder or audio recorder.

18. Learn how items and traditions have been preserved by families, librarians, conservationists, archivists, or family and public historians.

19. Gather family folklore, recipes, superstitions, or traditions.

20. Record family rites of passage, celebrations, or traditions.

21. Search genealogy records on the Internet

22. Read published genealogy information online.

23. Survey genealogy published materials.

24. Enter family information and print-out computer-generated charts and family trees.

25. Learn how to use vital records, divorce and cemetery records, jurisdictions records, original records, Social Security Death Index records online, and specific localities searches of historical groups for an area. Look for transcriptions of original documents.

26. Understand handwriting changes and how to interpret early American handwriting. Translate documents recorded in early American handwriting.

27. Find out where to obtain court records used in genealogy research.

28. Use church data to fill in missing information.

29. Use newspapers in genealogy research

30. Trace ancestor's lives using a city directory.

31. Research information on the Family History Library, Salt Lake City, Utah. Locate the nearest Branch Family Center and research an ancestor or friend.

32. Learn to research immigration, emigration, and migration records, ships' passenger lists, Naturalization records.

33. Investigate the reason why your ancestor immigrated to America. Trace the migration patterns used. Use passenger lists and naturalization records and find out where these records are located.

34. Use land and tax records, school records, and ethnic records.

35. Research what records are available in the National Archives. Find out what military records are available to genealogists for research. Find out the addresses to write to for military, pension, and bounty land records.

36. Plan for and/or attend a genealogy-related seminar, research-oriented field trip, family reunion, or a meeting of a heritage, historical, or lineage association. Read an article on or view a documentary on a family reunion. Research what grants are available from various societies related to genealogy research.

37. Read an article on how to look at medical histories and genograms. A genogram is a schematic representation (drawing) of a family's medical history. A genogram describes the medical and/or genetic history of a family and includes family boundaries, attitudes, values, beliefs and related psychological history of family members.

38. Look at a Web site or surname group online researching DNA-driven genealogy for deep ancestry research. Read an article or handout on the psychological aspects of studying one's own family history. Start a genogram of your family. Does DNA-driven genealogy appeal more to anthropologists or to genealogists?

## Libraries and Field Trips

Visit a library that has records related to genealogy and/or oral history research or archives. Record in your notebook in two paragraphs what you learned from the field trip and what most interested you there.

## Method of Instruction

Class discussion, lectures, field trips, video documentaries, class participation, individual Internet computer research, collaborative projects, handouts, videos, and personal history recording projects is used. This course may be taught online or in person.

## Evaluation

Class participation and completion of projects/assignments is due by the end of the course. Assignments are due by the due date specified in the handout.

## Equipment

Access to the Internet, a personal computer and printer, a tape or other audio digital recorder or camcorder using either tape or DVDs, and a DVD or CD recorder/R/RW disk drive in your computer or other device that saves a computer file to a CD and/or a DVD. Save your recorded projects on DVDs or CDs. Instruction will be provided on how to save any recorded material to a DVD or CD. Technical help will be available.

## Length of Course

Adjust the syllabus content and assignments to the length of your own course. Genealogy courses may run for a 12, 16 or 18-week semester in adult education unified school districts or in extended studies or community college classes.

*Every life story has four seasons and twelve stages, like the months in a year. The four seasons are infancy, childhood, adulthood and grace-age."—How to Write Plays, Monologues, or Skits from Life Stories, Social Issues, or Current Events (for All Ages). ISBN: 0-595-31866-5*

# 6

## *How to Open Your Own DNA-Driven Genealogy Interpreting Company*

You may be a genealogist, historian, or entrepreneur with no science background. That's okay as long as your laboratory contacts or partners are scientists. The most important contact and contract you would have would be with a DNA testing laboratory. Your business would be to report the interpretations from the scientists in plain language to your genealogy or surname group clients. The DNA tests are for ancestry or genealogy, such as checking surname groups.

Find out who your competitors contract with as far as testing laboratories. For example, Family Tree DNA at the Web site: http://www.familytreedna.com/faq.html#q1 sends its DNA samples to be tested by the DNA testing laboratories at the University of Arizona.

Genealogy researcher, Bennett Greenspan, President and CEO of Family Tree DNA founded Family Tree in 1999. Greenspan is an entrepreneur **and** life-long genealogy enthusiast. He successfully turned his family history and ancestry hobby into a full-time vocation running a DNA testing-for-ancestry company. Together with Max Blankfeld, they founded in 1997 GoCollege.com a website for college-bound students which survived the .COM implosion.

Max Blankfeld is Greenspan's Vice President of Operations/Marketing. Before entering the business world, Blankfeld was a journalist. After that, he started and managed several successful ventures in the area of public relations as well as consumer goods both in Brazil and the US. Today, the highly successful Family Tree DNA is America's first genealogy-driven DNA testing service.

At the University of Arizona, top DNA research scientists such as geneticist, Mike Hammer, PhD, population geneticist Bruce Walsh, PhD, geneticist Max F. Rothschild, molecular anthropologist, Theodore G. Schurr, and lab manager,

Matthew Kaplan along with the rest of the DNA testing team do the testing and analysis.

So it's important if you want to open your own DNA for ancestry testing company to contract with a reputable laboratory to do the testing. Find out whether the lab you're going to be dealing with will answer a client's questions in case of problems with a test that might require re-testing. Clients will come to you to answer questions rather than go to the busy laboratory. Most laboratories are either part of a university, a medical school, or are independent DNA testing laboratories run by scientists and their technicians and technologists.

Your business will deal with genealogy buffs testing their DNA for ancestry related to surnames. You wouldn't link with a lab that tests DNA for genetic risk markers in order to tailor a special diet or foods to someone's genetic risk markers. Many independent laboratories do test genes for the purpose of tailoring diets to genes. The new field is called nutrigenomics. Check out the various Web sites devoted to nutrigenomics if you're interested in this type of DNA testing business. For example, there is Alpha-Genetics at http:// www.Alpha-Genics.com.

According to Dr. Fredric D. Abramson, PhD, S.M., President and CEO of AlphaGenics, Inc., "The key to using diet to manage genes and health lies in managing gene expression (which we call the Expressitype). Knowing your genotype merely tells you a starting point. Genotype is like knowing where the entrance ramps to an interstate can be found. They are important to know, but tell you absolutely nothing about what direction to travel or how the journey will go. That is why Expressitype must be the focus." You can contact AlphaGenics, Inc. at: http:// www.Alpha-Genics.com or write to: Maryland Technology Incubator, 9700 Great Seneca Highway, Rockville, MD 20850.

Why open any kind of a genealogy-related DNA test reporting business? It's because the entrepreneur is at the forefront of a revolution in our concept of ancestry, diet, and medicines. Genes are tested to reveal how your body metabolizes medicine as well as food, and genes are tested for ancient ancestry or recent relationships such as paternity. Genes are tested for courtroom evidence.

"Each of us is a unique organism, and for the first time in human history, genetic research is confirming that one diet is not optimum for everyone," says Abramson. Because your genes differ from someone else's, you process food and supplements in a unique way. Your ancestry is unique also.

For genealogists seeking to expand into putting the 'genes' in genealogy, clients would receive a report on only surnames and ancestry connections. You would be the middle person who interprets the DNA-driven genealogy reports. This means explaining how the surname is related or not related to the maternal and/or paternal sequences. For a woman, it's the mtDNA that's tested. You're testing the maternal lineages. It's ancient and goes back thousands of years. For the man, you can have a lab test the Y-chromosome, the paternal lineages and the mtDNA, the maternal lineages.

What you supply your clients with is a printout report and explanation of the individual's sequences and mtDNA group called the haplogroup and/or the Y-chromosome ancestral genetic markers. For a male, you can test the Y-chromosome and provide those markers, usually 25 markers and the mtDNA. For a woman, you can only test the mtDNA, the maternal line for 'haplogroup' letter and what is called the HVS-1 and HVS-2 sequences. The Lab testing DNA and matching them to surnames will define these terms that also are found genetic terminology glossary, free online at The Human Genome Project at: http://www.genome.gov/glossary.cfm.

mtDNA haplogroups show sequences of the maternal lineages back thousands of years. Y chromosome haplogroups and haplotypes show the paternal sequences of ancestors who lived thousands of years ago in specific geographic areas. To get started, look at the Web sites and databases of all the companies that test for ancestry using DNA.

What most of the DNA testing entrepreneurs have in common is that they can do business online. People order the DNA testing kit online. The companies send out a DNA testing kit. The client sends back DNA to a lab to be tested. The process does not involve any blood drawing to test for ancestry. Then the company sends a report directly to the customer about what the DNA test revealed solely in regard to ancient ancestry—maternal or paternal lines.

Reports include the possible geographic location where the DNA sequences originated. Customers usually want to see the name of an actual town, even though towns didn't exist 10,000 years ago when the sequences might have arisen. The whole genome is not tested, only the few ancestral markers, usually 500 base pairs of genes. Testing DNA for ancestry does not have anything to do with testing genes for health risks because only certain genes are tested—genes related to ancestry. And all the testing is done at a laboratory, not at your online business.

To get started, contact genealogists and genealogy online and print publications. You'd focus on specific ethnic groups as a niche market. The major groups interested in ancestry using DNA testing include Northern European, Ashkenazi, Italian, Greek, Armenian, Eastern European, African, Asian, Latin American, and Middle Eastern.

Many successful entrepreneurs in the DNA testing for ancestry businesses started with a hobby of looking up family history records—genealogy. So if you're a history buff, or if your hobby is family history research, oral history, archaeology, or genealogy, you now can turn to DNA testing.

What you actually sell to customers are DNA test kits and DNA test reports. To promote your business, offer free access to your Web site database with all your clients listed by important DNA sequences. Keep names private and use only assigned numbers or letters to protect the privacy of your clients. Never give private and confidential genetic test information to insurance companies or employers. Clients who want to have their DNA tested for ancestry do not want their names and DNA stored to fall into the "wrong hands." So honor privacy requests. Some people will actually ask you to store DNA for future generations.

If you want to include this service, offer a time capsule. For your clients, you would create a time capsule, which is like a secure scrap book on acid-free paper and on technology that can be transferred in the future when technology changes. Don't store anything on materials that can't be transferred from one technology to another. For example, have reports on acid-free paper.

You can include a CD or DVD also, but make sure that in the future when the CD players aren't around any longer, the well-preserved report, perhaps laminated or on vellum or other acid-free materials that don't crumble with age can be put into the time capsule. You can include a scrap book with family photos and video on a CD if you wish, or simply offer the DNA test report and comments explaining to the customer what the DNA shows.

Use plain language and no technical terms unless you define them on the same page. Your goal is to help people find other people who match DNA sequences and to use this knowledge to send your customers reports. If no matches can be found, then supply your clients with a thorough report. Keep out any confusing jargon. Show with illustrations how your customer's DNA was tested. In plain language tell them what was done.

Your report will show the results, and tell simply what the results mean. You can offer clients a list of how many people in what countries have their same DNA sequences. Include the present day city or town and the geographic location using longitude and latitude.

You're going to ask, with no science background yourself, how will you know what to put in the report? That's the second step. You contact a university laboratory that does DNA testing for outside companies. They will generate all the reports for you. What you do with the report is to make sure the language is easy to understand by non-scientists and promote it by making it look visually appealing. Define any words you think the customer won't understand with simpler words that fully explain what the DNA sequences mean and what the various letters and numbers mean. Any dictionary of genetic terms will give you the meaning in one sentence using plain language. Use short sentences in your reports and plain language.

Your new service targets genealogists who help their own customers find lost relatives. Your secondary market is the general public. Most people taking a DNA test for ancestry want information on where their DNA roamed 20,000 years ago and in the last 10,000 years. DNA testing shows people only where their ancient ancestors camped. However, when sequences with other people match exactly, it could point the way to an ancient common ancestor whose descendants went in a straight line from someone with those sequences who lived 10,000 years ago to a common ancestor who lived only a few generations ago.

Inside, you'd have maps, charts, and locations for the client to look at. Keep the material visual. Include a CD with the DNA sequences if you can. The explanation would show the customer the steps taken to test the DNA.

Keep that visual with charts and graphs. Don't use small print fonts or scientific terminology to any extent so your customer won't feel your report is over his or her head. Instead use illustrations, geographic maps. Put colorful circles on the cities or geographic locations where that person's DNA is found.

Put a bright color or arrow on the possible geographic area of origin for those DNA sequences. Nobody can pinpoint an exact town for certain, but scientists know where certain DNA sequences are found and where they might have sat out the last Ice Age 20,000 years ago, and survived to pass those same DNA sequences on to their direct descendants, that customer of yours who has those sequences.

For example, when I had my mtDNA (maternal lineages) tested, the report included my DNA matches by geographic coordinates. The geographic center is 48.30N 4.65E, Bar sur Aube, France with a deviation of 669.62 miles as done by "Roots for Real," a London company that tests DNA for ancestry. The exact sequences are in the Roots for Real Database (and other mtDNA databases) for my markers. Applications for testing genetic signatures are growing, since this science is still in its infancy in regard to applications of genetic and genomic testing.

Some laboratories listed below test DNA only for ancestry and genealogy, including surname group project DNA and racial percentages testing. Other DNA companies test genes for personalized medicine and nutrigenomics, pharmacogenetics, and ancestry.

◆     ◆     ◆

## The Nutrition-DNA-Family History Connection

Check out the various Web sites devoted to nutrigenomics if you're interested in this type of DNA testing business. For example, there is Alpha-Genetics at http:// www.Alpha-Genics.com.

According to Dr. Fredric D. Abramson, PhD, S.M., President and CEO of AlphaGenics, Inc., "The key to using diet to manage genes and health lies in managing gene expression (which we call the Expressitype). Knowing your genotype merely tells you a starting point. Genotype is like knowing where the entrance ramps to an interstate can be found. They are important to know, but tell you absolutely nothing about what direction to travel or how the journey will go. That is why Expressitype must be the focus." You can contact AlphaGenics, Inc. at: http:// www.Alpha-Genics.com or write to: Maryland Technology Incubator, 9700 Great Seneca Highway, Rockville, MD 20850.

Why open any kind of a DNA testing business? It's because the entrepreneur is at the forefront of a revolution in our concept of ancestry, diet, and medicines. Genes are tested to reveal how your body metabolizes medicine as well as food, and genes are tested for ancient ancestry or recent relationships such as paternity. Genes are tested for courtroom evidence.

So you have the choice of opening a DNA testing service focusing on diet, ancestry, skin care product matches, or medicine. You can have scientists contract with you to test genes for risk or relationships. Some companies claim to test DNA in order to determine whether the skin care products are right for your genetic signature. It goes beyond the old allergy tests of the eighties.

"Each of us is a unique organism, and for the first time in human history, genetic research is confirming that one diet is not optimum for everyone," says Abramson. Because your genes differ from someone else's, you process food and supplements in a unique way. Your ancestry is unique also.

Do you want to open a business that tunes nutrition to meet the optimum health needs of each person? If so, you need to contract with scientists to do the testing. If you have no science background, it would be an easier first step to open a business that tests DNA only for ancestry and contract with university laboratories who know about genes and ancestry.

Your client would receive a report on only the ancestry. This means the maternal and/or paternal sequences. For a woman it's the mtDNA that's tested. You're testing the maternal lineages. It's ancient and goes back thousands of years. For the man, you can have a lab test the Y-chromosome, the paternal lineages and the mtDNA, the maternal lineages.

What you supply your clients with is a printout report and explanation of the individual's sequences and mtDNA group called the haplogroup and/or the Y-chromosome ancestral genetic markers. For a male, you can test the Y-chromosome and provide those markers, usually 25 markers and the mtDNA. For a woman, you can only test the mtDNA, the maternal line for haplogroup letter and what is called the HVS-1 and HVS-2 sequences. These sequences show the maternal lineages back thousands of years. To get started, look at the Web sites and databases of all the companies that test for ancestry using DNA.

What most of the DNA testing entrepreneurs have in common is that they can do business online. People order the DNA testing kit online. The companies send out a DNA testing kit. The client sends back DNA to a lab to be tested. The process does not involve any blood drawing to test for ancestry. Then the company sends a report directly to the customer about what the DNA test revealed solely in regard to ancient ancestry—maternal or paternal lines.

Reports include the possible geographic location where the DNA sequences originated. Customers usually want to see the name of an actual town, even though towns didn't exist 10,000 years ago when the sequences might have arisen. The whole genome is not tested, only the few ancestral markers, usually 500 base pairs of genes. Testing DNA for ancestry does not have anything to do with testing genes for health risks because only certain genes are tested—genes related to ancestry. And all the testing is done at a laboratory, not at your online business.

If you're interested in a career in genetics counseling and wish to pursue a graduate degree in genetics counseling, that's another career route. For information, contact The American Board of Genetic Counseling. Sometimes social workers with some coursework in biology take a graduate degree in genetic counseling since it combines counseling skills with training in genetics and in interpreting genetics tests for your clients.

## The American Board of Genetic Counseling.

9650 Rockville Pike
Bethesda, MD 20814-3998
Phone: (301) 571-1825
FAX: (301) 571-1895
http://www.abgc.net/

Below is a list of several DNA-testing companies. Some of these companies test DNA only for ancestry. Other companies listed below test genes for personalized medicine and nutrigenomics, and some companies test for nutrigenomics, pharmacogenetics, and ancestry.

You'll also find several companies listed that only test the DNA of animals. So you have a choice of testing DNA for a variety of purposes, for testing human DNA only, or for testing animal DNA. And the applications for testing genetic signatures are growing, since this science is still in its infancy in regard to applications of genetic and genomic testing.

**Roots for Real**
http://www.rootsforreal.com
address: PO Box 43708
London W14 8WG UK

**Family Tree DNA—Genealogy by Genetics, Ltd.**
World Headquarters
1919 North Loop West, Suite 110 Houston, Texas 77008, USA
info@FamilyTreeDNA.com
http://www.familytreedna.com/

**Oxford Ancestors**
Oxford Ancestors, London,
http://www.oxfordancestors.com/

**AncestrybyDNA, DNAPrint genomics, Inc.**
900 Cocoanut Ave, Sarasota, FL 34236. USA
Tel: 941-366-3400 Fax: 941-952-9770 Web site: http://www.
ancestrybydna.com/

**GeneTree DNA Testing Center**
2495 South West Temple
Salt Lake City, UT 84115
Toll Free: (888) 404-GENE
Phone: (801) 461-9757
Fax: (801) 461-9761, http://www.genetree.com/

**Trace Genetics LLC**
P.O. Box 2010
Davis, California 95617
info@tracegenetics.com
http://www.tracegenetics.com/aboutus.html

**Predictive Genomics for Personalized Medicine including Nutrigenomics**
**AlphaGenics Inc.**

9700 Great Seneca Highway
Rockville, Maryland 20850
Email: info@alpha-genics.com
http://www.alpha-genics.com/index.php
## Genovations™
Great Smokies Diagnostic Laboratory/Genovations™
63 Zillicoa Street
Asheville, NC 28801 USA
http://www.genovations.com/
## Centre for Human Nutrigenomics
http://www.nutrigenomics.nl/
According to its Web site, "The Centre for Human NutriGenomics aims at establishing an international centre of expertise combining excellent pre-competitive research and high quality (post)graduate training on the interface of genomics, nutrition and human health."
**Nutrigenomics Links**: http://nutrigene.4t.com/nutrigen.htm
## Veterinary DNA Testing
## Veterinary Genetics Laboratory
University of California, Davis
One Shields Avenue
Davis, CA 95616-8744
http://www.vgl.ucdavis.edu/
According to their Web site, "The Veterinary Genetics Laboratory is internationally recognized for its expertise in parentage verification and genetic diagnostics for animals. VGL has provided services to breed registries, practitioners, individual owners and breeders since 1955." The Veterinary Genetics Laboratory performs contracted DNA testing.
Alpaca/Llama
Beefalo
Cat
Cattle
Dog
Elk
Goat
Horse
Sheep

DNA Testing of Dogs and Horses:
VetGen, 3728 Plaza Drive, Suite 1, Ann Arbor, Michigan, 48108 USA
http://www.vetgen.com/

We read numerous ways that you can use your training in family or public history and genealogy journalism to preserve the documents, records, and photos of different immigrant groups, seek internships or start your own online family history research or videography businesses. Now let's look at heritage through the Web sites and online databases of various social and family history area studies, groups, and genealogy sites and publications.

# 7

# *Preserving the Family History of Many Different Immigrant Groups*

For the Baltic Sea nations, there's an excellent site on Basic Registers in the Baltic countries at: http://www.kada.lt/regno2001/presentations.php. Whatever area studies you apply to family and social or public history research, there's almost always a niche or hidden corner of business that makes excellent use of training in family history/genealogy research techniques, writing, and languages. You can include studies of the future along with studies of the past, ethnography, and area studies and behavior. This niche includes trend research. You might also consider working for think tanks or developing your own similar services linking with businesses or libraries.

## Finland

The Finnish American Heritage Center (FAHA) has the distinction of housing the most comprehensive Finnish-American archival collection in the world. The mission of the FAHA is to collect and preserve the multifaceted history of North American Finns. Check out its archive with more than 20,000 items at the Finnish American Heritage Center at: http://www.finlandia.edu/fahc.html, including old newspapers. Excellent sources of information on individuals are newspaper articles on Finnish-Americans.

In the past, the law of inheritance focused Finnish genealogy on legal matters. Special provisions made genealogical research necessary. Today, you also can start your ancestor search with the Genealogical Society of Finland at: http://www.genealogia.fi/indexe.htm. It's in English and includes articles on the Finnish communities in various US cities, including grave markers.

The site also offers links to church records, parishes, libraries, family indexes, research directories, societies, mailing lists, other genealogical societies, photo galleries, biographical indexes, abbreviations, and personal names. The site also has a database on men who didn't report for military service without reason. Check out their article on Karelians. The Genealogical Research Agency Radix is situated in Turku, Finland, but its activities cover the whole of Finland.

Also contact The Institute of Migration at: http://130.232.32.230/index.php. Click on the site's English translation icon. The Institute of Migration researches, compiles, stores, and documents ethnic research and migration materials relating to Finland's international and internal migration and serves as a major resource site for genealogists. Another excellent online database is the Finnish Genealogy site at: http://www.canadianfriendsoffinland.ca/genfin.htm. For information on Finnish immigration to the USA, try the Suomen Sukututkimusseura at: http://www.genealogia.fi/. The site is in Finnish. It also lists cemeteries where ancestors from the Finnish immigrations to the USA are buried.

These cemeteries include the following areas in the USA: Savo Cemetery (Savo Township, Brown County, South Dakota); Finnish Apostolic Lutheran Cemetery (Savo Township, Brown County, South Dakota); Toledo Cemetery (Toledo, Lewis County, Washington); Eglon Cemetery (Kingston, Kitsap County, Washington); Winlock Cemetery (Winlock, Lewis County, Washington). Lisätty hautausmaaluetteloita (USA): St. Paul's Lutheran Cemetery, Moe Township, Douglas County, Minnesota; Holmes City Lake Finnish Apostolic Lutheran Church Cemetery, Moe Township, and Douglas County, Minnesota.

You can find genealogy articles and links at the Sukututkimus Web site at: http://www.engr.uvic.ca/~syli/geneo/. Also see the article on *Changing Uses of Genealogical Research in Finland* at: http://www.genealogia.fi/emi/art/indexe.htm. Also try the Scandinavian and Nordic Genealogy site at: http://www.cyberpursuits.com/gen/scandlist.asp. See the Evangelical Lutheran Church of Finland site at: http://www.evl.fi/english/. The Swedish Finn Historical Society is at: http://sfhs.eget.net/welcome.html, since so many Swedes migrated to Finland. The Finns on the Titanic site is at: http://www.migrationinstitute.fi/index_e.php.

You'll find an excellent article on Finnish surnames at: http://www.genealogia.fi/emi/art/article104e.htm. For example, an excerpt from the article states, "The most prevalent form has been the shortening of the Finnish patronymic, usually by clipping either a prefix or suffix. This process abbreviated the surname in the interests of American phonology yet retained for it an unmistakable Finnish identity. Thus, by dropping the prefix, Kaunismäki, Kauramäki,

Koivumäki, Myllymäki, Palomäki, Lamminmäki, Rautamäki, Peramäki, Hako-mäki, Kortesmäki, Hautamäki, Niinimäki, Katajamäki, etc., became simply Maki;[2] or then again, by deleting the suffix, Mäkelä, Mäkinen, Mäkitalo, Mäki-vuori, etc., were similarly transformed into Maki." The article explains in foot-note [2] that, "The Finnish vowels ä and ö are inevitably rendered jo this country as the English a and o. The Finnish v and w are interchangeable."

Also see the publication, *American Speech. A Quarterly of Linguistic Usage*, Vol-ume XIV, p. 33–38, 1939. A patronymic is a personal name based on the name of one's father. A personal name based on the name of one's mother is a matro-nymic. The present trend in Finland is from Swedish to Finnish patronymics. Read the article titled, Surnames in Finland on the threshold of the new millen-nium by Sirkka Paikkala at: http://www.genealogia.fi/nimet/nimi82s.htm.

According to Kate Monk's Onomostikon at: http://www.gaminggeeks.org/ Resources/KateMonk/Europe-Scandinavia/Finland/Surnames.htm "Originally Finns had only one forename followed by a patronymic taken from the genitive form of their father's first name with the suffix 'poika'—son, or 'tytär'—daugh-ter. For example, Jussi Pentinpoika—Jussi, Pentti's son, or Ulla Pentin-tytär—Ulla, Pentti's daughter."

There's a Web site researching the Saari surname at: http://members.aol.com/ dssaari/saarinam.htm and a tutorial on Finnish surnames along with farm names. The Finnish surname Korela Web well-researched site is at: http://www.cs.tut.fi/ ~jkorpela/korpela.html.

You can consult the Population Register Center of Finland, or look at the Web site of the international Porvoo Group that seeks to support the deployment of electronic identity in Europe. The Porboo Group's site (in English) is at: http://www.vaestorekisterikeskus.fi/vrk/home.nsf/pages/ 20710B02C6C5B894C2256D1A0048E290.

According to its Web site, "The Porvoo Group is a pro-active, European-level electronic identity 'interest group', widely recognized as a significant and relevant contributor to informed public dialogue in this area."

To register a child born in the United States (to Finnish parents/ Finnish par-ent) to the population registry in Finland, the parent would ask the Finnish Embassy in Washington DC or the Consulate General in New York or Los Ange-les (http://www.finland.org/doc/fi/usamap/ to send the parent a "birth registra-tion" form.

Also see the pdf file titled, *250 Years of Population Statistics in Finland* by Mauri Nieminen, Statistics Finland, Population Statistics, Työpajakatu 13, Hels-inki, Finland. The Web site is at: http://www.stat.fi/isi99/proceedings/arkisto/

varasto/niem1020.pdf. For other population statistics, also see Register Based Statistics Production, Statistics Finland, by Riitta Harala. The site is at: http://www.stat.fi/tk/ys/roundtable/sefdrha.html.

Development of electronic government transactions in Finland site is at http://europa.eu.int/idabc/en/document/966/334. The site notes, "Many transactions between the government and its citizens are largely automated using databases and electronic data transfer." In 1998, the Finnish *government* decided to create a generic system for electronic identification, data transfer encryption and digital signatures for electronic transactions.

The Population Register Center offers PKI-based certification services, where a citizen can buy an electronic identification card the size of a credit card. The private key and certificates are installed on the smart card, see http://www.fineid.fi/. If you're looking to the future of electronic genealogy, it's going to follow government and banking authentication tools for population registers, passenger lists, migrations, and other historical information. Finland is advanced in developing technology for electronic identification authentication.

Check out the future and development of electronic government transactions in Finland at: http://europa.eu.int/idabc/en/document/966/334. According to an E Government News site dated Sept. 19 2002 titled, Development of electronic government transactions in Finland, it states that according to Olavi Köngäs, Chief Information Officer, Finnish Ministry of Finance, "Finland's strength in electronic government lies in a good and efficiently employed information infrastructure. "In developing the infrastructure, it is essential that the citizens rely on confidentiality, protection of privacy and high standard of information when administration handles personal information.

According to surveys, citizens' have good trust in government information processing. The government continues to enhance its information security in order to keep this trust." How do you feel about your genealogy, population registration, or even the futuristic concept of your DNA sequences on a smart card in your own country? With visionary technology, balance is the key.

## Finnish Genes and Genealogy

Check out the Discover magazine article, *Finland's Fascinating Genes, Learning Series: Genes, Race, and Medicine [Part 2]*, According to the article, "The people in this land of lakes and forests are so alike that scientists can filter out the genes that contribute to heart disease, diabetes, and asthma," by Jeff Wheelwright, DISCOVER Vol. 26 No. 04 | April 2005 | Biology & Medicine.

The UCLA study also might help you learn more about your Finn-American medical heritage. For example, Karelians from Eastern Finland and Karelia are being compared in studies to people from Western Finland to see whether or not there are any genetic predispositions in the Eastern Finns and Karelians compared to the Western Finns. The article notes that Karelians and Eastern Finns with short arms and legs may have genes for different genetic predispositions compared to Western Finns with longer arms and legs, but all this is currently under study. Gene hunters described in the spring 1999 UCLA magazine article at: http://www.magazine.ucla.edu/year1999/spring99_03.html and http://www.magazine.ucla.edu/year1999/spring99_03_02.html state that Leena Peltonen, of the world's foremost geneticists, helped to put Finland on the map as a global powerhouse in genetic research. She hopes to do the same for UCLA.

Finland has a small population, isolation, and less immigration than other European nations. The government kept meticulous tax records. As a result, Finland has medical records on individuals that go back more than three hundred years. With carefully written medical and genealogical records, it's one way to trace familial health and ailments as well as family surnames. According to the UCLA 1999 magazine article, "Finland also has a system of free, high-quality health care in which patients trust their doctors and are highly willing to participate in medical research."

According to the UCLA magazine article, "In the 20 years that she has been studying genetic defects, Peltonen has identified no fewer than 18 genes related to such common disorders as multiple sclerosis and schizophrenia as well as more obscure diseases like AGT, a rare and horrific brain disorder found almost only among children in Finland."

In 1998, Peltonen localized the gene for familial combined hyperlipidemia, or FCHL, in a group of Finnish families. According to the UCLA magazine article, "the condition leads to the early onset of coronary-artery disease, which remains one of the leading causes of death in the industrialized world."

Check out the UCLA Human Genetics Web site at: http://www.genetics.ucla.edu/home/future.htm. Or if you're in the Los Angeles area, you can hear guest speakers presented by the Department of Human Genetics, David Geffen School of Medicine at UCLA. In your own area, go the many free lectures on genetics open to the public and learn what scientists are talking about in the fields of human genetic variation, population structure, or temperature sensation.

How can you (as a general consumer) apply what scientists have learned yesterday to benefit humanity today? For example, Peltonen's findings on FCHL coincided with a study by UCLA geneticist Jake Lusis, who localized the same gene using a mouse model. "The two scientists, who only learned of each other's research when each published a paper in the same issue of Nature Genetics, are now working together," according to the UCLA magazine article of 1999 titled *Gene Hunter*. You'll find the entire article on the Web site at: http://www.magazine.ucla.edu/year1999/spring99_03.html.

Check out this 1999 article as well as the more recent April 2005 issue of *Discover* magazine article which also describes Peltonen's more recent work at UCLA in genetic research and particularly with Finnish genes. You'll find that the Internet's Web can act as a springboard to motivate you as a consumer with no science background to read about what is being done in the evolving field of genetic testing.

If several scientists can collaborate, so can a world of consumers. Your goal would be to find out how to interpret and apply the results of any genetic tests to improve your quality of life and health. You don't need a science degree to move into new areas. Scientists are doing this daily.

Consumers need to observe the proliferation of information available online and in libraries. Federal research and the Human Genome Project have been mapping human genes since 1990. Ever since the human genome code was cracked in 2000, a flood of publications, articles, books, DNA testing companies, DNA testing kits, and DNA-driven genealogy services proliferated. What's offered as a result of testing is information. For every gene hunter, there is or could be a consumer seeking practical applications of such research.

Genetics is about preventive medicine. As a consumer, you've got breadth. Scientists have depth. They are only beginning to collaborate with one another and get the breadth that general consumers always had without much science knowledge. Genetics is a horizontal expression of a vertical desire. The consumer represents the horizontal breadth of knowledge.

The scientist's hierarchy sits amidst the vertical tower of scientific terminology. It's about language and communication as much as it's about science. Consumers want tests interpreted in plain language so they can readily apply the results to change their lifestyle.

Do scientists working in different disciplines really collaborate with one another? They have to now that the consumer is involved in the practical side of genetics—information dissemination. Collaboration means understanding how to interpret your test results and apply the research to what nourishes your body.

## Finnish and Baltic Genealogy Research Starting Points
## List of Items to Research:

For more information on Finnish ethnology and ethnography, see the Information Center (Centre) of Finno-Ugric Peoples. The Web site is at: http://www.suri.ee/index.html.

At the Web site you can learn about the "The Fenno-Ugria Foundation, established by a group of Estonian scientists, politicians, economists in Tallinn in 1927 with the aim of supporting the organizing of Finno-Ugric cultural congresses and promoting relations between Estonia and other Finno-Ugrian peoples."

**Click on the link to the** Finno-Ugric Peoples' Consultative Committee. There are links to its statutes and rules. Members include the following ethnicities: Erzyas, Estonians, Finns, Hungarians, Ingrian Finns, Ingrians, Karelians, Khants, Komis, Mansis, Maris, Mokshas, Nenetses, Permian Komis, Saamis, Tver Karelians, Udmurts, and Vepsians. Observers include: Livonians, and Setos.

## Start with Dates

1.  Dates: Several hundred thousand Finnish immigrants arrived in the USA between 1880 and 1920, settling throughout the country.

2.  Look for census documents with names, dates, and places when personal history information from relatives runs dry. Trace women's as well as men's lineages by looking at birth, marriage, and death certificates.

3.  Family Bibles provide notes and names. Ask living relatives for any information, photos, or other memorabilia.

4.  Ask for naturalization papers and petitions for the intention to be naturalized as well as final papers after naturalization.

5.  Visit cemeteries and ask from sexton's records.

6.  Were any letters kept from older relatives or from Finland or any other former country? Many Finnish people came to Finland from Sweden or had Swedish names.

7.  Do you have any old passports?

8.  Get maps and find addresses of churches. Contact churches for a Parish Membership Transfer Certificate. In Finnish, it's called a Muuttokirja. If your ancestor belonged to a Swedish-speaking parish, ask for in Swedish a Utflyttnings betyg.

9.  In the US, use city directories and census for various decades for data on birth, marriage, and death information or addresses in the case of city directories. These vital records are indexed by state, but were originally recorded by city or town. You'll find these city or town records indexed by county. In the US, marriage records were the earliest to be indexed. The western states didn't organize birth and death records until the beginning of the 20th century.

10. Contact your State Department of Health and your State Vital Records Office. Ask to purchase a certificate. If you need various years searched, the offices usually charge a fee. Some states have privacy laws.

11. Look for various states' and counties' microfilm and microfiche copies of vital records at the Family History Library in Salt Lake City. The library's Web site is at: www.familysearch.org. Or write to them at: Church of Jesus Christ of Latter-Day Saints the: Family History Library, 35 N West Temple, Salt Lake City, UT 84150. Phone (801) 240-2331.

12. Learn to read old handwriting. Before 1920, most vital records in the US were kept in hand-written ledgers. If you're searching in Finland, you'd need to find someone who reads Finnish unless you can take a language course at least to get reading ability. In the US, the handwritten indexes are typed onto a certificate.

13. How many ways were your ancestor's named spelled? Clerks who have to type certificates reading from misspelled handwritten entries and poor writing may take a long time. At least at the Family History Library, copies of the originals may already be on microfilm or microfiche and easily printed out.

14. Search the census records. Those records may have the names of members of a family unknown to living descendants. Also names on pages just after or just before the name you want may also be relatives. Certain censuses list everyone in the household. US Federal Census records for 1880, 1900, 1910 and 1920 do list everyone in the same residence.

15. In Finland, you can access the national registry. In the US, Finnish immigrant names (and names of other nationalities) are microfilmed and available in the genealogy sections of some local libraries, State Libraries / Archives, university libraries. First try the Family History Library in Salt Lake City, Utah and LDS branch libraries. Then look at the files or books with genealogy names on loan from the National Archives.

16. On census records, look for full names, ages, genders, relationships, number of children, name of the mother, the state or country of birth for the head of household and the name and country of birth for the parents, year of immigration. You'll also find categorized whether the immigrant is an alien, petitioned or naturalized. You'll find the head of household's occupation; language spoken if not English. If you need phonetic indexes, use the partial Soundex index. It's available for the years1880 and 1910. A complete Soundex index is available for the years 1900 and 1920.

17. What indexes are most likely to contain the records of Scandinavian, particularly Finnish immigrants? It's the various state Censuses. Check them on microfilm at the Family History Library, Salt Lake City, Utah. Most Finns went to Minnesota, Michigan, North and South Dakota, Colorado, and Wisconsin. Some went to Canada. **The Family History Library** lists the following **Censuses**:

    1. Minnesota: 1875, 1885, 1895, 1905. Complete.

    2. Michigan: 1884 & 1894. Only a few counties' records exist.

    3. North Dakota: 1915 & 1925. Complete.

    4. South Dakota: 1885 & 1895. Partial census. 1905, 1915, 1925, 1935, 1945. Complete. State Historical Society.

    5. Colorado: 1885.

    6. Wisconsin: 1875, 1885, 1895, 1905. Complete.

    At the Family History library, you also can check the Canadian Census records as they have them on file open to the public for the years 1881, 1891 and 1901. Canada also put an individual's religion in the Census, whereas the US didn't include any affiliation.

18. Visit courts to find old US naturalization records processed before 1906. Look for your ancestor's Petition for Naturalization and/or Intention for

Naturalization. This petition contains the name of applicant, country of origin / monarch to whom allegiance was previously owed, and date of application. Check the records by county.

19. After 1900, numerous counties added more data on each applicant. Also after 1906, the district courts included places of birth, dates, physical descriptions, when and where the applicant first entered the US, the port; occupation, spouse, and children. Photos and comments went into the various district courts handling naturalization. Gradually, the county courts handed naturalization processing over to the district courts.

20. New England towns kept records as well as district courts. There's a master index dated from 1791–1906 for Maine, New Hampshire, Vermont, Massachusetts, Connecticut and Rhode Island.

21. Check county draft registrations for the World Wars. You have 3,000 counties to paw through, but luckily only two or less draft boards—unless your relative lived in a large city. Registration for World War 1 required US citizen and foreign males living in the US to register for the draft on three specified dates. Look for registrations for the draft on June 5 1917, September 12 1917 and September 12 1918. The birthdates of the men fell between 1873 and 1900.

22. What you're searching for are the registration forms. On these forms you'll find listed full name, birth date, birth place, citizenship, residence, age, occupation, employer, name of relative and address of relative to contact in case of emergency, some physical description, signature, date and any other registration number(s).

23. Finnish immigration to the US at its highest count coincided with World War 1 draft registrations. If you locate the registration cards or forms, at least you'll have a birth date and place of birth.

24. You'll know whether the ancestor had US citizenship at that time or was classified as an 'alien' living in the US. Since the applicant had to put down who to contact in case of emergency—usually a relative, you might be able to track the name of a parent or wife and that relative's address.

25. Then you can turn to a city directory as well as a census to compare the information for that date. When you see someone's city of birth on a regis-

tration card, you have a lead when visiting that place in whatever country to track down other descendants. For example, if the city listed is in Finland or Sweden (or any other country) you can visit that town and begin research at the local parish.

26. Church records of marriages offer new information. Before visiting the National Archives of the particular country, first track what microfiche or microfilm copies are retained in the Family History Library, Salt Lake City, Utah (or any of the Family History Library branches).

27. Check US passport applications. They are available to the public up to the year 1925. Scandinavian, particularly Finnish immigrants may have obtained passports to visit the old country.

28. If you are searching for passport applications for other countries, the US Federal Government began issuing passports in 1790. Many 18<sup>th</sup> century residents visited their former country, particularly England and Western Europe. Passports actually were not required to go back and forth to the 'old' country until World War 1 began.

29. When you check out passport history, in 1900 information on passport applications required full names, birth dates, places of birth, dates of entrance to the US, date of naturalization, physical descriptions of hair and eye color, destinations. You even had to explain why you were going to another country and had to list spouses, children, where you worked, and provide photographs. So you can see all this historical information up to the year 1925, which is now public information.

30. Use information on passport applications to locate church parishes in the old country. For other religions, check records of religious schools and houses of worship with the information obtained from 1790 to 1925 passport applications.

31. Indexes: For Finland and Sweden, check the index for 1906–1925, unless you know your relatives came from Sweden with an early immigration to New England or Virginia.

32. A few Swedes settled in New England in the 17<sup>th</sup> century. In checking Finnish names, the index lists applicants by the first two alphabet letters of a last name. However, the Finnish passport applications index lists the year of

application and passport number. The index leaves out the person's address and state. To save time, all these indexes mentioned above for Finland already have been microfilmed at the Family History Library, Salt Lake City, Utah.

33. Look for maps of parishes. In the parishes—Scandinavians and Finnish peoples registered vital records with their home parish of the Lutheran Church. Records date from the late $17^{th}$ century. You can obtain microfilmed records from the mid $19^{th}$ century from the parishes. What you're looking for is the *Rippikirjat.* Translated, you want to see the "Main Books," also known as the "Communion Books." These are Lutheran Church records that began to appear early in the $17^{th}$ century.

34. Indexing: The "Main Books" are organized by **farm name** first with the name of the **owner of each farm** listed second followed by any other resident of the farm listed by relationship. Each farm is then indexed by the name of each **village**, and the records are accurate, particularly for the 1600s.

35. Other parish records. You'll see registration for births, baptisms, confirmations, banns, marriages, membership transfers, parish minutes, deaths, burials, and detailed information on parish business. Once through that, you have the military and court records that have been microfilmed in Finland.

36. Don't forget tax and property records, notary records on farm ownership, and whatever else has been microfilmed and then transferred to electronic databases. Check to see whether any census data has been put on smart cards or in electronic databases.

37. Research the records of other religious groups living in Finland. Was your Finnish ancestor a member of the Russian Orthodox Church in Finland or the Finnish Jewish community? Jewish community records in synagogues and religious schools date back to the mid $19^{th}$ century.

38. Recorded Finnish Jewish history began in the first half of the 19th century. Jewish soldiers (called cantonists) that had served in the Russian Army stationed in Finland continued to live in Finland. Note any Finnish residential records that followed the decree of 1858, under which discharged Russian soldiers and their families, without regard to their religion, were encouraged to live in Finland. On Jan. 25, 1782, the government passed a special regula-

tion so the Jews could possess synagogues in Stockholm, Göteborg, and Malmöhus.

39. Many Jews had Swedish names. In 1862 a law concerning passports was enacted in Finland. Note that a few retired Jewish soldiers and sailors from Sweden and Russia lived in Finland. Some adopted Finnish names, and others kept their Swedish, Germanic, Yiddish, or Russian surnames. See the Helsinki Jewish Community's site at: http://www.jchelsinki.fi/home.htm#hometext and The Jewish Encyclopedia for Finland site at: http://www.jewishencyclopedia.com/view.jsp?artid=147&letter=F. The sites are in English.

40. During the Finnish-Russian War of 1939–40 (the Winter War), Finnish Jews fought alongside their non-Jewish fellow countrymen.

41. During the Finnish-Russian War of 1941–44, in which Finnish Jews also took part, Finland and Nazi-Germany were co-belligerents. Despite strong German pressure, the Finnish Government *refused* to take action against Finnish nationals of Jewish origin who thus continued to *enjoy full civil rights* throughout the War. There are many anecdotes from this period, concerning, among others, the presence of a Jewish prayer tent on the Russian front under the Nazi's noses and the food help given to Russian-Jewish POWs by the Jewish communities of Finland. See "A Short History of Finnish Jewry" Web site at: http://www.jchelsinki.fi/history.htm. Also view the Jewish Community of Helsinki, Finland Web site at: http://www.jchelsinki.fi/home.htm#hometext.

42. Russian Orthodox Church records also have some Finnish members. About one percent of the Finnish population follows the Russian Orthodox faith. In addition, thousands of Karelian (Eastern Finnish) immigrants moved into Finland when Karelia in Eastern Finland became part of Russia. There also are some Estonians living in Finland. Most Finns belong to the Lutheran Church. Also look at records of other religious groups and military service records. Read the records in various houses of worship.

43. Microfiche information on Finnish records dating to 1900 is at the Family History Library, Salt Lake City, Utah. Lutheran Parish Records microfilmed at the Family History Library listed below are available at the Family History Library, Salt Lake City, Utah for the following Finnish surnames:

Bötom / Karijoki
Eno
Forssa
Ilmajoki
Joroinen / Jorois
Jorois / Joroinen
Jämsä Kaarlela / Karleby
Kalajoki
Kangasala
Kangaslampi
Kangasniemi
Kannus / Yli-kannus
Karijoki / Bötom
Karjala / Mynämäki
Karjalohja
Karkkila
Karinainen
Karleby / Kaarlela
Karuna / Sauvo
Karvia
Kauhajoki
Kauvatsa
Kemi (rural)
Kivennapa
Kivijärvi
Kjulo / Köyliö
Korsnäs
Kuhmo(oinen)
Kuopio

Kuortane
Kurikka
Kymi
Kälviä
Kärsämäki
Kärkölä
Köyliö / Kjulo
Laihia
Laitila / Letala
Lammi
Lapinlahti
Lappajärvi
Lappee
Lappfjärd / Lapväärtti
Lappi (Turku-Pori)
Lapvärtti / Lappfjärd
Lapua Larsmo / Luoto
Lavia
Lemi
Lempäälä
Leppävirta
Lestivirta
Letala / Laitila
Lieto / Lundo
Liminka
Lohja
Lohtaja
Loimaa / Metsämaa
Loppi

Lundo / Lieto
Luoto / Larsmo
Längelmäki
Marttila
Masku
Merikarvia / Sastmola
Merimasku
Metsämaa / Loimaa
Mietoinen
Mouhijärvi
Muhos
Multia
Mynämäki / Karjala
Mäntsälä
Mäntyharju
Naantali
Nivala
Pirttikylä / Pörtom
Pörtom / Pirttikylä
Sastmola / Merikarvia
Sauva / Karuna
Solf / Sulva
Sulva / Solf
Tohmajärvi
Vimpeli / Vindala
Vindala / Vimpeli
Virrat
Yli-kannus
/ Kannus

If you're looking for an expert team of genealogists specializing in the US, Canada, Finland, Denmark, Sweden, Norway, and England, I highly recommend Family Sleuths, PO Box 526163 Salt Lake City, Utah 84152-6163.

The above information found in the Family History Library, Salt Lake City, also is explained in much further detail with excellent resources, such as a link to the <u>Kennecott Utah Copper Corporation Employment Records: 1909–1920 in Bingham Canyon, Utah</u> containing a complete listing of all Finns and Scandinavians on the Family Sleuths genealogy Web site at: http://www.familysleuths.com.

The link at: http://www.migrationinstitute.fi/db/articles/art.php?artid=9 #Journal#Journal takes you to the site of the Institute of Migration. There you can see the list of surnames from the Family History Library, Salt Lake City, and also buy the book, *The Journal of Pastor Johan Wilhelm Eloheimo from the Evangelical Lutheran Parishes from Calumet, Michigan and Ironwood, Michigan.*

You can order the various Finnish genealogy books at the Family Sleuths Web site. The site also contains an excellent bibliography of books you can order on Finnish genealogy research and also a link to a Journal of Baptisms, Confirmations, Marriages and Deaths: 1891–1910 in the States of Michigan, Wisconsin, Wyoming and Idaho and Others. I highly recommend their research, Web links with articles on genealogy research, and bibliography if you're interested in Finnish genealogy. They have research material explained and books available on subjects ranging from collected employment cards of Finns to parish addresses.

## Resources on Finnish Genealogy

### Finnish, Scandinavian and U.S. Research
http://www.feefhs.org/FI/FRG-FS.HTML

### Family Sleuths
http://www.familysleuths.com

### Finnish Genealogy Group
http://www.feefhs.org/MISC/frgfinmn.html

### Institute of Migration
http://www.migrationinstitute.fi/db/articles/art.php?artid=9

## Finno-Ugric Peoples

*In a press release dated April 27, 2005, posted at the Information Center of Finno-Ugric Peoples at:* **http://www.suri.ee/press/eng/050427.html**, *members of the European Parliament passed an action plan to improve the situation of Finno-Ugric minorities in Russia. According to the media release: "On 26th of April, members of the Finno-Ugric Forum at the European Parliament approved an action plan to help Finno-Ugric minorities of Russia to improve their situation.*

*"Pointing at the goals set by the World Congress of Finno-Ugric Peoples, the action plan provides for measures to improve the linguistic and cultural situation of these peoples, bringing it into accord with international standards. The Finno-Ugric Forum urges the official bodies of European Union to enter a dialogue with the Russian authorities on the issues of linguistic and cultural rights of Finno-Ugric minori-*

*ties. It also stipulates for cultural and youth exchanges and co-operation on the grass-root level.*

"The Forum decided to send its delegation to the next meeting of the Consultative Committee of the Finno-Ugric Peoples scheduled for this November in Syktyvkar, the capital city of the Komi Republic (Russia). Members of the European Parliament also agreed to draw a resolution on the continuing violation of human rights in the Republic of Mari El and in the territories of Finno-Ugric peoples of Russia in general. The Finno-Ugric Forum includes 44 delegates of the European Parliament, mostly from Finland, Hungary and Estonia."

For more information, you can read the appendix: English text of the Action Plan approved by the Finno-Ugric Forum of the European Parliament (passed 26.04.2005 in Brussels) at the center's Web site at: http://www.suri.ee/press/eng/050427ap.html. Additional information is at: http://www.suri.ee

## Back Door Genealogy

Due to changing borders, a popular back-door method of finding Baltic genealogy records is to contact *English-speaking* real estate agents and lawyers or students' associations. The real estate agents sell online Latvian, Lithuanian, Estonian, Finnish, Swedish, German, or Polish houses to Americans and also search property, tax, and court records.

There also are student associations at various universities that have numerous bilingual students from Baltic countries with academic contacts such as librarians and government archive researchers. Also contact the International Lawyers' Association, Finland at: http://www.forum-legal.com/ilaf/ if you want to search court records.

Contact the Association of Finnish Culture and Identity at: http://www.suomalaisuudenliitto.fi/sl-english.htm. There's a Baltic and Finnish Student Association at Indiana University. Click on http://webdb.iu.edu/InternationalServices/scripts/ois/record.cfm?id=673 for the updated email address. Baltic students speak English and can screen and put you in touch with real estate agents, lawyers, archivists, librarians, and genealogists in the various countries.

## Tracing Baltic Genealogy

Let's look at tracing family history online for some of the other nations bordering the Baltic Sea. A few centuries ago, 70 Baltic Sea cities formed the most dominating trading bloc in the world resulting in genealogy 'logs' archived in Swedish or Finnish or in a common 'records' language—Russian or German.

If you come from any of the lands bordering the Baltic Sea, start your ancestry search with the microfiche of Latvian, Lithuanian, Estonian, Swedish, Finnish, Polish or German records and sources at the LDS Family History Library Center or any of its branches in the US, Canada, Britain, Australia, and New Zealand. The Family History Library Center online is at: http://www.genhomepage.com/FHC/fhc.html.

At the LDS Family History Library Center, you'll find a microfiche file for each Baltic nation. Other online sites include the East European Genealogical Society at: http://www.eegsociety.org/Index.html or the Federation of East European Family History Societies. Both societies have maps, surname, ethnic, religious, and village databases. Check out their archives, and the Federation's journal. Their Baltic genealogy sites and databases include BLITZ (Baltic-Russian Research from St. Petersburg), Dags' Latvian Home Page, Latvia Jewish Special Interest Group (Latvia SIG), Lietuvos Bajoru Karaliskoji Sajunga (LBKS)—Royal Lithuanian Nobility Society, and the Lithuanian-American Genealogy Society

# 8

# *Latvia*

Many Latvian genealogy records are in German. The microfiche of Latvian resources at the LDS Family History Library Center contains a section on where to begin your search in Riga, which includes the Central State *History* Archives called the Centralais Valsts, the Central State Archives, the Lutheran Church, the Catholic Church, and the Orthodox Church. In the other Baltic countries, you'd begin by writing to the same type of central state archives and various churches in each of the other countries bordering the Baltic.

Online, for Latvian genealogy research links, try Dags' Latvian Genealogy Page at: http://feefhs.org/BALTIC/LV/frg-dag.html. There are links to Latvian and Baltic genealogy search contacts such as the Roots Location List Data or addresses for searching church records.

If you want to search genealogy in Latvia, try Latvians Online at: http://latviansonline.com/index.php. and at: http://latviansonline.com/search/index.php. Also see Latvian Research at: http://maxpages.com/poland/Latvian Research. Check out at the site the Latvia Roots Location List Data, Ancestral File, International Genealogical Index (IGI), and Family Registry. These links include names of researchers working on a particular name. Materials are on microfiche.

## The Languages of Land Ownership

Genealogy records from around 1905 in Latvia actually separate the German nobility of Latvia and Estonia from the Latvian-speaking Baltic peoples. The 1905 police were mostly Czarist. German nobility owned most of the land in Latvia and Estonia in the 19th and early 20th century. In Latvia, the genealogy records witness the 1905 first socialist revolution in the Russian empire pitting poverty-stricken Baltic peasants against the German land owners.

Many genealogy records felt the impact of the riots that ended with thousands deported to Siberia. If you trace the maps of the wealthy manor houses and a variety of large buildings in Latvia, you'll see the property changing hands from the German nobility to the Latvian peasants around 1905.

You might be interested in researching land grants, tax records, deeds to property, and notary recordings to see whether your ancestors owned one of these manor houses or ended up in Siberia. A Trans-Siberian genealogy site actually exists at the Trans-Siberian Railway Forum (genealogy and railway history) at: http://www.transsib.ru/cgi-bin/UBB/ultimatebb.cgi?ubb=forum&f=4. For Latvian genealogy, contact Latvian Research at: http://maxpages.com/poland/Latvian_Research.

## Searching Female Genealogy

The Baltic lands have been putting their matriarchs on genealogical pedestals since ancient times, and genealogy folklore often follows women's maiden names aggrandized through folk songs and nature. Finns and Latvians have female presidents. The Latvian president is Vaira Vīķe-Freiberga, and the Finnish president is Tarja Halonen. Finland is the first European country to grant women the right to vote (1906). Genealogy is a part of the Māra—the material world and the feminine. In Latvia, genealogy incorporates *dievturība*, the folk religion of genealogy based on folk verses.

You'll find folkloric genealogy alive in the Baltic countries. Folkoric genealogy is about tracing your ancestry and surname origins based on the concept of young people taking advice from older people who get their wisdom from nature. The focus of family history research is that genealogy enriches *dievturība*.

*Dievturība* allows each individual to understand family folklore according to his own needs and abilities. All new information and research in the fields of genealogy, science, history, folklore and religion serve to further develop dievturība.

## Vintage Railroad Maps as a Guide to Genealogy

An old Livonian, Finnish, and Estonian proverb about the Baltic Sea peoples states, "*Genetically, they are related, and so are their railroads.*" So look at a vintage railroad map dated to the year that your relatives or clients lived there. To find a *detailed* old map of the Baltic countries, a great place to start is with former editions of Encyclopædia Britannica dated to the year of your ancestor's residence in one of the Baltic countries.

A good starting point with a map also is the Latvian GenWeb site at: http://www.rootsweb.com/~lvawgw/. At this site you'll see a link for a variety of resources.

John Bartholomew & Son, Ltd, Edinburgh, Scotland, published an excellent 9 ¾" by 7 ¼" *Baltic Railroad Map* that includes only three Baltic nations—Estonia, Latvia, and Lithuania. Those countries had been under Soviet rule since World War II. However, they were independent at the time of the map's publication in 1929.

If you want to learn about the cultural components or history of each country bordering the Baltic that once belonged to the Soviet Union, try the The Red Book of the Peoples of the Russian Empire. Click on various groups such as the Latvians (Livonians) at http://www.eki.ee/books/redbook/livonians.shtml or for special groups within Lithuania, such as the Tatars, try the link to the Polish or Lithuanian Tatars at: http://www.eki.ee/books/redbook/lithuanian_tatars.shtml.

In tracing family history, it's important that you find a vintage map like this one showing details of cities, small towns, railroads, steamship routes, and natural features. It's like finding a map of the old neighborhoods, streets, and houses.

A vintage map will show major cities where you can begin your search in the various halls of records in cities such as Riga, Latvia, Tallinn, Estonia, Jelgava, towns along the Dvina River, Kaunas, Rakwere, Port Kunda, Klaipeda, and other cities whose names have changed since the twenties. For example, Kaunas used to be called Kovno, Rakwere had been Vezenbert, and Klaipeda used to be called Memel.

Depending upon the era, Latvian genealogy records could be recorded in German, Russian or Latvian. Dundaga, Latvia, had been written in German, as Dondangen, and Mitau is now called Jelgava.

The eastern Baltic lands, Latvia, Lithuania, and Estonia witnessed a 1910 dialect struggle that ended with the development of standard national languages. As a result, some genealogy records are archived in the Russian language, even in Poland. Germany, Sweden, and Finland have genealogy records archived in the language of each country. Jewish genealogy records in Poland are recorded and archived in Russian.

# 9

# *Poland*

A mailing list of surnames for anyone researching genealogy in the former historical borders of Poland including Estonia, Latvia, Lithuania, East Prussia and other Eastern European areas is called PolandBorderSurnames-L. To subscribe to this list, click on their surnames link above and type the word subscribe in the message box or email: polandbordersurnames-l-request@rootsweb.com. Archived records may be in Russian or German rather than in Latvian, Estonian, or Lithuanian.

The Polish Genealogical Society of America's site is at: http://www.feefhs.org/POL/frg-pgsa.html. The site contains maps, ethnic and religious databases, a Polish cross-index, and a link to the Federation of East European Family History Societies.

**The Polish-Jewish genealogy** Web site is at: http://polishjews.org/. More than 3 million Jews lived in Poland in 1939. One of the provinces with a large Jewish population in Poland was Bialystock, and for genealogy research, an excellent travelogue, cultural, and genealogical history book, *Jewish Bialystok*, by Tomasz Wisniewski (see http://www.zchor.org/BIALISTO.HTM) lists surnames from tombstone rubbings and walking guides. Also, general Polish genealogy sources are at Distant Cousin.com at: http://distantcousin.com/Links/Polish.html. Also see the Web site titled New Poland Genealogy at: http://www.newpoland.com/genealogy.htm.

## Jewish Communities in Poland Today

View the Web site, Jewish Life in Poland Today at: http://www.diapozytyw.pl/en/site/zycie/po_1989/. The Ronald S. Lauder Foundation runs several cultural centers in Poland. They are located in Warsaw, Krakow, Lodz and Gdansk, and serve as centers for individuals interested in becoming acquainted with Jewish culture and religion.

According to the Web site, Poland today has two Jewish schools funded by the Lauder Foundation in Wroclaw and Warsaw. In Krakow, the first Jewish religious school, the Pardes Lauder Yeshiva, is open. Three publications for the Jewish audience are published: *Dos Yidishe Vort/Slowo zydowskie*, a bilingual, Polish-Jewish magazine published under the auspices of the Jewish Social and Cultural Association; the cultural and literary magazine *Midrasz*, and *Szterndlech*, which is for young children. There's also the Festival of Jewish culture, organized yearly in Kraków. It includes lectures and concerts, as well as courses in Yiddish and dance, and workshops on calligraphy and traditional paper cutouts.

Check out the Immigration and Ships' Passenger Lists Research Guide at: http://home.att.net/~arnielang/ship05.html#search. Also click on the link to the National Archives if your relatives arrived in New York. The National Archives has passenger arrival records for the port of New York dating from 1820 to 1957. When there are no more written records, perhaps you can find a long-lost descendant of cousins or great grandparents by learning to interpret your DNA-driven genealogy report or DNA test for ancestry.

## Polish DNA-Driven Genealogy

Learn to interpret the results of your own DNA test and expand your historical research ability to trace your ancestry. "An interesting idea was expressed by a colleague from Canada, Dr. Charles Scriver," explains geneticist, Dr. Batsheva Bonné-Temir. "At a meeting which I organized here in Israel on Genetic Diversity Among Jews in 1990, Dr. Scriver gave a paper on 'What Are Genes Like that Doing in a Place Like This? Human History and Molecular Prosopography.' Dr. Charles Scriver is founder of the DeBelle Laboratory of Biochemical Genetics in Canada.

He also established screening programs in Montreal for thalassaemia and Tay Sachs Disease. He claimed that "a biological trait has two histories, a biological component and a cultural component."

Most biologists would call DNA a biological component and consciousness of a core identity a trait. The conscious trait of the whole person rather than the molecular level DNA would be the cultural component. A cultural trait would be the environmental familiarity of the whole person's relation to his or her family and community.

According to Bonné-Tamir, at the 1990 meeting in Israel on Genetic Diversity Among Jews, Dr. Charles Scriver stated, "When the event clusters and an important cause of it is biological, the cultural history also is likely to be important because it may explain why the persons carrying the gene are in the particular place at the time."

The term, "when the event clusters" refers to an event when genes cluster together in a DNA test because the genes are similar in origin, that is, they have a common ancestral origin in a particular area, a common ancestor.

"When I look at my own papers throughout the years," says Bonné-Tamir. "I find that I have been quite a pioneer in realizing the significance of combining the history of individuals or of populations with their biological attributes. This is now a leading undertaking in many studies which use, for example, mutations to estimate time to the most recent ancestors and alike."

What lines of inquiry are used in genetics? Dr. Charles R. Scriver wrote a chapter in Batsheva Bonné-Temir's book, titled *What are genes like that doing in a place like this? Human History and Molecular Prosopography*. The book title is: *Genetic Diversity Among Jews: Diseases and Markers at the DNA Level.* Bonné-Tamir, B. and Adam, A.

Oxford University Press. 1992. With permission, an excerpt is reprinted below from page 319:

"When a disease clusters in a particular community, two lines of inquiry follow:

1.  Is the clustering caused by shared environmental exposure? Or is it explained by host susceptibility accountable to biological and/or cultural inheritance?

2.  If the explanation is biological, how are the determinants inherited? These lines of inquiry imply that a disease has two different histories, one biological, the other cultural. One involves genes (heredity), pathways of development (ontogeny), and constitutional factors; the other, demography, migration and cultural practice.

Neither history is mutually exclusive. Such thinking shifts the focus of inquiry from sick populations and incidence of disease to sick individuals and the cause of their particular disease. The person with the disease becomes the object of concern which is not the same as the disease the person has." (Page. 319).

After hearing from Dr. Scriver by email, I then emailed Stanley M. Diamond. He contacted writer, Barbara Khait, and got permission for me to reprint in this book some of what she wrote about Diamond's project. It's the chapter, "*Genetics Study Identifies At-risk Relatives*" from *Celebrating the Family* published by Ancestry.com Publishing. Check out the Web site at: http://shops.ancestry.com/product.asp?productid=2625&shopid=128.

Here's the reprinted article. Persons interested may go to the Web site for more information. I found out about Stanley M. Diamond from Dr. Scriver, since he mentioned Stanley M. Diamond's project in the book chapter Scriver wrote for Batsheva Bonné-Temir's book, *Genetic Diversity Among Jews: Diseases and Markers at the DNA Level.* Barbara Khait's chapter follows.

◆        ◆        ◆

"In 1977, Stanley Diamond of Montreal learned he carried the betathalassemia genetic trait. Though common among people of Mediterranean, Middle Eastern, Southeast Asian and African descent, the trait is rare among descendants of eastern European Jews like Stan. His doctor made a full study of the family and identified Stanley's father as the source.

"Stan was spurred to action by a letter his brother received in 1991 from a previously unknown first cousin. Stan asked the cousin, "Do you carry the beta-thalassemia trait?" Though the answer was no, Stan began his journey to find out what other members of his family might be unsuspecting carriers.

"Later that year, Stan found a relative from his paternal grandmother's family, the Widelitz family. Again he asked, "Is there any incidence of anemia in your family?"His newfound cousin answered, "Oh, you mean beta-thalassemia? It's all over the family!"

"There was no question now that the trait could now be traced to Stan's grandmother, Masha Widelitz Diamond and that Masha's older brother Aaron also had to have been a carrier. Stan's next question: who passed the trait onto Masha and Aaron? Was it their mother, Sura Nowes, or their father, Jankiel Widelec?

"At the 1992 annual summer seminar on Jewish genealogy in New York City, Stan conferred with Or. Robert Desnick, who suggested that Stan's first step should be to determine whether the trait was related to a known mutation or a gene unique to his family. He advised Stan to seek out another Montrealer, Dr. Charles Scriver of McGill University-Montreal Children's Hospital. With the help of a grant, Dr. Scriver

undertook the necessary DNA screening with the goal of determining the beta-thalassemia mutation.

"During this time, Stan began to research his family's history in earnest and identified their nineteenth century home town of Ostrow Mazowiecka in Poland. With the help of birth, marriage, and death records for the Jewish population of

Ostrow Mazowiecka filmed by The Church of Jesus Christ of Latter-day Saints (LOS), Stan was able to construct his family tree.

"Late in 1993, Dr. Scriver faxed the news that the mutation had been identified and that it was, in fact, a novel mutation. Independently, Dr. Ariella Oppenheim at Jerusalem's Hebrew University-Hadassah Hospital mad e a similar discovery about a woman who had recently emigrated from the former Soviet Union.

"The likelihood that we were witnessing a DNA region 'identical by descent' in the two families was impressive. We had apparently discovered a familial relationship between Stanley and the woman in Jerusalem, previously unknown to either family," says Dr. Scriver.

"It wasn't very long ago when children born with thalassemia major seldom made it past the age of ten. Recent advances have increased life span but, to stay alive, these children must undergo blood transfusions every two to four weeks. And every night, they must receive painful transfusions of a special drug for up to twelve hours.

"The repeated blood transfusions lead to a buildup of iron in the body that can damage the heart, liver, and other organs. That's why, when the disease is misdiagnosed as mild chronic anemia, the prescription of additional iron is even more harmful. Right now, no cure exists for the disease, though medical experts say experimental bone-marrow transplants and gene-therapy procedures may one day lead to one.

"Stan's primary concern is that carriers of thalassemia trait may marry, often unaware that their mild chronic anemia may be something else. To aid in his search for carriers of his family's gene mutation of the beta-thalassemia trait, he founded and coordinates an initiative known as *Jewish Records Indexing-Poland*, an award-winning **Internet-based index of Jewish vital records in Poland**, with more than one million references. This database is helping Jewish families, particularly those at increased risk for hereditary conditions and diseases, trace their medical histories, as well as geneticists."

Says Dr. Robert Burk, professor of epidemiology at the Albert Einstein College of Medicine at Yeshiva University, and principal investigator for the Cancer Longevity, Ancestry and Lifestyle (CLAL) study in the Jewish population (currently focusing on prostate cancer), "Through the establishment of a searchable database from **Poland**, careful analysis of the relationship between individuals will be possible at both the familial and the molecular level.

"This will afford us the opportunity to learn not only more about the

Creator's great work, but will also allow (us) researchers new opportunities to dissect the cause of many diseases in large established pedigrees."

Several other medical institutions, including Yale University's Cancer Genetics Program, the Epidemiology-Genetics Program at the Johns Hopkins School of Medicine, and Mount Sinai Hospital's School of Medicine have recognized Diamond's work as an outstanding application of knowing one's family history and as a guide to others who may be trying to trace their medical histories, particularly those at increased risk for hereditary conditions and diseases.

In February 1998, in a breakthrough effort, Stanley discovered another member of his family who carried the trait. He found the descendants of Jankiel's niece and nephew—first cousins who married—David Lustig and his wife, Fanny Bengelsdorf. This was no ordinary find—he located the graves by using a map of the Ostrow Mazowiecka section of Chicago's Waldheim Cemetery and contacted the person listed as the one paying for perpetual care, David and Fanny's grandson, Alex.

"It turned out Alex, too, had been diagnosed as a beta-thalassemia carrier by his personal physician fifteen years earlier. The discovery that David and Fanny's descendants were carriers of the beta-thalassemia trait convinced Stan, Dr. Scriver, and Dr.Oppenheim that Hersz Widelec, born in 1785, must be the source of the family's novel mutation.

"'This groundbreaking work helps geneticists all over the world understand the trait and its effects on one family,' says Dr. Oppenheim. "A most important contribution of Stanley Diamond's work is increasing the awareness among his relatives and others to the possibility that they carry a genetic trait which with proper measures, can be prevented in future generations. In addition, the work has demonstrated the power of modern genetics in identifying distant relatives, and helps to clarify how genetic diseases are being spread throughout the world."

For more information about thalassemia, contact Cooley's Anemia Foundation (129-09 26th Avenue. Flushing, New York, 11354; by phone 800-522-7222; or online at www.cooleysanemia.org). For more about Stanley Diamond's research. visit his Web site (www.diamondgen.org). Thalassemia is not only carried by people living today in Mediterranean lands. **The first Polish (not Jewish) carrier of Beta-Thal** was discovered in the last few years in Bialystok, Poland. Stanley Diamond met with the Director of the Hematology Institute in Warsaw in November 2002, and the Director of the Hematology Institute in

Warsaw indicated that they now have identified 52 carriers. Check out these Web sites listed below if the subject intrigues you.

**"Genealogy with an extra reason"…Beta-Thalassemia Research Project.**
http://www.diamondgen.org

**JTA genetic disorder and Polish Jewish history**
www.jta.org/page_view_story.asp?intarticleid=11608&intcategoryid=5

**IAJGS Lifetime Achievement Award**
http://www.jewishgen.org/ajgs/awards.html

**Jewish Records Indexing—Poland**
http://www.jri-poland.org

For more Polish genealogy links, try the Polish Genealogy Links site at: http://www.geocities.com/SiliconValley/Haven/1538/Polishpg.html. The Polish Genealogical Society of America's (PGSA) Web site is at: http://www.pgsa.org/. As of May 2, 2005 there were 878,700surnames in PGSA's databases. If you're searching Polish genealogy, attend some of the Polish genealogical conferences.

Digital Library of Wielkopolska Web site with 3971 publications at the time this book went to press is at: http://www.wbc.poznan.pl/ gives you access to the oldest Polish writing relics. The Web site is in English. According to the site, "You also can read scientific scripts and monographies and see exhibitions with unique resources from various Wielkopolska libraries." Also at the upper right hand corner of the site, click on the flag of language you want—English or Polish.

Also try The Association of Professional Genealogists at: http://www.apgen.org/directory/index.php to find someone who specializes in your particular town or surname research. American military sources links are at the Military Links and Record Sources Web site at: http://www.pgsa.org/MilitaryRec.htm.

The article, Genealogy and Poland—a Guide, is at: http://www.polishroots.com/genpoland/index.htm.

The excellent *Guide* at the Web site notes that, "Millions of people all around the world trace their roots to the territory of present-day Poland. Their ancestors might have been of Polish, German, Jewish, Ruthenian or other ethnic backgrounds and they might have belonged to the Roman Catholic, Greek Catholic, Lutheran, Orthodox, Calvinist or Mennonite Churches, or professed Judaism."

What's great about this site is that has a link to Polish directories at: and answers frequently asked questions with links such as the following questions and links to the answers: For example, the site called: *How to Start my Search for*

*Ancestors* is at http://www.polishroots.org/genpoland/start.htm. It contains information you need for the compilation of data. The next question on How to locate my ancestors' place of origin site is at: http://www.polishroots.org/genpoland/where.htm, and contains the names of localities in Poland and the history of administrative divisions. Many cities in Western Poland retained their German names until 1945.

The link titled, My ancestors were Germans (Jews, Russians etc.) Why should I look for them in Poland? is at: http://www.polishroots.org/genpoland/polhistory.htm and contains a map of central Europe in 1772 and a 200 year brief history.

The Web site's article explains that during the second half of the 18th century the Kingdom of Poland included all of what we now call Lithuania, Belarus and half of contemporary Ukraine. Nearly half of the contemporary area of Poland then belonged to Prussia (Germany). Historic Prussia on an old map is found in Eastern Germany.

The boundary changes section on what 19th century provinces now belong to Poland is at: http://www.polishroots.org/genpoland/changes.htm.

See the link on What kind of records are available in Poland for my ancestors? Where can I find them?, Investigative research site is at: http://www.polishroots.org/genpoland/records.htm. Note that you can find records of births, deaths, and marriages in parishes.

The site notes that, the Civil Codex of Napoleon Bonaparte required religious clergy of all religions to make duplicates of their registers and to deliver them to the local authorities (the district courts). All of the countries formerly governing the present territory of Poland had to deliver the registers. According to the Web site, "After the fall of Napoleon this practice continued." The Civil Registration Offices (*Standesämter*) in Prussia, established on Oct 1, 1874, controlled the registers. Therefore, registrations of births, marriages and deaths for all religions after 1874 were filed in the Civil Registration offices.

Also, check out the link answering the frequently-asked question of How to obtain a birth/marriage/death certificate from Poland. at: http://www.polishroots.org/genpoland/certif.htm. The link shows you how to deal with archivists, officials, and pastors,

If you're looking for meanings of names, click on the site titled, What does my surname mean? It's at http://www.polishroots.org/genpoland/surnames.htm. You'll find helpful hints on etymology.

# 10

## *Estonia*

Numerous English language links for genealogy research, history, language, culture, and message boards of Estonia are at the Estonian Research site at: http://maxpages.com/poland/Estonian_Research. Estonian genealogy links also are at the Estonian Genealogy Page at: http://www.genealoogia.ee/English/links.html. Estonian family trees online are at: http://www.genealoogia.ee/English/links.html#eestivosa. For information on World War II casualties in Estonia, try the Museum at: muuseum@okupatsioon.ee which is called the Okupatsioonide Muuseum which will also include a virtual museum online.

Also search online at the Kistler-Ritso Foundation at: http://www.ngonet.ee/db/ngo?rec=00758. The Foundation's task is to document the catastrophes of the last fifty years and to find detailed proof about the past based on facts and analysis. The Kistler-Ritso Web site states that, "We are interested in the life of Estonians, and also of Russians, Germans, Jews, Swedes and other minorities under the totalitarian regime of the second half of the XX century."

Articles about Estonian genealogy in the Estonian language are posted online at: http://folklore.ee/rl/folkte/pere/pere6.htm. You might want to invest in Web-translating software from Estonian (or any other language of the Baltic areas) to English. Or to read information in English about Estonian genealogy, see the Estonian Family Registry offices online at: http://www.genealoogia.ee/English/fro.html.

The materials in their archives are births, marriages and deaths of the corresponding county since July 1, 1926 and personal registers for the years 1926–1940 (1949) for persons who lived in those years in Estonia. After 1940 (in some places 1949) the registers were not used and the births, marriages and deaths for Estonia need to be researched separately.

Research can't be done, according to this Web site, in the central Family Registry Office where there are family registers and metrics since 1830s until 1926.

Instead, check Estonian local registry offices. The mailing addresses of the local registry offices are listed at: http://www.genealoogia.ee/English/fro.html.

Also check out Estonian Genealogy Links in English at: http://www. genealoogia.ee/English/links.html#artiklid for Estonian genealogy links.

A unique way to link to old genealogy, tax, and property records other than church-archived marriage records in Estonia is by searching "Baltic Real Estate." Try the English-speaking agents of Sunshine Estates—International Real Estate at: http://www.sunshineestates.net/reg_sum/tallinn.html to inquire about real estate in Tallinn, Estonia. Or if you read Estonian, click on the Estonian Real Estate Center at: http://www.kinnisvarakeskus.ee/.

Foreigners in Estonia can freely buy and sell residential real estate with no restrictions, and completion can take less than a month. For genealogy searches, your purpose in talking to an English-speaking real estate agent located in the Baltic country would be to make knowledgeable contacts who can find and translate hidden maps, titles, tax, notary, zoning records and other data such as old institutional, military, dental, medical, school, marriage, divorce, birth, death, business, census, street directories, and residential property sale certificates or names of former property owners.

To make contact with genealogists, curators, archivists, librarians, or government records administrators who may not speak English is through a liaison from foreign student associations in the US, such as the various Latvian, Lithuanian, Polish, Estonian, Swedish, German, or Finnish student societies at universities that draw large numbers of students from Baltic countries. The Estonian Association of Teachers of English at: http://www.ngonet.ee/db/ngo?rec=00339 may be able to help you find a bilingual translator of your genealogy records.

# 11

## *Sweden*

Swedish resources are at: http://www.tc.umn.edu/~pmg/swedish.html. See the Master Index to Swedish Genealogical Data (by surname) at: http://www3.dcs.hull.ac.uk/genealogy/swedish/. An excellent source also is the book titled, R.W.Swanson, '*The Swedish Surname in America*', *ibid.*, 3 (1927–1928), 468–477.

Find information about original records in public archives at SVAR (Swedish National Archives). The Web site is at: http://www.svar.ra.se/. Click on the English language icon. You'll find databases and indexes. Search for Swedish archive documents, scanned or on microfiche and book titles with books covering the Swedish census of 1890, parish records, and genealogy books.

Swedish genealogy publications and archives are highly organized, in multi-media, and available in English and Swedish. You'll also find books on family patterns in 19th, the Saami, and genealogy publications. The book descriptions and lists I check out were in English.

The Federation of Swedish Genealogical Societies Web site is at: http://www.genealogi.se/roots/. This is the English version. There's a Swedish language site at: http://www.genealogi.se/. Check out the Swedish Soldier's Register at: http://www.genealogi.se/roots/. This site is in English and recounts some history of how men were assembled and recruited for the military.

See also the Sweden Genealogy Forum at: http://genforum.genealogy.com/sweden/ (from Genealogy.com). A Review of Swedish Immigration to America site is at: http://www.americanwest.com/swedemigr/pages/emigra.htm. Swedes started to come in 1638, just eighteen years after the landing of the *Mayflower*. According to the Web site, the "tidal wave of Swedish immigration began in the mid-1840s." The site also mentions the 17th century history of Swedish immigrants to the US and notes that, "Swedes were not religious dissenters but rather an organized group of colonizers.

"They had been sent out by the government in Stockholm in order to establish a colony under the Swedish crown in Delaware. The era of New Sweden ended in 1655, when the colony was lost to the Dutch."

Interestingly the Web site reports that the "original settlers remained and kept up their language and culture for a long time." Also noted is that "Many of the descendants of the Delaware Swedes became distinguished fighters for freedom in the war against England in 1776." The site mentions John Morton, "who gave the decisive vote for independence at the Continental Congress in Philadelphia."

An excellent list of links with numerous articles on Swedish genealogy and history is at the Swedish Resources Web site at: http://www.tc.umn.edu/~pmg/swedish.html. Also check out the English language link to the Immigrant Institute in Sweden at: http://www.immi.se/portale.htm. The site states that, "The Immigrant institute is a non-governmental organization which aim is to be a research and documentation centre about immigrants, refugees and racism, with an archive, a library and a museum."

For genealogy information on the Jewish community of Sweden, contact the Jewish Genealogical Society of Sweden. Click on http://www.ijk-s.se/genealogi/index_en.html. The history of Jewish immigration to Sweden link is at: http://www.ijk-s.se/genealogi/index_en.html.

All Jews who were Swedish citizens were allowed to reside anywhere in Sweden. Jews began immigrating to Sweden in the 18th century. By 1850 Jews began to immigrate to Sweden from Mecklenberg, Germany and a few other towns. At the same time, Jews also arrived from Russia and Poland. At first Jews settled in Stockholm, Göteborg (Gothenburg), Norrköping and Karlskrona. Later they moved also to newly-founded Jewish settlements in Malmö, Lund, Kristianstad, Landskrona, Helsingborg, Sölvesborg, Kalmar, Oskarshamn, Växjö, Halmstad, Visby, Karlstad, Sundsvall, Härnösand, and Östersund.

According to the site, "Jewish Immigration to Sweden" at: http://www.ijk-s.se/genealogi/index_en.html, a historical note states that "During the final years of World War II and just afterward, many thousands of Jewish refugees arrived in Sweden, some of whom stayed. During the war more than 7000 Danish Jews and about 925 Norwegian Jews found asylum in Sweden."

In the decade following the war, Jews arrived from Hungary, Czechoslovakia, Poland, and other former Soviet republics. It's estimated that 17,000 Jews live in Sweden currently. That's less than 0.2 percent of the total population. Because of many intermarriages, the number of Swedes with Jewish genealogical roots is much higher. For more information, click on the Web site of the Scandinavia Special Interest Group (SIG) of the Jewish Genealogy site called JewishGen, Inc.

at: http://www.ijk-s.se/genealogi/index_en.html. The site links cover the Jewish communities and/or Jewish genealogy and some history in Sweden, Finland, Norway, Denmark, former Danish colonies, Danish Virgin Island, the Faroe Islands, Guinea, Tranquebar, Iceland, and Greenland.

# 12

## *Denmark*

You'll find excellent computerized genealogy resources for Denmark. For starters, try the Web site at: http://www.geocities.com/aitkenms/denmark.html, and click on the link titled Genealogy Resources on the Internet at: http://www-personal.umich.edu/~cgaunt/dk.html. You'll find more resources for Danish-American genealogy sources at Portals to the World, Resources Selected by the Library of Congress, titled Genealogy: Denmark at: http://www.loc.gov/rr/international/corc.oclc.org/WebZ/XPathfinderQuery7244.html.

For emigration records, click on Danelink.com (linking Danes everywhere) at: http://www.danelink.com/locations/intgenealogy.html.

Danish Emigration Archives site is in English and is at: http://www.emiarch.dk/home.php3. Click on the link to bring up the *Dansk Demografisk Database* and enter the name you wish to research. The Danish Archives (in Danish) site comes up first. So you need to click on the English flag icon at the top right hand corner to bring up the Web site in English. The English language site is at: http://ddd.sa.dk/ddd_en.htm. The Danish language site is at: http://ddd.sa.dk/. Also click on the addresses button. For further information, write to the: **Top of From The Danish Emigration Archives,** Arkivstræde 1, P.O. BOX 1731, 9100 Aalborg, Denmark.

# 13

## *Norway*

The Velkommen to Norway Genealogy site is at: http://www.rootsweb.com/~wgnorway/index2.htm. There are links to everything from genealogy resources to links to searching the white or yellow pages of the phone books of Norway at the link at: http://www.gulesider.no/gsi/whiteSearchFront.do?spraak=3 (White pages) or the Yellow Pages at: http://www.gulesider.no/gsi/index.do?spraak=3

The Web site (in English) for maps showing boundaries for parishes is at: http://digitalarkivet.uib.no/norkart/index-eng.htm. The links for Norwegian sources online are well-organized. You can find almost all your resources compiled as links on one site. The Digital Archives database (*Arkivverket Digitalarkivet*) for census and parish information is in English. Click on the *Arkivverket Digitalarkivet* at: http://digitalarkivet.uib.no/cgi-win/WebFront.exe?slag=vis&tekst=meldingar&spraak=e.

What's great about this Norwegian genealogy research site is that almost everything you want to begin your search is at this site's many links. Try the Norwegian farm names site (in English) called *Oluf Rhygh* at: http://www.dokpro.uio.no/rygh_ng/rygh_form.html. Search for farm names as they were used during the years past.

Norwegian genealogy research may have already been done with results published results in a book. In Norway such a book is called a 'bygdebok'. (In this context 'bygd' means 'parish'). Check out the Bydgebok site (in English) at: http://www.nndata.no/home/jborgos/bygdeen.htm. Also look at land records information on finding resources on the Norwegian Land Records site at: http://www.rootsweb.com/~wgnorway/NorLinks8.htm. It includes census, church books, emigrants, farms information, and land information in Norwegian, a tax and land records link, and more sites and links in English.

# 14

## *Iceland*

The site for Emigration from Iceland to North America is at: http://www.simnet.is/halfdanh/vestur.htm. Settlers generally went to Alberta, Manitoba, Saskatchewan, in Canada, and in the USA to Minnesota, North Dakota, Utah, Washington, and Wisconsin. The site also published as newsletter. Genealogy.com's Iceland Forum is at: http://genforum.genealogy.com/iceland/. Genealogy in Iceland has excellent documentation with some surnames recorded in Icelandic sources dating from 1560.

Iceland Genealogy Links are at: http://iceland.vefur.is/Education/Genealogy/. Also click on the Iceland surnames site (Virtually Virtual Iceland) at: http://www.simnet.is/gardarj/family.htm. More genealogy links for Iceland is at the Genealogy site at: http://www.samkoma.com/cgi/links.pl.cgi?061. Also try the Emigration from Iceland to North America map site at: http://www.isholf.is/halfdanh/islmap.htm. According to the site, "As each Icelander's name is an individual property, the names do not change in marriage." Women keep their names.

For example, according to the Web site sample names explanation, Sveinbjörg Sigurðardóttir is a woman. Her name ends in 'dóttir.' That means and sounds like the word 'daughter.' She is married to Þórður Hannesson. Note that their daughter, Halldóra

Þórðardóttir has taken as her surname the first name of her father, which is Þórður and adds the word dóttir to the ending. That becomes her surname that she will carry throughout her life and will not change when she marries.

A man takes his father's first name and adds 'sson' to the ending. For example, Haraldur Sveinsson has a son named Jóhann Már Haraldsson. Note that the son has taken as his surname his father's first name, Haraldur and shortened it to Harald and then added 'sson.' He's Harald's son.

Also, according to the Icelandic surnames Web site, when Jóhann Már Haraldsson marries Halldóra Þórðardóttir, their son could be named Gestur Þór

Jóhannsson, and their daughter could be named Bára Sif Jóhannsdóttir. Note their son's middle name is taken from the wife's father's first name. Their daughter's last name, Jóhannsdóttir is taken from her father's surname with the 'dóttir' ending added to Jóhanns, whereas her brother's surname is Jóhannsson (that is, 'Jóhanns' with 'son' added.) Because Icelandic lettering is different, if an Icelander moves to the USA or Canada, (or any English-speaking country), English typefonts may change spelling, but frequently not pronunciation.

# 15

## *Lithuania*

The Lithuanian Global Genealogical Society is at: http://www. lithuaniangenealogy.org/databases/. There are vital records for most states and Lithuanian Parishes of the Roman Catholic Diocese in America at: http:// www.lithuaniangenealogy.org/databases/churches/lt_churches-us.html. The Lithuania Genealogy Forum of Genealogy.com is at: http://genforum. genealogy.com/lithuania/.

Also check out the Lithuanian Research site at: http://www.maxpages.com/ poland/Lithuanian_Research. You can contact Chicago's Balzekas Museum of Lithuanian Culture, Immigration History & Genealogy Department, 6500 South Pulaski Road, Chicago, IL 60629. The Global Resources for Lithuania Web site is at: http://www.angelfire.com/ut/Luthuanian/index.html. The Lithuanian Global Genealogical Society at: http://www.lithuaniangenealogy. org/organizations/index.html#poland lists the address of the **Poland-Lithuanian Community, as the following:** Chairperson: Juozas Sigitas Paransevièius, ul.Mickiewicza 23, 16-515 Punsk, woj.Suwalki, Poland.

The Web site discussion forum called *'About'* has a Lithuanian Genealogy site of article and resources at: http://genealogy.about.com/od/lithuania/. The site reports that, "The largest Lithuanian resource center outside Lithuania, the Chicago museum offers searches of major Lithuanian-American genealogy sources, as well as an on-staff genealogist of Lithuanian ancestry. Home to the Lithuanian Americal Genealogy Society."

Check out the archives of the museum. To find ancestors in Lithuania, there's a site from 'About' called How to Find Relatives in Lithuania at: http:// genealogy.about.com/gi/dynamic/offsite.htm?zi=1/XJ&sdn=geneal-ogy&zu=http://www.lfcc.lt/howfind.html. Some addresses recommended for inquiry include the following:

1. **Lithuanian National Historical Archive:**
   Lietuvos valstybinis istorijos archyvas

Gerosios Vilties g. 10
2015 Vilnius, Lithuania

**Registry department of Lithuanian National Historical Archive:**
Lietuvos valstybinis istorijos archyvas, Metriku skyrius
K.Kalinausko g. 21, 2000 Vilnius, LITHUANIA

2.  Write a **letter of inquiry** to:
    **Bureau of Addresses**
    Adresu Biuras
    Vivulskio g. 4a, 2009 Vilnius, LITHUANIA

Phone numbers are included on the Web site. I've left them out in this book because phone numbers could change by the time the book went to press. So check first by writing. Contact each institution at the level of local administration, that is the municipality of each district in Lithuania that you want to search, and direct your questions to the archives department.

There's a link to Lithuanian organizations collected from a variety of countries. The site is at: http://genealogy.about.com/gi/dynamic/offsite.htm?zi=1/XJ&sdn=genealogy&zu=http://www.lfcc.lt/howfind.html. Click on the Lithuanian Folk Center at: http://genealogy.about.com/gi/dynamic/offsite.htm?zi=1/XJ&sdn=genealogy&zu=http://www.lfcc.lt/howfind.html. Or check out the mirrored link at the Lithuanian Global Genealogical Society at: http://genealogy.about.com/gi/dynamic/offsite.htm?zi=1/XJ&sdn=genealogy&zu=http://www.lfcc.lt/howfind.html.

◆      ◆      ◆

**Genealogy Research Archives**
**Estonia**
**Central Family Registry Office**

Pikk 61
15065 Tallinn
Ph (0) 612 5164
Executive Svetlana Toots, *svetlana.toots@mail.ee*
Main specialist Piret Põldmäe
Specialist Mare Verma, *mare.verma@mail.ee*

## Tallinn City family registry office

Pärnu mnt 67
10135 Tallinn
(0) 646 3364, *prksa@tallinnlv.ee*
Reception Mon-Fri 9-17

## Latvia
## Latvian Archives

Central State History Archives
Centralais Valsts vestures arhivs
Slokas iela 16
Riga, LV 226007

Central State Archives
Centralais Valsts vestures arhivs
Bezdeligu iela 1
Riga, LV 226007

Central State Cine-Phono-Photo Document Archives
Centralais Valsts Kino-Foto-Fono-Dokumentu arhivs
Skuna iela 11
Riga, LV 226007

Lutheran Church
Latvijas ev. lut. baznicas konsitorija
Lacplesa iela 4-4
Riga, LV 226010

Catholic Church
Katolu baznicas metropolijas Kurija
M. Pils iela 2a
Riga, LV 226047

Orthodox Church
Krievu pareizticiga baznicas parijas parvalde
M. Pils iela 2a
Riga, LV 226047

## Published Latvian, Lithuanian, and Polish Genealogy & Related Information

Latvijas Ideja Amerika by Osvalds Akmentins. Boston, Massachusetts, USA c 1969.

Lielas Liesmas Atblazma by Margers Stepermanis. Riga 1971.

**Jewish Baltic & E. European Communities**: Shtetl Finder: Jewish Communities in the 19th and Early 20th Centuries in the Pale of Settlement of Russia and Poland, and in Lithuania, Latvia, Galicia, and Bukovina with Names of Residents: Heritage Books, Bowie, Maryland, USA 1989.

**Latvian language Web sites:**

http://www.sil.org/ethnologue/families/Indo-European.html

**The Latvian alphabet**

Uldis Balodis' t Web page on the Latvian language is at: http://www.goodnet.com/~vanags/valoda.html.

**Latvia, Dundaga—Church Records on Microfiche and Microfilm**

Seuberlich, Erich.

Kurland: Auszug aus dem Kirchenbuch: Dondangen, 1710–1870.—

|EUROPE |

Salt Lake City: Gefilmt durch The Genealogical Society of

|FILM AREA |

Utah, 1992.—auf 1 Mikrofilmrolle; 35 mm.

Mikrofilm aufgenommen von Manuskripten in der Zentralstelle für Genealogie, Leipzig. Extracts of parish registers (marriages, deaths) from the Protestant community of Dondangen, Courland, Russia; now Dundaga, Latvia. Text in German.

Heiraten 1711–1836

----------------------------1858061

Taufen 1710–1839

item 5.

Konfirmanden 1718–1838

Tote 1712–1844

Kommunikanten 1751–1839

Vereidigungen 1819–1870

# 16

## *Genealogy in the Balkans, Eastern Europe & the Middle East*

Have any of your ancestors ever lived under the former Ottoman Empire? The Ottoman Empire lasted from 1300 until 1922. In 1924 Kemal Ataturk abolished the Muslim caliphate and founded the Republic of Turkey. So regardless of the language spoken by your ancestors—Slavic, Arabic, Greek, Judezmo, Uralic, Yiddish, Romanian, or Turkish, the Ottoman Empire controlled and kept careful census records in Turkish using Arabic script in the following countries of Europe and the Middle East known today, but not necessarily before 1924 as the following names:

Hungary, Yugoslavia, Croatia, Bosnia, Albania, Macedonia, Greece, Romania, Moldova, Bulgaria, southern Ukraine, Turkey, Georgia, Armenia, Iraq, Kuwait, Cyprus, Syria, Lebanon, Israel/Palestine, Jordan, Eastern and Western Saudi Arabia, Oman, Bahrain, eastern Yemen, Egypt, northern Libya, Tunisia, and northern Algeria.

In addition, more recent records in Arabic or in the language of the country emphasized are kept in the national archives and in the courts dealing with property-related issues, assets left behind, divorce decrees, and other legal documents. Often when a population is forced out, the individual country, such as present-day Egypt, may then determine that assets, property, and religious items taken away or left behind such as Judaica, Hellenica, and Armenica are declared antiquities of that country that cannot be removed.

You can approach genealogy by running a teen genealogy camp for foreign travel. If you get enough tourists, you can go free and emphasize genealogy research. Another approach is to collect memorabilia from your ethnic group such as Hellenica, Judaica, Armenica, Arabica, and other objects. Every object you collect in genealogy as far as records or actual objects opens a door. As you step over the threshold, you can see time and place in the context of that culture.

# 17

## *Middle Eastern & East European*

Genealogy opens portals to the artistic, cultural, religious, social, historical, and economic environment in which a particular item was designed and brought forth, from people to their icons. Genealogy is cultural geography as well as a history and ethnography of human genes.

Look at ethnic objects along with the census or other genealogy records. There are so many locations to cover the settlement of your peoples, the human race. Genealogy allows you to view a juxtaposition of demography with memorabilia and ethnic or religious items. Learn how to research your own group and show others about the life of the people you choose to study, their history and design.

That's why running a teen (or other age group) genealogy camp is fun, especially in researching the former Ottoman Empire—or any other location that you want to emphasize, perhaps your own ethnic history.

How do you start? The Family History Library (Salt Lake City, UT) has a catalog that can give you rewarding and rich research ideas. So if it's the former Ottoman Empire you want to emphasize, or how the world of antiquity blends into your relatively modern genealogy, first check the Family History Library catalog (Salt Lake City, UT) for books, microfilms, civil registration, localities and jurisdictions.

Then search the Ottoman Census and Population Registers by country named in Turkish the Nüfus Defter. Check the online library catalog at Bogaziçi University (a.k.a. the University of the Bosphorus). See http://www.geog.port.ac.uk/hist-bound/country rep/ottoman.htm. Also check out the flyer: http://www.hanover.edu/haq center/Bogazici-Flyer.html

Records are found in the Ottoman Census archives in Turkey pertaining to tax collection during the Ottoman rule. Moslems weren't taxed. Before 1881, each census focused on tabulating male names to find Moslem men to conscript into the military service and non-Moslem men to pay personal tax. Search records according to the religion and ethnic group. Start your search with the list of countries under the Ottomans and pick your ancestor's homeland.

Egypt was under the former Ottoman Empire. Therefore, if you are a Jew from Egypt (regardless of whether your family members are Ashkenazim, Sepharadim, or Mizrahi), check out The <u>Historical Society Of Jews From Egypt</u>. Their Web site is at: <u>http://hsje.org/</u>. This site is designed to gather, and provide historical and current information on the <u>Jews From Egypt,</u> one of the most ancient established societies in the world."

According to their Web site, "We will attempt to cover the period from <u>Joseph Saadia el Fayoumi</u> (Saadia Gaon) to the present day." The Web site notes that, "This organization shall be known as Historical Society of Jews from Egypt, and not of Egypt or of Egyptian Jews, but from Egypt for the purpose will be to include all our co-religionists whose lineage have sojourned in the <u>Jewish Communities</u> of Egypt."

Contact them if you had relatives who lived in the Jewish communities of Egypt. Some Romanian and Greek Jews also lived in the Jewish communities of Egypt and some Ashkenazim also. According to their Web site, "The aims of this <u>society</u> are to preserve, maintain, coordinate the implementation, and to convey our rich heritage to our children and grand children's, using all educational means at our disposal to bring into being the necessary foundations."

Referring to Romania and in particular, Bessarabia, some Romanian Jews migrated to Palestine in the Ottoman era. This migration included Ashkenazim and Sephardim. Numerous Sephardim and Mizrahi had migrated to Palestine in earlier times and a smaller number of Ashkenazim. Your genealogy source here could be to consult a Jewish genealogy journal such as Avotaynu at: <u>http://www.avotaynu.com</u>.

According to the Jews of Egypt Web site at: <u>http://www.us-israel.org/jsource/anti-semitism/egjews.html</u>, "In 1979, the Egyptian Jewish community became the first in the Arab world to establish official contact with Israel. Israel now has an embassy in Cairo and a consulate general in Alexandria. At present, the few remaining Jews are free to practice <u>Judaism</u> without any restrictions or harassment. Shaar Hashamayim is the only functioning <u>synagogue</u> in Cairo. Of the many synagogues in Alexandria only the Eliahu Hanabi is open for worship.[4]." The source of this information on their Web site is listed as <u>Jewish Communities of the World</u>.

According to researcher, Kahlile Mehr, "For searching the Ottoman period in most countries under the former Ottoman Empire, the researcher would have to read Turkish in Arabic script. The Family History library was able to film some

Christian church records in Israel during the 1980s. But for most of the populace, the commonly known genealogical sources of the West simply do not exist. The best known source is the Nufus registers."

All the articles and information on Bulgaria, Macedonia, and Croatia written by former staff writer for the Family History Library, Salt Lake City, UT, Khalile Mehr, are copyrighted by The Family History Library.

"The Family History Library filmed the Nufus registers in the Israeli State Archives for Israel, parts of Jordan and Egypt. A description of these can be found in the catalog at www.familysearch.org.

"If you're searching various ethnic groups in Bessarabia, it was not part of Romania except during the period between World War I and II. It was historically part of the Ottoman and then the Russian Empire. Today, it is Moldova."

There was a time in the late 18$^{th}$ century and early 19$^{th}$ century when Bessarabia fell out of the Ottoman Empire and became under the rule of the Russians. At that time a large immigration of German Christians and German Jews as well as Jews from Poland, Ukraine, Belarus, and surrounding areas flocked to Bessarabia. So you have a community of Protestant Germans in Bessarabia along with German and Polish Jews. The immigration took place as soon as Bessarabia fell into Russian hands and out of Ottoman hands for that period of time.

You can trace names that show up in Poland such as Herkowicz to Romanian, where the spelling changes to Herkowitz and later to the Romanian spelling, Herkovici, in some cases. Countries change names. Bessarabia, once a place with its own name rather than a province in a country, then becomes an area within a country, and finally today, falling in the borders of Moldova and Romania.

# 18

## *Translating Names*

Don't skip generations. Each generation is a vital link in countries where thousands have the same name. Check out the Middle EastGenWeb Project at: http://www.rootsweb.com/~mdeastgw/index.html.

Some religious names are used by Moslems and Christians. Christian European names are translated into Arabic in Arabic-speaking countries. For example, in Lebanon, Peter becomes Boutros and George becomes Girgis or Abdul Messikh, meaning servant of the Messiah (Christ). Shammout (strong), Deeb (wolf), or Dib (bear). Nissim (miracles) is used by Jewish Levantines, and Adam is used by Jewish, Christian, and Moslem families.

Women had the choice of taking their husband's surnames or keeping their maiden names. Neutral names, used by Moslems, Jews, and Christians such as Ibrahim (Abraham) or Yusef (Joseph) came from the Old Testament. In Lebanon, Christians often used neutral names such as Tewfik (fortunate).

Arabic-speaking and Turkic-speaking countries didn't use surnames until after the end of the Ottoman Empire. Then in Lebanon and Syria many Christians took as their surnames European or Biblical first male names such as the Arabic versions of George, Jacob, Thomas, and Peter which were in Arabic: Girgis, Yacoub, Toumas, and Boutros. Others took popular surnames describing their occupations such as Haddad meaning 'smith.'

After 1928 in Turkey, but not in any of the other Middle Eastern nations, a modified Latin alphabet replaced Arabic script. Four years later (1932) the Turkish Linguistic Society simplified the language to unify the people. Surnames were required in 1934 and, old titles indicating professions and classes were dropped. (See "Turkey" Web site at: http://www.kusadasitravel.com/turkey.html.)

In Middle Eastern countries under the former Ottoman Empire, such as Lebanon/Syria, each child was given a first name but most people in the Middle East had no surname until 1932. Also the father's given name was given as a middle name such as Yusef Girgis, meaning Yusef (Joseph), son of George. It came in handy in the days before surnames were required. Now it's used as a middle name.

Many Syrian and Lebanese families, particularly Christians, after 1932 took similar names such as Peter Jacobs or George Thomas. The name 'Thomas' in Lebanon is spelled in translation as either Touma or Toumas. Many Assyrian males in Northern Iraq took the popular name Sargon, an ancient king.

When surnames in Lebanon became a requirement, you have very popular names such as Peter George Khoury in America being Boutros Girgis Khouri in Lebanon or Syria when translated into Arabic. In the Levant, daughters have a first name and their father's given name meaning "daughter of Yusef" "'bint' Yusef" where bint and binti means 'daughter.' Outside the home, females would be called with the proper respect "daughter of Yusef or "Bint Yusef." Inside the home to immediate family, a female would be known by her first name, which could be Ayah. She would be registered as Ayah Yusef. She'd be known by a first name, Ayah and a surname, Yusef. Translated into English at Ellis Island, it could have become Aya Joseph.

When surnames became a requirement, many included professions or place names, especially Halaby (from Aleppo) or Antaky (from Antioch). The largest Lebanese community in America is in Dearborn, Michigan.

In Lebanon, most names were Christian prior to 1870, and the Christian names could also be European, especially Greek names like Petros (Peter) which later becomes Boutros in Arabic. If you're searching Assyrians, check out the Assyrian Nation Communities Web site at: http://www.assyriannation.com/communities/index.php.

# 19

# *Researching Assyrian Genealogy*

## Assyrian Presbyterian Genealogy Records Research

According to the Public Services and Outreach division of the Presbyterian Historical Society, while the Presbyterian Church sent missionaries to the Middle East, materials at the Presbyterian Historical Society document their activities there and do not contain any information about individuals from the Middle East who immigrated to the United States. To get an idea of the types of materials at the Presbyterian Historical Society useful for genealogists, review the following sections of their website at: http://www.history.pcusa.org/famhist/ or http://www.history.pcusa.org/collect/. This second page also provides links to their on-line finding aids, http://www.history.pcusa.org/finding/index.html, and catalog, CALVIN, http://www.history.pcusa.org/dbtw-wpd/WebOPACmenu.htm.

Search each to see what they might have for your area of interest.

Records of individual congregations are the main resource for family history research at the society. There are no centralized denominational registers of church memberships, baptisms, or marriages; nor is there a comprehensive index to the thousands of family names included in the records in our holdings.

To start a search, it is essential to know both the location (city and state) and the full and correct name of the congregation associated with the individual you are researching. They do not have lists of churches by township, city, or county, or street name cross indexes.

Research genealogy records of members of the Assyrian Presbyterian Church in the US or in Iraq and Iran. Search Assyrian colonies in various US cities for genealogy records related to the Presbyterian Church.

If you are searching Assyrian records, and your family belonged to the Presbyterian Church, check out the Presbyterian Church Historical Society at: http://history.pcusa.org/finding/phs%20379.xml#scopecontent where you can find book titles and/or records such as the Assyrian and National Church History, volumes 1 and 2. Look up Isaac B. Moorhatch (1880– ) Papers, 1938, Finding Aid to Record Group 379, © Presbyterian Historical Society, Philadelphia, PA 19147.

From the early 20$^{th}$ century, many Assyrians immigrating to the US joined the Presbyterian church. This is due to the missionaries in Persia and Iraq in the early 20$^{th}$ century. For example, In 1910 Isaac Moorhatch established the Assyrian Presbyterian Church of Gary, Indiana.

In 1923 he arrived in Philadelphia, where the Assyrian colony asked him to serve as their pastor. After ordination, he took charge of the Persian/Assyrian Presbyterian Mission. He served this mission until retirement in 1950.

So your first step is to find out where the Assyrian colonies were in the US. Was one of your relatives a missionary in a country then under the former Ottoman Empire?

Isaac Moorhatch was born in Urumia, Persia, the son of Presbyterian missionaries. He grew up in Iran and attended the Presbyterian college in Urumia. In 1897 he began working as an evangelical and educational missionary for the Board of Foreign Missions (PCUSA).

So search the Presbyterian colleges in various Middle Eastern countries when they were under the Ottoman Empire. In 1909 Moorhatch arrived in the United States with the intention of entering a Presbyterian seminary and returning to work among the Persian Moslems after graduation. In the end he enrolled in the Baptist Theological Seminary in Kansas City, KS in 1912.

According to the Web site of the Presbyterian Church History records at: http://history.pcusa.org/finding/phs%20379.xml#scopecontent,     "In     1910 Moorhatch established the Assyrian Presbyterian Church of Gary, IN. In 1923 he arrived in Philadelphia, where the Assyrian colony asked him to serve as their pastor. After ordination, he took charge of the Persian/Assyrian Presbyterian Mission. He served this mission until retirement in 1950."

If you research the collection of Presbyterian Church History records, you can read Moorhatch's two-volume manuscript work titled: Assyrian and National Church History: History of Iran: Rise of Islam. The work is written in Aramaic. Each volume includes a table of contents. So if you come from an Assyrian family or any other ethnic group that is able to read Aramaic, such as numerous Jews and a few groups in Syria, you can read or even translate the Aramaic to English.

If you're searching the collection of Presbyterian Church history, records less than 50 years old are restricted. Contact the archivist. The collection was processed in 1993. Your reference point would be: Finding Aid to Record Group

379, Box 1 Folder 1. Assyrian and National Church History, volumes 1 and 2. Folder 2-3.

After 1870, in Lebanon and Syria names in Christian families became Arabic rather than European due to increasing pressure by the Ottoman Empire on Christians to use Arabic instead of Greek names. After the demise of the Ottoman Empire at the close of World War I, Hellenistic names such as Kostaki (Constantine) became popular in Beirut.

The distinctly Christian Lebanese surnames Khoury (priest) or Kourban sprang up again when Lebanon became a French protectorate. Neutral, Greek, and Old Testament names also return. You see many French first names in Christian families between 1914 and 1950.

After the 1950s, Christian and French first names dwindle, and Arabic names appear. If your ancestors were Moslem, instead of a surname prior to 1932, you were known as "son of" (Ibn) as in Ibn Omar, for a male, and for a married woman with children called, "mother of" (om) as in Om Kolthum, (mother of Kolthum).

You'd be called mother of your first born son, (Om___Name of first born son) (Om Ahmed). If you had no sons, you'd be called mother of your first born daughter (Om Rania) (Om___Name of first born daughter). Single women often were called "daughter of" as in Bint Ahmed (daughter of Ahmed).

Arabic women's first names were plentiful, popular, and used at mainly at home. Examples include Samara, Zobaida, Rayana, Rania, Anissa, Dayala, Azma, Aya, or Salwa. Children had first names.

If your ancestors were Armenian living in the Levant you might have the name Ter or Der before a surname designating descent from an Armenian Apostolic priest followed by a name ending in ian or yan meaning "son of" such as Manvelian or a place name such as Halebian (from Aleppo) when translated into English. If you're Armenian searching Turkish census records, the pre-1920 border of Armenian habitation usually was south of Lake Van, near Mush (in Armenia), and Bairt and Dersim (in Turkey). Each religion had a different status under the former Ottoman Empire—Moslems first class and conscripted into the military; all other religions, not conscripted, but taxed.

## Narrow the Categories

Categorize the religion—not only Catholic, but Melkite Catholic or Maronite Catholic. Antiochian Syrian Orthodox or Roman Catholic? Byzantine Catholic (Byzantic) or Greek Orthodox? Lebanese immigrant to Cairo, Egypt and Coptic Orthodox? Moslem? Jewish? Druze? Armenian Apostolic? Sephardim? Ashkenazim? Protestant? Greek Orthodox? Greek Catholic? Bulgarian or Romanian Orthodox? Serbian? Croatian?

Color-code cards or files noting the date, religion, ethnic group, and town. When did the immigrant arrive in the US from a Middle Eastern country? Was it before or after the end of the former Ottoman Empire? For example, Antioch, now in Turkey used to be in Syria before World War II. And before 1918, Syria and Lebanon was one province under the Ottoman Empire. So use old and new maps to see what country to emphasize at which dates.

## National Archives in the Country of Origin

Maps of old neighborhoods show locations of houses. Start with the national archives in the country of origin. For Syria that would be the Syrian National Archives in Damascus, Aleppo, Homs, or Hama where court records are archived for the years 1517 to 1919. If the relatives lived before the end of the Ottoman Empire or before World War I, also search the census records of the former Ottoman Empire in Turkey rather than the archives in the country of origin that may not have existed before the end of the Ottoman Empire.

Records stand alone rather than in groups of catalogs. Check separate Jewish genealogy sources and synagogue documents for the Jewish records of Mizrahi and Sephardim, such as marriage ketubim, bar mitzvah records, births, deaths, rabbinical documents such as a 'Get' for a divorce or a pedigree called a Yiccus.

If you're checking Sephardic (Jewish) records of the former Ottoman Empire, there's an excellent article on Jewish genealogy published in Los Muestros magazine, a publication of Sephardic and Middle Eastern Jewish genealogy titled Resources for Sephardic Genealogy at: http://www.sefarad.org/publication/lm/010/cardoza.html. Also see the magazine, Los Muestros at: http://www.sefarad.org/publication/lm/010/som10.html for archived Sephardic genealogy articles.

Another excellent publication of Jewish genealogy, Avotaynu maintains a Web site at: http://www.avotaynu.com/. If you're looking for Jewish records in the Middle East, also check the Sephardic associations, for example, Sephardim.com at http://www.sephardim.com/. Look for memorabilia, diaries, house keys, and maps of neighborhoods.

For Sephardic genealogy in the former Ottoman Empire, contact the Foundation for the Advancement of Sephardic Studies and Culture Web site at: http://www.sephardicstudies.org/cal2.html to learn how to interpret calendars and how to read birth certificates. You'll learn how to decipher the handwritten entries using Arabic script. Regardless of the religion of the individual, this site shows you how to read the certificates written with certain types of scripts.

The site also shows the dialects spoken in the various areas of the Ottoman Empire. Also there is information on how to read the Arabic script but Turkish language writing on gravestones, especially in Turkish cemeteries. The site shows you how to read the alphabet encountered in genealogical research in the former Ottoman Empire. Emphasis is on interpreting Sephardic birth certificates.

# 20

## *How to Translate and Locate without Surnames*

What's in the census? Ottoman census records for the period 1831–1872 were compilations of male names and addresses for fiscal and military purposes. Instead of population counts, the Ottoman records contain the name of the head of household, male family members, ages, occupation, and property.

You won't find surnames in old records. Most Middle Eastern countries didn't require surnames until after the fall of the Ottoman Empire. If you're searching Middle Eastern genealogy before 1924, begin by familiarizing yourself with the record keeping and social history of the Ottoman Empire.

Turkish language written in Arabic script is the key to searching genealogy records in European and Middle Eastern areas formerly ruled by the Ottomans. You'll need an Arabic-English dictionary or instruction guide that at least gives you the basic Arabic script alphabet.

You'll also need the same type of phrase book with alphabet translation for modern Turkish written using Latin letters. You can put the both together to figure out phrases.

Find in your town a graduate student or teacher from abroad who reads Arabic script and modern Turkish. Hire the student or teacher to copy the records you want when overseas. Barter services. Or contact the Middle East history and area studies, archaeology, or languages departments of numerous colleges.

Who teaches courses in both Turkish and Arabic? Contact private language schools such as Language School International, Inc. at: http://www.languageschoolsguide.com/listingsp3.cfm/listing/4092.

### What Religious Group Will You Search?

Social history is the key to genealogy. Records that existed under the Ottoman Empire listed names of the head of household and parents, residence, dates and places of birth and baptism, marriage, death and burial. Records also have entries for ages for marriage and death.

Baptisms included names of the godparents. Deaths sometimes included the cause of death. For Christians, entries sometimes identified residence for those not of the parish. Check the state archives in the country of your ancestors and also in Turkey. Then check the court, notary, and property records.

Contact the parish churches to look at parish registers and synagogues to look at the Jewish registers. If you're checking Bulgaria, Macedonia, or Greece, numerous pre-1872 registers are located in Greece. "The Bulgarian Orthodox Church was subordinate to the Patriarchate in Greece before 1872," notes researcher, Khalile Mehr. Find out whether a country had its state church subordinate to another country's church with records archived in a different language. Check Business, School Alumni, Medical, Military, Marriage, and Property Records

Research wills and marriage records in order to track down property records. Search medical and dental records, hospitals, orphanages, prisons, asylums, midwives' records, marriage certificates, business licenses, work permits, migration papers, passports, military pensions, notaries, sales records of homes or businesses, or any other court, military, or official transaction that might have occurred.

Other sites: For the Balkans, look at the Center for Democracy and Reconciliation in Southeast Europe's Web site at: http://www.cdsee.org/ teaching_packs_belgrade_bio.html.

## Search the 'Annual' Census and the Population Registers

Check recorded births and deaths in the first Ottoman census of 1831. Each census focused on tabulating male names to find Moslem men to conscript into the military service known as "The Army." Before 1881, the annual census registered only the male population. Search the names of committee members. Committees were set up each year to register the males in order to keep tabs on migrations in and out of each district. When the census wasn't taken, the Population Register of Moslem males kept careful records of migrations.

Find out in which local district or 'kaza' your ancestor lived. Ottomans called their annual census the sicil-i nüfus after 1881 or the nüfus between 1831–1850. You can research the Ottoman Census and Population Registers named in Turkish the Nüfus Defter. Ottoman population demographics and statistics adjusted to satisfy tax desires, since the non-Moslem population was taxed but not conscripted into military service.

The annual census didn't cover every year. Check the Ottoman census for the years1881–1883, and 1903–1906. Family historians can search each census as well as separate registers to view supplemental registration of births, marriages, divorces, and deaths. After 1881, the census takers counted all individuals (not only Moslem males) in the census and in the population registers.

Sometimes people who thought all genealogy records were destroyed in fires in their native country are surprised to learn that census records may be archived far away in Turkey. If you need text or a Web site translated into numerous languages, check out the Systran Web site at: http://www.systranbox.com/systran/box. You can translate free an entire Web site or 150 words of text.

# 21

## *Armenian Genealogy*

Check out these resources on the Web: The Armenian Research List is an on-line posting of Armenian genealogy and family history questions and answers at: http://feefhs.org/am/frg-amgs.html. Go to the Armenia Genealogy Forum. Check out this small group of dedicated Armenian-Americans that are actively engaged in seeking out Armenian records for preservation through microfilming and in assisting the formation of the first Armenian Family History Center (in-country) at Yeravan. If you want to research resources about Jews in medieval Armenia, check out the Web site at: http://www.khazaria.com/armenia/armenian-jews.html.

Then go to the Armenian Research List at: http://feefhs.org/am/amrl.html. The Armenian Research List is an on-line posting of Armenian genealogy and family history questions and answers. If you have Armenian ancestry, you are encouraged to submit your own summary genealogy and your questions. Go to the Armenian surnames as well as given male and female names at: http://feefhs.org/am/frg-amgs.html.

Search the Armenian Apostolic Church Parish Records. Then click on the online Armenia Genealogy Forum at: http://genforum.genealogy.com/armenia/. You can also search Armenian genealogy resources at http://www.DistantCousin.com. Check out genforum.genealogy.com/Armenia/ and also http://www.distantcousin.com/Links/Ethnic/Armenia/.

An Armenian genealogy Web site also is at: http:// www.geocities.com/Paris/Palais/2230/index2.html. Search Armenian genealogy at: genealogy.freewebsite-hosting.com/ links/armeniangenealogy. And links to Armenian genealogy resources Web sites are at: www.rootsweb.com/~armwgw/links.html. Then go to the Genealogy Register: Armenia at: http://genealogyregister.com/Asia/Armenia/. You'll find there these wonderful links to resources for searching Armenian genealogy such as the following: Family trees, the Armenia Genealogy Forum. It's a list of postings where Armenians having lost their relatives during the deportations and the genocide search members of their families and their descendants. The site features also a chat room.

The <u>Armenia Research List</u> contains postings by individuals who search information about lost family members during the genocide. There is also an archive. Click on <u>Armeniagenweb</u> at: <u>http://www.rootsweb.com/~armwgw/</u>. It has links to Armenian mailing lists and surname pages. You'll also find at the <u>Armenian Genealogical Society</u>. an Armenian research list and lists of Armenian names and surnames.

For passenger lists of ships transporting immigrations, check out the <u>Armenian Genealogical Web Page</u>. It also has a bibliography, and presents the book of a genealogist, cemetery data, maps, genocide survivor stories, information about Armenian legionnaires during World War I.

The <u>Distant Cousins: Armenian GenealogyResources</u> Features an Armenian surname search engine, a list of web resources and mailing lists, links for Armenian family historians including books and personal homepages. You can also read the <u>Family Questionnaire</u>. It's provided by the Armenian Historical Association of Rhode Island. The questionnaire is intended for determining the contribution of Armenians to the history of Rhode Island.

You need various personal and family data to answer the questionnaire. There's also a link to a genealogist specializing in Armenian research. All these informational links are at the Genealogy Register at: <u>http://genealogyregister.com/Asia/Armenia/</u>. There are surname lists and a home page.

Check it out. I highly rate and recommend this Web site for Armenian genealogy resources research. Click on the link to the Armenia Genealogy Forum at: http://genealogyregister.com/Asia/Armenia/. It has a list of postings where relatives may search for the descendants of lost and deported family members' names. If you're Armenian, also check out the Turkish Armenian Reconciliation Commission (TARC) at: <u>http://www.asbarez.com/TARC/Tarc.html</u>.

◆    ◆    ◆

**Web Resources and Books on Former Ottoman Empire Genealogy Web Sites**
**Albanian Research List: <u>http://feefhs.org/al/alrl.html</u>**
**Armenian Genealogical Society: <u>http://feefhs.org/am/frg-amgs.html</u>**
**Egyptian Genealogy: <u>http://www.daddezio.com/egypgen.html</u>**
**Egyptian Genealogy—Kindred Trails (tm): <u>http://www.kindredtrails.com/egypt.html</u>**

Egyptian Royal Genealogy: http://www.geocities.com/christopherjbennett/
Historical Society of Jews from Egypt: http://www.hsje.org/homepage.htm
Iranian: Persian Watch Center: Iranian-American AntiDiscrimination Council http://www.antidiscrimination.org/
The Iranian: http://www.iranian.com/Features/2002/December/LA2/index.html
Iran: Payvand's Iran News: http://www.payvand.com/news/00/aug/1054.html
Also see: Iranian American Jewish Federation and also the Council of Iranian American Jewish Organizations: P.O.BOX 3074, Beverly Hills, CA. 90212. See news article at Payvand's Iran News at: http://www.payvand.com/news/00/feb/1014.html
Excellent Genealogy and Related Books on Iran: Also see: http://payvand.com/books/
Another Sea, Another Shore: Stories of Iranian Migration
by Shouleh Vatanabadi, et all (2003)
Funny in Farsi: A Memoir of Growing Up Iranian in America
by Firoozeh Dumas (2003)
Wedding Song: Memoirs of an Iranian Jewish Woman
by Farideh Goldin (2003)
Exiled Memories: Stories of the Iranian Diaspora
by Zohreh Sullivan (2001)
Journey from the Land of No: A Girlhood Caught in Revolutionary Iran
by Roya Hakakian (2004)
Inside Iran: Women's Lives
by Jane Mary Howard (2002)
The National Iranian American Council: www.niacouncil.org
Jewish Genealogy: http://www.jewishgen.org/infofiles/
Lebanon Genealogy: http://genforum.genealogy.com/lebanon
http://www.mit.edu:8001/activities/lebanon/map.html
Lebanese Descendants of the Bourjaily Family (Abou R'Jaily): http://www.abourjeily.com/Family/index.htm
Descendants of Atallah Abou Rjeily, born about 1712
Lebanese Club of New York City:
http://nyc.lebaneseclub.org/
http://www.rootsweb.com/~lbnwgw/lebclubnyc/index.htm
Lebanese Genealogy: http://www.rootsweb.com/~lbnwgw/
Middle East Genealogy: http://www.rootsweb.com/~mdeastgw/index.html

**Middle East Genealogy by country:** http://www.rootsweb.com/~mdeastgw/ index.html#country

**Polish Genealogical Society of America:** http://feefhs.org/pol/frg-pgsa.html

**Sephardim.com:** http://www.sephardim.com/

**Syrian and Lebanese Genealogy:** http://www.genealogytoday. com/family/syrian/

**Syria Genealogy:** http://www.rootsweb.com/~syrwgw/

**Syrian/Lebanese/Jewish/Farhi Genealogy Site (Flowers of the Orient):** http://www.farhi.org

**Turkish Genealogy Discussion Group:** http://www.turkey. com/forums/forumdisplay.php3?forumid=18

**Turkish Telephone Directories Information: Türk Telekomünikasyon (Telecommunication)** http://ttrehber.gov.tr/rehber_webtech/index.asp

**Croatia Genealogy Cross Index:** http://feefhs.org/cro/indexcro.html

**Eastern Europe:** http://www.cyndislist.com/easteuro.htm

**Eastern European Genealogical Society, Inc.:** http://feefhs.org/ca/frg-eegs.html

**Eastern Europe Index:** http://feefhs.org/ethnic.html

**India Royalty:** http://freepages.genealogy.rootsweb.com/~royalty/india/ persons.html

**Romanian American Heritage Center:** http://feefhs.org/ro/frg-rahc.html

**Slavs, South: Cultural Society:** http://feefhs.org/frg-csss.html

**Ukrainian Genealogical and Historical Society of Canada:** http://feefhs.org/ ca/frgughsc.html

**Rom (Gypsies):** http://www.cyndislist.com/peoples.htm#Gypsies

**See: McGowan, Bruce William, 1933- Defter-i mufassal-i liva-i Sirem: an Ottoman revenue survey dating from the reign of Selim II. / Bruce William McGowan.**

**Ann Arbor, Mich.: University Microfilms, 1967.**

**See: Bogaziçi University Library Web sites:** http://seyhan.library.boun.edu.tr/search/wN{232}ufus+Defter/ wN{232}ufus+Defter/1,29,29,B/frameset&FF=wN{232}ufus+Defter&9,9, or http://seyhan.library.boun.edu.tr/search/dTaxation+--+Turkey. /dtaxation+turkey/-5,-1,0,B/exact&FF=dtaxation+turkey&1,57,

**Jurisdictions and Localities in Bulgaria:**

Michev N. and P. Koledarov. *Rechnik na selishchata i selishchnite imena v Bulgariia, 1878–1987* (Dictionary of villages and village names in Bulgaria, 1878–1987), Sofia: Nauka i izkustvo, 1989 (FHL book 949.77 E5m).

# 22

## *Greek Genealogy*

Greek Genealogy Web sites offer links to information on videos, publications, and rich oral history. Everybody becomes Greek for a day at Greek music and food festivals. At one Greek genealogy Web site at: http://www.daddezio.com/catalog/grkndx20.html, you'll learn that name days instead of birthdays are celebrated in Greece according to "fairly rigid conventions."

The Internet has numerous Greek genealogy Web sites, some helping to re-unite numerous adoptees with their original families through genealogy research. To start your Greek genealogy search, I highly recommend the book titled, A History of the Greeks in the Americas 1453–1938. You can find it online at Amazon.com at the Web site: http://www.amazon.com/exec/obidos/ASIN/1882792157/. You'll find an excellent publication on Greek genealogy titled: Greek Genealogy Publications by Lica H. Catsakis at the Web site: http://www.feefhs.org/misc/pub-lhc.html.

Also I highly recommend these books on Greek genealogy:

**The Greeks in America**
http://www.amazon.com/exec/obidos/ASIN/0822510103/
**The Family in Greek History**
http://www.amazon.com/exec/obidos/ASIN/0674292707/

### Check out these Greek genealogy Web sites:

**goGreece.com: Genealogy**
http://gogreece.com/society_culture/genealogy.html
**Hellenes-Diaspora Greek Genealogy**
http://www.geocities.com/SouthBeach/Cove/4537/Main1.html

- Begin your genealogy search with maps of your ancestor's town, city, and neighborhood. For example, you'll find an excellent source with Greek Genealogy Research, 2nd Edition (1993), 82 pages, with assistance from

119

Dan Schlyter, and Greek Gazetteer, Volume 1 (1997), 120 pages, by Lica Catsakis.

It's easier to find information on searching Greek genealogy than in some of the other countries of Eastern Europe and the Middle East that formerly were under the Ottoman Empire, except where fire destroyed records as it did in parts of Crete. At the Web site titled "Greece.com Society and Culture" at http://gogreece.com/society_culture/genealogy.html, you'll find "an extensive collection of links to web sites relevant to genealogical research, as well as, mailing lists, and articles relevant to Greek culture."

What's great about this Web site is that contains a description and list of the Greek genealogy sites. Also try the message board at: GreekFamilies.com at: http://www.greekfamilies.com/pages/138257/index.htm. Look at the Hellenic Genealogy Web site at: http://www.geocities.com/SouthBeach/Cove/4537/. Also, you'll find excellent Web sites on Greek (Hellenic) genealogy at Dimitri's Surname Database at: http://www.dimitri.8m.com/surnames.html. You can search many Greek surnames there and their ancestral origins. For example, the Greek surname, Fotiadis comes from Thessalonikis in Macedonia. So to look up the origins, note that the variant spellings of Photiadis and Fotiadis are variations of the same name and search in both the "F" and the "P" files. On this surname database, it's listed under "F."

If you're ancestors are Greek, chances are you've kept in contact with other Greek family members, unless you're an adoptee or come from a family that has intermarried several generations back. Then here's your chance to get in touch again. Go to the Greek Roots Center at: http://www.butterbox.gr/. Roots Research Center is a non-profit, voluntary, non governmental organization, helping adults adoptees with Greek roots to discover their origins.

The Roots Research Center has information on orphanages in Greece. Write to them at: Roots Research Center, P.O Box 71514, Vyron, 16210, Athens, Greece. They cooperate with all Founding houses of Greece, Red Cross reunion section, International Social Service Greek section, Hellenes Diasporas and every other willing Organization and offer "an independent mediation service where prospective adoptive parts, birth relatives can be helped to make cooperative arrangements about contact."

There are many Greek children who were adopted by families in many different countries, including the USA. Some of them don't have written records or adoption files. If you want to meet your birth family or find out more about your Greek roots, you should know that some Greek families who want to find descendants of adopted children can't find missing members because they can't afford to pay for research in other nations. If this is your genealogy research project, feel free to contact the Roots Research Center at: 56 PANEPISTIMIOU STR 104 31, in Athens, or at their Confidential Address, P.O Box 71514, 16210 Gr.

# 23

## *Macedonia of the Ottoman Empire Era*

Start with parish registers. Then proceed to civil registration and the censuses. Since most of the Christian population of Macedonia is Macedonian Orthodox, which is similar to Serbian Orthodox, if you're searching parish registers from 1800 to the present, you can probably find records from 1800 forwards in time in the parish registers. You'll find the parish registers in the national, historical, and community archives as well as in various churches.

If you're looking for civil registration, there wasn't any until 1946. For dates before 1913, look to the Ottoman population registers, because after 1913 Macedonia was then part of Serbia. Write to the Ministry of Internal Affairs to look through civil registration materials. The Ministry of Internal Affairs is not the state archives.

Your next step would be to turn to the censuses. They were under the Ottoman population registers before 1913. When the Ottoman Empire fell, Macedonia became part of Serbia. Therefore, 1921 became the year of the first national census at the time that Macedonia then became an area within Yugoslavia.

Next you'll want to turn to the Ottoman population registers. You can find the census returns/population registers from 1829 or 1831. When you skip to 1881–1889, you'll find that by that time the records have been meticulously swept within a single system. You'll view the census returns at the district level (kaza).

At first only Moslem males were registered, but the information portrays a vivid picture as described because not only are the birth dates recorded or the migrations in and out, but also eye color and complexion down to the freckles. You'll note that what was recorded included whether they moved, date of death, and military service dates.

When you get to the 1881 census and later tabulations of population, you'll see that the goal was to establish a demography or population figures for political and social history. Not only Moslem males, but all people were then counted in both the census and the population registers after that date.

The registers listed all family members; sex; birth date; residence; age; religion; craft or occupation; marital status, marriage date; health; military status. It's a good way to find out the religion or occupation of family members.

Your third step would be to turn to records in the Family History Library collection. According to the Library, "Virtually no manuscript materials have been filmed by the Family History Library." If your family comes from one of the countries under the former Ottoman Empire, it would be great if you can donate manuscript materials to be filmed. Ask them first if they are accepting materials and in what form.

## Research Procedures

The catalog of the Family History Library may have records listed by the name of the district or the town. According to the Family History Library, look for jurisdictions and localities in Slovenia by consulting a book of place names in the former Yugoslavia. The Family History Library in Salt Lake City refers researchers to the book titled: *Imenik mesta u Jugoslaviji* (Places names in Yugoslavia). Beograd: Novinska Ustanova Sluñbeni List SFRJ, 1973. (949.7 E5u; film 874,462 item 2)

Have you researched records at the national level? If so, look for records from a specific town or area. The films are not housed in the Family History Library. Order films prior to arriving in Salt Lake City by calling or writing: Family History Library, Attn: Library Attendants, 35 N. West Temple Street, Salt Lake City, UT 84150-3400, telephone: 801-240-2331.

War, earthquakes, and fire have destroyed lots of Macedonian archives and records. You have to tend with the destruction of documents from the Balkan wars as well as World War I and II. What if you had to search the ancient library at Alexandria? Yet all is not lost.

Between 1918 and 1941, you can search the state archive in Beograd for genealogy records in what was called Macedonia when your relatives lived there.

World War II devastated the archives of Skopje. The Archive of Macedonia was established in 1951. It has a website at http://www.arhiv.gov.mk/Ang1.htm. You'll have to allow for the 1963 earthquake that demolished the facility, but a new building rose in 1969. What you can search there are nine regional archives located in Bitola, Kumanovo, Ohrid, Prilep, Skopje, Strumica, Tetovo, Titov

Veles, and Stip. What genealogy records that remain at the Archive of Macedonia includes mostly material from after 1969. Therefore, it's wise to check with them to see whether anything exists from a former period.

If you're researching religion, In 1870 the newly established Bulgarian exarchate received the support of Macedonians, mainly because of its Slavic character. In 1958, the Macedonian Orthodox Church was reestablished in Ohrid. So Macedonia broke free of the Ottoman Empire during the Balkan wars of 1912–1913. Searching records could include tracking relatives to Greece, Bulgaria, or Serbia as Macedonia was divided between Serbia and Greece with a tiny part going to Bulgaria.

Find out whether your relatives lived in Aegean Macedonia (Greece), Vardar Macedonia (Serbia), or Pirin Macedonia (Bulgaria). After 1991, land-locked Macedonia became a small, independent nation. Records could be difficult to find, but also may be hidden in church parishes and family keepsakes. Some records along with religious items were sewn inside of clothing, quilt, and drapery hems. So check out your relatives' oral histories and traditions.

# 24

## *Croatia Genealogy Research*

First look at the Family History Library's microfilm collection on Croatia. They have about 2,600 rolls of microfilm that were sent in from Croatia since filming began there in 1985. Filming has occurred at the central state archive and regional archives of Osijek, Varañdin, Zadar, Split, Dubrovnik, Rijeka, and Pazin.

If you're looking at parish registers, they start in the 1700s and are archived until the present. Roman Catholic parishes kept registers earlier than Orthodox parishes which were required to keep them only after 1777.

According to the Family History Library, "Civil transcripts of registers were mandated during the 19$^{th}$ century. A tabular format was adopted after 1848. In 1946, civil registration replaced parish registration of vital events.

As of 1945 most registers were turned over to civil authorities and deposited in the local city hall. Older registers have been and continue to be transferred to the district historical archives or the Croatia State Archive."

To find the registers, contact the Civil Registry offices. If you need post World War Two material from the Civil Registers—after 1946, they are there. However, civil registration before May 1946 contains the names and data on Moslems only. After 1946, civil authorities in Croatia and the rest of Yugoslavia began universal registration.

Next, look at the censuses that start in the year 1785 and continue until the present. During the Ottoman Empire, the census followed the usual name-taking for taxation or conscription and to provide a demography of the people in Croatia.

If you want military records of ancestors, the first military census began in 1785. By 1804–5, you have the civil census. Regular censuses were conducted in 1857, 1869, and every ten years, 1880–1910. Go to the archives of each district or city to find a name lists if it is available.

The Family History Library in Salt Lake City recommends for searching gene-alogy records of Croatia the book titled: *Imenik mesta u Jugoslaviji* (Places names in Yugoslavia). Beograd: Novinska Ustanova Sluñbeni List SFRJ, 1973. (949.7 E5u; film 874,462 item 2)

This book will help you to identify the jurisdictions and localities. If you can't read the place names in Yugoslavia, then check out the Family History Library Catalog to see if any records are listed under the name of the town or the district.

Your next step would be to search records on a national level. Look for specific towns or villages and cities. The films are not housed in the Family History Library. Order films prior to arriving in Salt Lake City by calling or writing: Family History Library, Attn: Library Attendants, 35 N. West Temple Street, Salt Lake City, UT 84150-3400, telephone: 801-240-2331.

If you've exhausted the Croatian social associations in the US, then turn to the Croatia State Archive, Hrvatski Dravni Arhiv, Maruliev Trg. 21, 10000 Zagreb, telephone: 385-01-4801-930, fax 385-01-4829-000, email hda@arhiv.hr, web http://zagreb.arhiv.hr/.

Instead of actually going to the country in person, email first to set up appointments where you'll go if you actually make a trip over there. Old books were transferred to the archives in 1957—that means books more than 1000 years old. Check out the town halls because they have registers dating before World War II.

After the war, the churches kept registers. There was a census in 1957. If you're looking for old records before 1857, then go to archives at the church reg-isters as well as the state archives. A lot of registers remain in parishes.

Look for transcripts in the Archbishopric Archive. According to the Family History Library, "Pedigrees are scattered in the collection. Though censuses were conducted in 1857, 1869, 1880, 1890, and 1900, there are no census records in the archive."

The charge 88 kuna/hour for research. There are twelve district historical archives and contact information is available on the web site. Check out the Zagreb Historical Archive. Historijski arhiv Zagreb, Opati?ka 29, 10000 Zagreb, telephone: 385-01-4551-375, fax 385-01-4851-374, povijesni-arhiv-zg@zg.tel.hr, open 9:00–14:00 daily. The Family History Library notes that "A good genealogy website is found at: http://www.croatia-in-english.com/gen/index.html."

There are numerous Croatian social halls and associations in the USA and other countries because more than a quarter of all Croatians lived outside of Croatia by 1970. Check these social and fraternal or family associations for genealogy connections and books, published or unpublished, written by individuals for their own families.

Croats are mainly Roman Catholic, and speak Croation, and Serbs are mostly Orthodox and speak Serbian. The language of the records is either Latin, Croatian, Hungarian, or Italian. Besides Roman script, there is also Glagolitic script.

# 25

# *Bulgaria*

Check out the Bulgaria Genealogy forum at: http://genforum.genealogy.com/bulgaria/. If you're Jewish, also check out the Sephardi Connection Discussion Forums People Finder at the Sephardi Connection. Their Web site is at: http://sephardiconnect.com/webx/webx.cgi?sephard-13@%5E185@.ee6c850.

If you're Christian, look at the Orthodox and Catholic records which date back to around 1850. A few Catholic books go back to slightly before 1797. These genealogy records have the names of the head of household and parents, residence, dates and places of birth and baptism, marriage, death and burial; as well as ages in entries for marriage and death.

According to the Family History Library in Salt Lake City, baptisms include names of the godparents. Deaths sometimes include the cause of death.

Entries sometimes identify residence for those not of the parish. Some parish registers have been sent to the state archives or the national museum. Visit the parish churches to look at parish registers.

Some pre-1872 registers are in Greece. Before 1872 the Bulgarian Orthodox Church was subordinate to the Patriarchate in Greece. If you're looking for civil registration, the records begin around 1893 when the process of civil registration began.

According to the Family History Library, "Birth, marriage, and death records have the exact date of the event, including time of day for births; name of the principal and parents' names; occupation and religious preference of parents; name of informant for births and witnesses for marriages; residence for parents of new born, of the groom and bride for marriages, and of the deceased for deaths; age at death, cause of death, and burial place in death records."

Go to the district archives in each of the 26 districts of Bulgaria to find specific records for particular areas. To record all the vital information in the same building, in 1920 family registers came into practice.

To find these family registers before 1920, look to the national census. It began in 1880. The first national census took place right after Bulgaria's liberation from Ottoman rule.

Because 19th century name lists are not available, you'd have to turn to the Ottoman census records for the period 1831–1872. Only these records were enumerations of males for tax, fiscal, and military purposes. They contain the name of the head of household, male family members, ages, occupation, and property.

To start with the Family History Library, go to their small book collection and microfilms of civil registration, 1893–1906, for the Bulgarian districts of Sofia and Pazardzhik. You're going to have to list the local areas or jurisdictions to narrow down your search. To find these jurisdictions, you need the book by Michev N. and P. Koledarov. *Rechnik na selishchata i selishchnite imena v Bulgariia, 1878–1987* (Dictionary of villages and village names in Bulgaria, 1878–1987), Sofia: Nauka i izkustvo, 1989 (FHL book 949.77 E5m).

Once you have the name of the district and town, go to the Family History Library Catalog (Salt Lake City). There may be records listing under the name of the district in Bulgaria. If you can't find anything, then check national level records of a specific town rather than the district.

You can see some of these towns on films. The films are not housed in the Family History Library. Order films prior to arriving in Salt Lake City by calling or writing: Family History Library, Attn: Library Attendants, 35 N. West Temple Street, Salt Lake City, UT 84150-3400, telephone: 801-240-2331.

To narrow down the districts, there are only twenty six. In each of the districts, there is an archive. In that archive you have church records and civil registration records. Then narrow down still more as you go to the churches and monasteries.

You won't find vital records in the National Historical Archive in Sofia, according to the Family History Library research. A guide exists to the holdings of this archive: *Putevoditel na Tsentralniia Durzhaven Istoricheski Arkhiv*, Sofia: Nauka i izkustvo, 1970 (FHL book 949.77 A5p).

To research deeper, turn to the Ottoman census records at the Oriental Department of the Cyril and Methodius National Library, Sofia. What if you don't read Bulgarian? If you get to the records at the Cyril and Methodius National Library, find a translator or translation manual and then go onto the next nation in nearby Istanbul.

Once in Istanbul, look at the archives of the Ottoman Empire. You've now reached the core of the former Ottoman Empire. It seems everything lands up in Istanbul, or does it? That depends on what else is in the various churches or synagogues depending upon your ethnic identity or religion. Check out the genealogy site on the Web at: www.rootsweb.com/~bgrwgw/index.html#NEW.

When searching Bulgaria, understand it was the first state to join the Ottoman Empire and the last to be liberated. Bulgaria was under the former Ottoman Empire from 1396–1878, only to be liberated by the Russian army. Another country was added to Bulgaria called Eastern Rumelia, in the southeast.

More territory was added by 1913 during the Balkan wars. A lot of records were hidden because Bulgaria allied with Germany in both World Wars. So if you're of ethnic groups whose records were hidden, such as Sephardic Jews, you need to go to synagogues and Sephardic organizations to find links and leads to where the records can be found. In 1990 Bulgaria became an independent country.

Records are kept in different places for different ethnic groups. You have besides Bulgaries, the Rom people (Gypsies), Turks, Macedonians, Armenians, Russians and Sephardic Jews. If you need to learn Bulgarian before searching records, the Slavic language is written in Cyrillic script.

When you search records, the languages will change with the ethnicity of the people being recorded. Records are found not only in Bulgarian, the main language, but also in Turkish, Greek, and Old Church Slavonic as well as the Sephardic records of synagogues and Jewish schools in Hebrew and Judezmo/Ladino.

Acknowledgement and credit for all the information in this book on Bulgaria, Croatia, and Macedonia is given to the Family History Library, Salt Lake City, UT. Thanks to researcher/writer, Kahlile Mehr. All the articles and information on Bulgaria, Macedonia, and Croatia written by former staff writer for the Family History Library, Salt Lake City, UT, Khalile Mehr, are copyrighted by The Family History Library.

# 26

## *Hungary*

Start your search of genealogy records for Hungry when it was under the former Ottoman Empire by going to the Hungarian Bookstore site on the Web at: http://www.hungarianbookstore.com/. They have links to many Hungarian sites and publications. Join various Hungarian associations.

These include the American Hungarian Foundation, the American Hungarian Library and Historical Society, and the various Hungarian Genealogy Societies in your locality. Contact the Carpatho-Rusyn Society. Gather your maps.

You can also contact the Hungarian Genealogy of Greater Cleveland and the Cleveland Hungarian Heritage Museum, if you're visiting Ohio. Then look at the Hungarian Phone Book if you can read Hungarian. Search for familiar surnames. Look in the Budapest City Archives, the National Archives of Hungary, the HungaryGenWeb, and the Map pages of Eötvös University, Department of Cartography. If you go to the Hungarian Bookstore Web site at: http://www.hungarianbookstore.com/, you'll find links to various genealogy Web sites and even a Hungarian language radio station.

It's a good start to join a Hungarian or Hungarian-American group and also to subscribe to a magazine from your ancestor's town. Check out the Web site on East European genealogy at: http://www.feefhs.org/. Or if you can write in Hungarian, consider joining soc.culture.magyar, a Google newsgroup online. It's at: http://groups.google.com/groups?hl=en&lr=&ie=UTF-8&oe=UTF-8&group=soc.culture.magyar.

According to email from Anthony Trendl, community editor, The Hungarian Bookstore, I asked the following question:

Where would be the best place to start to search Hungarian genealogy if one only speaks English? Mr. Trendl's answer by email is the following:

Anne,

That's a big question. :)

My caveat is I'm not a professional genealogist. We're still getting into this ourselves. My dad's side is Hungarian (I'm American), and my fiancée is from Hungary. I only speak English, and have the same handicap as those in your book..

The wars and such have chopped up the country, and in some cases, destroyed records. Don't be discouraged. There is still hope.

Some of what it takes to research Hungarian genealogy is logical, and useful in any genealogical project. Here's what's off the top of my head.

- The most obvious start is to talk to everyone in your family. This isn't always easy, since most have never been interviewed and aren't used to thinking what you, the reporter might want to know. Bring a tape recorder. Follow-up with new questions.

- Watch History Detectives on PBS. These sharp sleuths have little to do with genealogy, but they do research in the same kind of creative manner that you will find helpful.

- Be organized in your research. Label things, scan things, and start connecting the dots. As your work grows, so will your files. Good organization can keep a researcher from going batty later on.

- Make copies of everyone in your family's baptismal, wedding, and death records.

- Do some reading on the communities from where you think you came from. There are plenty of good resources for history out there.

- Remember communism revised some of the history books to suit their views. Look at the book's copyright date. Suspect anything before 1989.

- Remember religion in Hungary is largely cultural. Don't presume that just because someone claims to be Catholic, for example, that they've ever been actually involved in the parish serving that area. Also, some Jews converted rather than be killed.

- As country lines have change, recognize sometimes city names have changed as well. In doing some reading...even starting with the local library's travel guides, you'll start to get a feel for an area. Some are more English-speaking than others.

- Remember the Holocaust hit Hungarians hard. It wasn't just Jews, but those suspected of being Jewish, and those who simply were Hungarian.

- Go to Hungary. Research your tail off, save all of it on a CD, and come on over to Hungary to do more. Plan ahead, and have an itinerary and meetings planned. If it is a social trip, just be sure to be disciplined. Hungary is beautiful, and it is easy to get sidetracked.

- When you go to Hungary, bring your camera and have unlimited film. Ask permission when inside places.

- Take pictures of your relatives.

- Churches can be a great asset. Baptisms, weddings, all that sort of thing often are recorded. Even though you may not read Hungarian, learning a few key words to understand headings can help.

- Buy a dictionary that covers both languages. Get a real one, not one of those travel ones. You want to learn the word for "baptism' not 'bathroom' :)

- Find a Hungarian friend willing to help.

- Consider hiring a translation service. We used one here in Chicago to translate medical records while we prepared papers for INS.

- When surfing the web, you can still use Hungarian sites. Many have English versions. Look for the little Britiish flag.

- Google has a Hungarian version. That's no small thing, since it can help you isolate your research.

- Surnames change. Not only do people drop accents from their name, but occasionally, the spelling changes. In America, you might find Kovach, but in Hungary, it is likely spelled Kovacs. Same pronunciation, different spelling.

- Join a genealogy club. Eastern Europe is more than just Hungary, but there are lots from Eastern and Central Europe roots who have already tread the path you are starting on. Don't be shy. Ask questions.

My site has a genealogy section that includes lots of links to official city sites in Hungary, like for Pecs and Szeged. You'll also see a number of useful books, software applications and magazines, all available for purchase.
http://www.hungarianbookstore.com/genealogy.htm (Genealogy links—including online discussion boards, plus a short essay)
http://www.hungarianbookstore.com/language.htm (Dictionaries, tips, and some online dictionary links readers can use for free)

http://www.hungarianbookstore.com/news.htm (Magazines, newspapers...very useful for the researcher looking to know the culture. Many are in English).

http://www.hungarianbookstore.com/groups.htm (Listing of Hungarian social clubs in the USA, including online discussion boards. Very useful for researchers trying to learn about the ins and outs of the country. They can also be a great resource to find professional assistance.)

I'm interested in reading your book when is ready. I also review on Amazon, and am ranked among their top reviewers. The link below will take you to my area on Amazon. Contact me again to get a current address if you'd like to send a review copy. I review nonHungarian-related books as well, so don't be surprised to see my thoughts on the latest bestseller next to a book on Hungarian poetry. :)

About HungarianBooks editor@hungarianbookstore.com

I hope this helps you Anne. Feel free to quote me as you like, and reference our site when you do.

Anthony Trendl

community editor

editor@hungarianbookstore.com

**The Hungarian Bookstore**

http://www.hungarianbookstore.com


The Hungarian Bookstore connects Hungarians with their culture by providing a directory of churches, restaurants and grocery stores. We sell books, DVDs, CDs, music, videos, magazines, newspapers and more.

# 27

## *Searching Several Areas Formerly Under the Ottoman Empire*

If your relatives lived under the former Ottoman Empire in the following areas: Hungary, Yugoslavia, Croatia, Bosnia, Albania, Macedonia, Greece, Romania, Moldova, Bulgaria, southern Ukraine, Turkey, Georgia, Armenia, Iraq, Kuwait, Cyprus, Syria, Lebanon, Israel/Palestine, Jordan, Eastern and Western Saudi Arabia, Oman, Bahrain, eastern Yemen, Egypt, northern Libya, Tunisia, and northern Algeria, the first step to take after gathering your own family or client's materials such as birth, marriage, and death certificates, military service, or maps of old addresses and towns is to join associations and subscribe to magazines about that area of the world.

Whether your relatives or clients had ancestors who came from Albania, Romania, Moldova, Cyprus, Syria, Egypt, Yemen, Libya, Tunisia, Northern Algeria or any of the European countries under the Ottoman Empire before 1914, you gather your materials and start your search in pretty much the same way.

You look at church parishes, synagogues, mosques, religious schools, public schools, marriage licenses, death certificates, birth certificates, passports, ship passenger registries, dates entered the US or Canada or any other country, and you contact people in ethnic associations. Online you search for magazines published in the town or near the city of your ancestor's or client's birth.

You look at material in the Family History Library if it's there, or you go to the various genealogy groups for Eastern European or Middle Eastern genealogy and ancestry research. If you belong to a particular ethnic or religious group you go to records kept by your ethnic or religious group.

Jewish genealogy records would be kept in different places than Christian records in most of the countries under the Ottoman Empire, but not always and not in every country. So check out individual town registers as they may not have classified always by religion. Some countries had population registers for all males or heads of households and for all family members.

Other countries recorded the migrations in and out of the country, and still other countries kept a record of what the person looked like, military service, and property ownership for tax collection purposes or notary recordings. So check notaries and court records as well as wills and recorded marriages.

Some people migrated from one country that was under the Ottoman Empire to a country that wasn't. For example, back-migration from Romania to Poland or Ukraine. If you're Sephardic, a good source is Sephardim.com at: http:// www.sephardim.com/. Search their engine for surnames.

The Sephardic names search engine lists names going back to the 14th century and beyond by alphabet letter. For example, the name Leven, a Sephardic name in the 14th century, shows up later as an Ashkenazi name (Levin/Levine/Lewin) in Poland in the 18th century and also showing a migration to Bessarabia, Romania, in the late 18th century coming from Poland.

Another excellent site is Sephardic Genealogy Forum at: http://www. orthohelp.com/geneal/sources2.HTM. At that Web site you might want to check out the passenger lists of Spaniards and/or Sephardim sailing to the Americas between 1500 and 1800. The archive of passengers is still in Seville. You'll find the records in the Archivo General de Indias.

The list of passengers from each ship sailing to America up to1800, the records state each passenger name and place of birth, name of parents and their brithplaces, the job and destination of the passenger after arrival in the Americas. If you write to the archives in Seville, include the following: passenger name and the approximate date of the trip to America. Address your inquiry addressed to: Archivo General de Indias, Avda. Constitucion s/n, SEVILLA—SPAIN. Phone: +34-95-4500530. Fax: +34-95-4219485. Consult also the Sephardic Forum: http://www.jewishgen.org/sefardsig/SefardForum.htm

For information on other Jewish migrations to Palestine/Israel, write to: Batya Unterschatz, Director, Jewish Agency Bureau of Missing Relative, P.O.Box 92, Jerusalem 91000. Also see: Avotaynu, Publishers of Works on Jewish Genealogy (Journal and Books) at: http://www.avotaynu.com/

◆     ◆     ◆

## Books to Research recommended by the Web site at Sephardim.com:

Assis: Jews in the Crown of Aragon (Part II 1328–1493); Regesta of the Cartas Reales in Archivo de la Corona de Aragon. Ginzei am olam: Central Arch Hist of Jewish People, Jerusalem

Beinart: Conversos on Trial. The Inquisition in Ciudad Real. Magnes Press, Hebrew University, Jerus. 1981

Raphael: Expulsion 1492 Chronicles. Carmi House Press

Tello: Judios de Toledo—2 Vols. Instituto B Arias Montano. Consejo Sup de inverstigacions Cientificas.

# 28

# *DNA-Driven Genealogy and the Molecular Revolution*

Geneticists today are making inroads in new areas such as phenomics and ancestral genetics. Batsheva Bonné-Tamir, PhD, http://www.tau.ac.il/medicine/USR/bonnétamirb.htm or http://www.tau.ac.il/medicine/ at Tel-Aviv University, Israel, is Head of the National Laboratory for the Genetics of Israeli Populations (with Mia Horowitz) and Director of the Shalom and Varda Yoran Institute for Genome Research Tel-Aviv. She is also on the faculty of the Department of Human Genetics and Molecular Medicine, Sackler School of Medicine.

Dr. Bonné-Tamir states that "One of my most impressive conclusions from the advancement in the last few years and the accumulation of knowledge in the fields of genetics and medicine, is the molecular revolution based on immense sophistication of lab techniques. This is really responsible for the recent increased emphasis on the human-socialanthropological aspects that affect biological diversity."

Bonné-Tamir explains, "At a meeting in 1973, in my paper on Merits and Difficulties in Studies of Middle Eastern Isolates, I said that 'The Middle Eastern isolates have emphasized again the fertile and necessary interrelationship between history and genetics.'"

Do historical events influence genes? "Comparative studies in population genetics are often undertaken in order to attempt reconstruction of historical and migratory movements based on gene frequencies," says Bonné-Tamir. "The Samaritans and Karaites offer opportunities in the opposite direction, for example, to learn the influence of historical events on gene frequencies."

In another paper in 1979 on *Analysis of Genetic Data on Jewish Populations*, Dr. Bonné-Temir wrote that "Our purpose in studying the differences and similarities between various Jewish populations was not to determine whether a Jewish race exists. Nor was it to discover the original genes of 'ancient Hebrews,' or to retrieve genetic characteristics in the historical development of the Jews.

"Rather, it was to evaluate the extent of 'heterogeneity' in the separate populations, to construct a profile of each population as shaped by the genetic data, and to draw inferences about the possible influences of dispersion, migration, and admixture processes on the genetic composition of these populations."

In 1999, Dr. Bonné-Temir organized an international symposium on Genomic Views of Jewish History. "And unfortunately, the many papers presented were never published," says Bonné-Temir.

## Molecular Genealogy Research Projects

Certain mtDNA haplogroups and mutations or markers within the haplogroups turn up in research studies of Ashkenazim when scientists look at the maternal lineages. For example, 9.0 of Ashkenazic (Jewish) women have mtDNA haplogroups that follow the Cambride Reference Sequence (CRS) (Anderson et al. 1981).

That means their matrilineal ancestry lines follow the reference sequence that all other mtDNA haplogroup markers are compared with. The CRS shows a specific sequence of mtDNA haplogroup H found in more than 46% of all Europeans and 6% of Middle Eastern peoples. You can view a table of mtDNA sequences titled "Frequently Encountered mtDNA Hapotypes" at Table 3 in the article, "*Founding Mothers of Jewish Communities: Geographically Separated Jewish Groups Were Independently Founded by Very Few Female Ancestors,*" Mark G. Thomas et al, American Journal of Human Genetics, 70: 1411–1420, 2002.

The only exception is that the Ashkenazic mtDNA haplogroup maternal ancestral lines, show up at only 2.6% with one mutation away from the CRS 343 creating U3 mtDNA haplogroup instead of the H mtDNA haplogroup. The CRS is H haplogroup.

Where does U3 mtDNA show up at the higher rate of 17%? In Iraqi Jews. Ashkenazi mtDNA shows up at 9.0 percent following the CRS with H mtDNA haplogroup. Yet 27.0% of Moroccan Jews have mtDNA following the CRS. So does more than 46% of all Europeans and 25% of all Middle Eastern people have MtDNA following the CRS. That's haplogroup H of the Cambridge Reference Sequence.

The table in the article mentioned above has many sequences of mtDNA listed. Ashkenazi mtDNA was compared to MtDNA in other Jewish groups—Moroccan, Iraqi, Iranian, Georgian, Bukharan, Yemenite, Ethopian, and Indian. These were compared to non-Jewish Germans, Berbers, Syrians,

Georgian non-Jews, Uzbeks, Yemenites, Ethiopian non-Jews, Hindus, and Israeli Arabs. The percentage of frequencies of HSV-1 mtDNA sequences were listed in the samples from sites 16090-16365.

Looking only at Ashkenazi mtDNA, the mutations 184 and 265T show up in 2.6% of the Ashkenazi mtDNA. Yet in Jews from Bukhara, these same mutations show up in 15.2% of mtDNA.

And 129 and 223 mutations show up in 2.6% of the Ashkenazi mtDNA. Yet in Bukharian Jewish mtDNA, this mutation shows up at 12.1%. The rest of the Ashkenazi mtDNA stands at 9.0% for matching the CRS. That's H haplogroup, the most frequent mtDNA haplogroup found in Europe. Only 1.3% of Ashkenazic mtDNA has one mutation at 274. Yet 20% of Yemenite Jewish mtDNA shows this same mutation at 274.

Be aware that not every Jewish person has been tested for mtDNA or Y-chromosomes. You first have to research how significant samples are in speaking for the majority of any population. They do have scientific credibility, but you must always look at the sample size.

DNA-driven genealogy is about tracing patterns—from patterns in the genes to patterns in the migrations. Where do the women—the founding mothers—of the Eastern European Jewish communities—the Ashkenazim—originate? How do their origins compare with the origins of the founding fathers, the paternal lines?

I asked genetic scientist, Dr. Mark Thomas, Department of Biology, University College London what his latest research findings were on Ashkenazi women as I had read his recent study.*

The article referred to in his letter is titled, *"Founding Mothers of Jewish Communities: Geographically Separated Jewish Groups Were Independently Founded by Very Few Female Ancestors,"* American Journal of Human Genetics. 70: 1411–1420, 2002. The study was researched by Dr. Mark G. Thomas, Martin Richards, Michael E. Weale, Antonio Toroni, David B. Goldstein, et al. Here is his reply.

---

**Dear Anne:**

**Our study did not conclude that they are not related to one another and not related to anyone in the Middle East. Neither did it conclude that they are wholly Slavic.**

**Our study presented evidence for strong independent female founding events in most Jewish communities. This evidence was**

*not as strong for Ashkenazi Jews and we proposed that Ashkenazi Jews were made up of a mosaic of different, independently founded communities that has since homogenised.*

*Because of the evidence for strong independent female founding events, assigning an origin to those founding mothers becomes a very difficult, if not impossible task. There was some suggestion in two communities, Indian Jews and Ethiopian Jews, of a local rather than a Middle Eastern origin for the founding mothers. I have enclosed a PDF version of our paper.*

*I hope this helps.*
 *Best wishes*

*Mark*
—

*Dr Mark Thomas*
*Department of Biology*
*University College London*
 *Web: www.ucl.ac.uk/tcga/*

◆      ◆      ◆

In January, 2006 another study was electronically published in the American Journal of Human Genetics. 2006; 78:000–000. _ 2006 by the American Society of Human Genetics, titled, *The Matrilineal Ancestry of Ashkenazi Jewry: Portrait of a Recent Founder Event.* You can read the article online as a PDF file at one of the Family Tree DNA Web site links at: http://www.familytreedna.com/pdf/ 43026_Doron.pdf#search=%22ashkenazi%20mtdna%22.

The abstract or summary of the study reported in part that "close to one-half of Ashkenazi Jews, estimated at 8,000,000 people, can be traced back to only 4 women carrying distinct mtDNAs that are virtually absent in other populations, with the important exception of low frequencies among non-Ashkenazi Jews."

What the study concluded with was that "four founding mtDNAs, likely of Near Eastern ancestry, underwent major expansion(s) in Europe within the past millennium."

Interestingly, the haplogroups of the four founding mothers fell into specific sequences of the "K" haplogroup (Hg) and the "N1b" haplogroup (Hg). The study found "a striking overrepresentation of Hgs K and N1b." What still is obscure is where did these four women originally come from and to what extent did they reproduce and expand. Further studies will open more doors to the history and expansions of Ashkenazi women.

What is known is that the women were part of families and followed the men. The early communities expanded, and what makes Ashkenazim fascinating to study by genealogy and genetics is that the demography is well-documented throughout history. The point of studying DNA-driven genealogy is to keep going further back in time when written records can not be located.

That's why DNA testing for ancestry is becoming a popular topic to learn more about for family historians and genealogists. Family historians also can work together with genetics counselors to help families understand their medical, genetic, or ancestral history. All this new information that is unfolding is perfect to put into a time capsule to hand to future generations so that they may better understand their past.

## DNA Testing for Ancestry

When written records cannot be found, is the next step DNA testing for deep paternal and maternal ancestry? Or further testing of more markers? The Y-chromosome is paternally inherited, and it's a non-recombining portion revealing gene genealogy of any ethnic group. Whether you're interested in human prehistory or your most recent common ancestor, that non-recombining portion of the Y-chromosome will in time show you accurate genetic genealogy.

It's the large stable non-recombining portion of the genome. You have many slowly and rapidly evolving markers. And your ancestry can be read in those markers from your prehistory to current yourself. The fields of DNA-driven genealogy, genomics, and genetic anthropology often come with the prefix 'geno' in front of another word as in "geno-geography" or "geno-journalism."

Men carry their mother's mtDNA but pass on to their sons their Y-chromosome. Women pass on their mtDNA haplogroup only to their daughters. Genomic views of any ethnic group's history are important for further study. Whether you are taking the skeptic's position or the genomic view of your cultural history, biology does have a cultural component that needs to be analyzed scientifically. Finding flaws or benefits in research studies of any kind is the way to find inroads to truths. How else can facts change and knowledge progress?

Molecular genealogy has joined efforts with molecular genetics. How can this information help you in family history research? Ugo A. Perego, MS. Senior Project Administrator, Molecular Genealogy Research Project, Brigham Young University, http://molecular-genealogy.byu.edu, says, "I believe that DNA is the next thing in genealogy—the tool for the 21st century family historians. In the past 20 years, the genealogical world has been revolutionized by the introduction of the Internet.

"An increasing number of people are becoming interested in searching for their ancestors because through emails and websites a large world of family history information is now available to them. The greatest contribution of molecular methods to family history is the fact that in some instances family relationships and blocked genealogies can be extended even in the absence of written records.

"Adoptions, illegitimacies, names that have been changes, migrations, wars, fire, flood, etc. are all situations in which a record may become unavailable. However, no one can change our genetic composition, which we have received by those that came before us.

"Currently, DNA testing is an effective approach to help with strict paternal and maternal lines thanks to the analysis and comparison of the Y chromosome (male line) and mitochondrial DNA (female line) in individuals that have reason to believe the existence of a common paternal or maternal ancestor.

"A large database of genetic and genealogical data is currently been built by the BYU Center for Molecular Genealogy and the **Sorenson Molecular Genealogy Foundation** at: http://smgf.org/. This database will contain thousands of pedigree charts and DNA from people from all over the world. Currently it has already over 35,000 participants in it.

"The purpose of this database is to provide additional knowledge in reconstructing family lines other than the paternal and maternal, by using a large number of autosomal DNA (the DNA found in the non-sex chromosomes). This research, known as the Molecular Genealogy Research Project is destined to take DNA for genealogists to the next level."

For additional reading, please visit the BYU's Molecular Genealogy Research Project's Web sites, the Sorenson Molecular Genealogy Foundation at: http://smgf.org/, or read an article in PDF file format titled, *Large Scale DNA Variation as an Aid to Reconstruction of Extended Human Pedigrees* at: http://smgf.org/PosterASHG2003.pdf. Another good source of information is the site at Relative Genetics, a company specializing in Y chromosome analysis for family studies at: http://www.relativegenetics.com. According to The Sorenson Molecular Genealogy Foundation's Web site, "The Sorenson Molecular Genealogy Foundation (SMGF) is a non-profit organization committed to developing the world's foremost database of correlated genetic and genealogical information, and making this information freely available to the public.

"DNA analysis is a powerful new tool for genealogical research. The SMGF database will allow genealogists to use their own genetic profile to identify possible genealogical links. This database is currently the largest of its kind in the world."

For further information on contributing your DNA to the worldwide database, contact the Sorenson Molecular Genealogy Foundation at the address below.

## Sorenson Molecular Genealogy Foundation

2511 South West Temple
Salt Lake City, UT 84115
Phone: (801) 461-9780
After hours phone: (801) 244-2542
Fax: (801) 461-9761
Email: info@smgf.org
Web site: http://smgf.org/

## What Are Your Genes Doing In That Temporary Container?

Have you ever wondered what your genes are doing in your "temporary container" before they move on and change and where they have traveled during the past 40,000 years or more? When you have your DNA tested, work with the lab and DNA testing company, and ask them to explain to you how the 37+ Y-chromosome markers you had tested as a male or mtDNA as a female help you determine your ancestry or find any matches similar to your DNA in a database. Read the frequently asked questions files of DNA testing companies online. Ask questions by email.

Sons inherit their mtDNA from their own mothers. Then mothers pass mtDNA on to their daughters. Sons also inherit the Y-chromosome from their fathers, but do not pass it to their daughters. Women don't have Y chromosomes.

The mtDNA is passed down from mother to son and mother to daughter through the cytoplasm (the cell contents surrounding the nucleus) in the egg. Only the daughters pass on their mtDNA to their daughters. And sons pass their Y-chromosomes to their sons, but those sons carry the mtDNA of their own mothers.

Even though both sons and daughters are formed from the union of a sperm and an egg, only the daughters will pass their mtDNA (which is the same as their great grandmother's on their maternal side and still further back to the first founder of their mtDNA group. Only daughters will pass the mtDNA on to the next generation.

Each lab has different methods of reporting their results, but you can use DNA test results as a tool for learning family history. Join DNA mailing lists and research or ask questions of the DNA testing firms specializing in genealogy by genetics about how many mutations occur in how many generations.

Do your own research independently of any laboratory that tested your own DNA if you're curious about Y-chromosome DNA tests. Males take Y-chromosome DNA tests to find out paternal ancestry lineages. Males also can have their mtDNA checked, but women don't have a Y chromosome. So women only can check their maternal lineages with mitochondrial (mtDNA) tests.

# 29

# *How to Be a Personal Historian or Documentarian 5–6 Week Course*

**Table of Contents**
**Also see http://www.newswriting.net for links to articles and helpful books.**
**Week 1**

1. Put Direct Experience In A Small Package And Launch It Worldwide. Make Time Capsules.

2. Write, Record, & Publish Purpose-Driven Personal History Dramatize, Package, Promote, Present, & Launch Your Purpose.

3. Edit, Dramatize, Package, Promote, Present, Publish, Record, Produce, & Launch Time Capsules of Personal Histories, Autobiographies, Biographies, Vignettes, and Eulogies: Launching the Inspiration-Driven or Design-Driven Life Story and Detailing Your Purpose.

## Week 2

Use Simplicity and Commitment in Personal History Writing, Time Capsules, and Videos. Here's useful insight to those who may someday write fiction, or their life stories, true experiences, or other people's life stories as vignettes or books created by linking a dozen or more vignettes together into a publishable book. Your aim is to produce time capsules or keepsake albums and other family history-related books, videos, audio projects, memory and/or prayer boxes, or memorabilia as heirlooms.

Look for insight, foresight, and hindsight. Mentoring is about pointing out what pitfalls to avoid. Instead of a formula, aim for simplicity, commitment, and persistence. Use simplicity in your writings.

## Week 3
## How to Motivate People to Interview One Another for Personal History Productions

People are "less camera shy" when two from the same peer group or class pair up and interview each other on video camcorder or on audio tape from a list of questions rehearsed. People also can write the questions they want to be asked and also write out and familiarize themselves with the answers alone and/or with their interviewers from their own peer group.

Some people have their favorite proverbs, or a logo that represents their outlook on life. Others have their own 'crusade' or mission. And some have a slogan that says what they are about in a few words…example, "seeking the joy of life," or "service with a smile."

A play can come from someone's slogan, for example. A slogan, logo, proverb, or motto can form the foundation for a questionnaire on what they want to say in an oral history or personal history video or audio tape on in a multimedia presentation of their life story highlights.

## Week 4
## How to Gather Personal Histories

Use the following sequence when gathering oral/aural histories:

1.  Develop one central issue and divide that issue into a few important questions that highlight or focus on that one central issue.

2.  Write out a plan just like a business plan for your oral history project. You may have to use that plan later to ask for a grant for funding, if required. Make a list of all your products that will result from the oral history when it's done.

3.  Write out a plan for publicity or public relations and media relations. How are you going to get the message to the public or special audiences?

4.  Develop a budget. This is important if you want a grant or to see how much you'll have to spend on creating an oral history project.

5.  List the cost of video taping and editing, packaging, publicity, and help with audio or special effects and stock shot photos of required.

6.  What kind of equipment will you need? List that and the time slots you give to each part of the project. How much time is available? What are your deadlines?

7.  What's your plan for a research? How are you going to approach the people to get the interviews? What questions will you ask?

8.  Do the interviews. Arrive prepared with a list of questions. It's okay to ask the people the kind of questions they would like to be asked. Know what dates the interviews will cover in terms of time. Are you covering the economic depression of the thirties? World Wars? Fifties? Sixties? Pick the time parameters.

9.  Edit the interviews so you get the highlights of experiences and events, the important parts. Make sure what's important to you also is important to the person you interviewed.

**Find out what the interviewee wants to**

# Week 5
# 1. Document Recovery for Personal History Time Capsules & Memorabilia
# 2. How to Open a DNA-Driven Genealogy Reporting and Production Service

How do you rescue and recover memories from mold using conservation techniques? You transport horizontally and store vertically. Store documents and photos in plastic holders, between sheets of waxed paper, or interleave with acid-free paper. Books are stored spine down. Archive DVDs and CDs in plastic holders and store in plastic crates. To conserve time capsules, according to the American Institute for Conservation of Historic and Artistic Works (AIC), in Washington, DC, neutralize that acid-wracked paper.

## Conclusions

If you decide to open an online, home-based DNA-driven genealogy reporting and production service, reports and time capsules could include the possible geographic location where the DNA sequences originated. Customers usually want to see the name of an actual town, even though towns didn't exist 10,000 years ago when the sequences might have arisen.

The whole genome is not tested, only the few ancestral markers, usually 500 base pairs of genes. Testing DNA for ancestry does not have anything to do with testing genes for health risks because only certain genes are tested—genes related to ancestry. And all the testing is done at a laboratory, not at your online business.

If you're interested in a career in genetics counseling and wish to pursue a graduate degree in genetics counseling, that's another career route. For information, contact The American Board of Genetic Counseling. Sometimes social workers with some coursework in biology take a graduate degree in genetic counseling since it combines counseling skills with training in genetics and in interpreting genetics tests for your clients.

## How to Be a Personal Historian or Documentarian and Make Time Capsules: 5-Week Course

### The Personal Historian as Journalist and Documentarian *by Anne Hart*

### Week One:

1. Put Direct Experience In A Small Package And Launch It Worldwide.

2. Write, Record, & Publish Purpose-Driven Personal History Dramatize, Package, Promote, Present, & Launch Your Purpose

3. Edit, Dramatize, Package, Promote, Present, Publish, Record, Produce, & Launch Time Capsules of Personal Histories, Autobiographies, Biographies, Vignettes, and Eulogies and/or DNA-Driven Genealogy Reports: Launching the Inspiration-Driven or Design-Driven Life Story and Detailing Your Purpose.

If you choose video, the newer camcorders such as Sony brand and others allow you to record directly onto a disk that can be played on a DVD or CD player or saved in the hard disk of a computer. The older camcorders still using tape allow you to save the video on digital high 8 tape and then save the tape in your computer. From there you can record the tape onto a DVD or CD disk.

Have the recording transcribed as text as a backup of information along with photos and other memorabilia for your time capsule. If you're working with tape, you'll need to attach a cable from your camcorder to your computer, such as a

1394 Firewire cable, or other cable device. The cable allows you to capture video and audio from your camcorder and save it in your computer. At the present I'm using Windows XP with Windows Media Player software to capture and edit video and audio.

What do you charge for video recording of personal history? You'd charge similar rates to wedding videographers. Shop around for the current rate in your area as to what wedding videographers charge per hour. Make an affordable, fair budget and present it to your clients. Video is for those who want to be remembered as they look at whatever stage of life they are being recorded.

Clients may also want to edit in youthful video clips, photos, or other memorabilia. Your goal is to make a time capsule with audio, video, photos, memorabilia, and other items such as diaries or DNA-driven ancestry information.

Some videographers charge $100 per hour, plus charges for transcribing video speech as text and saving the text on a CD along with other photo clips and memorabilia inserted into the video recording, such as photos of various stages of life and relatives' photos, video, images, diary excerpts read, or audio clips.

Some clients like to have music inserted. Be sure to obtain a written release from any musicians or composers for use of music on the videos, especially if copies are going to schools, libraries and museums. Check with the music publishers about music clips if the video is only for personal family use.

Some people like to be remembered as they looked when younger and prefer photos with audio. What do you charge for audio? You can charge anywhere from $10 or more to record a one-hour audio life story or oral history on a tape and 'burn' it to a CD or DVD. You can make time capsules by combining photos with the audio on the CD or DVD and make it a multi-media presentation. Or you can transcribe the audio into text.

It takes about five or six hours to transcribe a one-hour tape. Transcribers of tapes usually charge around $20 per hour. Therefore, a one-hour tape that takes five or six hours to transcribe would cost $100–$120 to transcribe. Before you can release a personal history, you'd need to have anyone on tape sign a release form.

Make sure your release form is signed and allows you to copyright the publishing rights to your production. You may not own the person's life story, but you want to make sure that you own the right to publish or produce the tape or disk for educational purposes.

The release form would specify where and how you would use the tape or disk, such as on Web sites or in library archives. Personal history used for educational purposes would be meant for librarians, teachers, students, public historians, and other educators, scholars and researchers. The idea is to share the personal history and create a time capsule—a container for memorabilia—to hand to future generations.

## Personal History Vignettes:

Put direct experience in a small package and launch it worldwide. Write your life story in short vignettes of 1,500 to 1,800 words.

Write anecdotes, eulogies, vocational biographies, elegies, and vignettes of life stories and personal histories for mini-biographies and autobiographies. Then condense or contract the life stories or personal histories into PowerPoint presentations and similar slide shows on disks using lots of photos and one-page of life story.

Finally, collect lots of vignettes and flesh-out the vignettes, linking them together into first-person diary-style novels and books, plays, skits, or other larger works. Write memoirs or eulogies for people or ghostwrite biographies and autobiographies for others.

If ghostwriting is too invisible, write biographies and vocational biographies, success stories and case histories, and customize for niche interest groups. Your main goal with personal history and life stories is to take the direct experience itself and package each story as a vignette.

The vignette can be read in ten minutes. So fill magazine space with a direct experience vignette. Magazine space needs only 1,500 words. When you link many vignettes together, each forms a book chapter or can be adapted to a play or script.

By turning vignettes into smaller packages, they are easier to launch to the media. When collected and linked together, they form a chain of vignettes offering nourishment, direction, purpose, and information used by people who need to make choices. Here's how to write those inspiration-driven, persistence-driven life stories and what to do with them. Use universal experience with which we all can identify.

Included are a full-length diary-format first person novel and a three-act play, including a monologue for performances. There's a demand for direct life experiences written or produced as vignettes and presented in small packages.

Save those vignettes electronically. Later, they can be placed together as chapters in a book or adapted as a play or script, turned into magazine feature, specialty, or news columns, or offered separately as easy-to-read packages.

**Put Direct Experience In A Small Package And Launch It Worldwide.**

*Here's How to Write, Edit, Dramatize, Package, Promote, Present, Publish & Launch Personal Histories, Autobiographies, Biographies, Vignettes, and Eulogies: Launching the Inspiration-Driven or Design-Driven Life Story and Detailing Your Purpose.*

## How to Write Personal History Essays: Text and Audio/Video

Use personal or biographical experiences as examples when you write your essay. Begin by using specific examples taken from your personal experience, personal history, or biographical resources.

Start with a general statement. Then relate the general to your specific personal experience. You don't have to only write about yourself. You can write about someone else as long as you have accurate historical facts about that person, and you state your credible resources.

Here's an example of two opening sentences that state the general and then give the specific personal experience. "Mom's a space garbage woman. She repairs satellites."

Let's analyze all the different parts of an informed argument essay. By analyzing the result in depth instead of only skimming for breadth, you will be able to write concretely from different points of view.

You'll learn how to construct an essay from bare bones—from its concept. You start with a concept. Then you add at least three specific examples to your concept until it develops into a mold. A mold is a form, skeleton or foundation. Think of concept as conception. Think of mold as form or skeleton. Think of awning as the outer skin that covers the whole essay and animates it into lively writing.

You don't want your essay to be flat writing. You want writing that is animated, alive, and able to move, motivate, or inspire readers. Finally, you cover the mold with an awning.

The mold is your pit, skeleton or foundation. Your mold contains your insight, foresight, and hindsight. It has the pitfalls to avoid and the highlights. You need to put flesh on its bones. Then you need to cover your mold with an awning. You need to include or protect that concept and mold or form by including it under this awning of a larger topic or category. The awning holds everything together. It's your category under which all your related topics fall. That's what the technique of organizing your essay or personal history is all about.

In other words, concept equals form plus details. Story equals form plus details. That's the math formula for writing an essay if you'd like to put it into a logical equation of critical thinking. $C = Fo + De$. That's what you need to remember about writing an essay: your concept is composed of your form (mold, foundation, or skeleton) and details. A concept isn't an idea. It's the application of your idea.

A concept is what your story is about. Your concept is imbedded in your story. A story can mean your personal history or any other story or anecdote in your essay, or any highlight of your life or specific life experience. A concept also can be a turning point such as rites of passage or take place at any stage of life.

When writing the informed argument, you will be able to give examples backed up with resources. That's what makes an essay great—knowing what examples to put into the essay at which specific points in time.

Gone will be general, vague, or sweeping statements. Therefore, I'd like each of you on this learning team to start planning your essay by analyzing and discussing the parts that chronologically go into the essay. That's how you organize essays in a linear fashion.

Take an essay apart just as you would take a clock or computer apart, and put it back together. Now all the parts fit and work. Taking apart an essay helps you understand how to plan and write your own essay-writing assignments or personal history as a time capsule.

Here's how to take an essay apart. To analyze an essay in depth, you break the essay down into its six parts: statement-of-position, description, argumentation, exposition, supplementation and evaluation. These parts of an essay also are explained in the book titled, *The Informed Argument.* (**ISBN:** 0155414593).

For more ideas, you also can look at some action verbs in another book titled, *801 Action Verbs for Communicators. (***ISBN***: 0-595-31911-4).

Before you even get to the expressive part of argumentation, you have to state your position and describe it by using specific examples. Then you get to the informed argument in the middle of your essay.

After you've finished arguing logically using critical thinking and your resources, you use exposition. Then you use supplementation, and finally evaluation.

To practice writing personal history essays in text or on video, define and analyze the words 'exposition' and 'supplementation.' Use exposition and supplementation in at least one sentence each as an example of how you would use it in your essay. Don't stick to only what is familiar.

My dictionary defines 'exposition' as "a careful setting out of the facts or ideas involved in something." The principal themes are presented first in a 'music' exposition. Apply it now to an essay. Present your principal themes first in your personal history. Supplementation means adding to your work to improve or complete it.

The goal of an essay is to analyze your informed argument in depth. That's why there are six parts to an essay. Knowing what those six parts are as well as showing examples gives you the experience you need to plan and organize your essay. The result is that once you have organized your plan in writing, the essay almost writes itself.

I keep an old saying in front of me when I write. It's about wanting you to know that I care. You probably want to know that I care more than you care what I know. It's a great saying to remind me why I'm writing how-to books, personal history, writing strategies, plays, and novels...because I care, and because everyone has a life story of great value.

How do you interpret family history as creative writing, and how do you interpret ancestry-related DNA tests?

◆      ◆      ◆

**Here Are 50 Strategies On How to Write Your Life Story or Anyone Else's:**
**Start with a Vignette....Link the Vignettes...Dramatize....and Novelize.**

1.  Contact anyone's family members to gain permission to write their family member's memorials.

2.  Write memoirs of various clerical or other religious or social leaders.

3.  Write two to four dozen memorials for houses of worship. Put these memorials in a larger book of memoirs for various organizations, religious groups, houses of worship, or professional associations.

4.  Find a model for your biographies.

5.  These could be based on a book of vocational biographies or centered on any other aspect of life such as religious or community service as well as vocations.

6. Read the various awards biographies written and presented for well-known people.

7. Focus on the accomplishments that stand out of these people or of you if you're writing an autobiography.

8. Use oral eulogies as your foundation. You'll find many oral eulogies that were used in memorial services.

9. Consult professionals who conduct memorial services to look at their eulogies written for a variety of people and presented at memorial services.

10. Stick to the length of a eulogy. You'll find the average eulogy runs about 1,500 to 1,800 words. That' is what's known as magazine article average length. Most magazines ask for feature articles of about 1,500 words. So your eulogies should run that same length.

11. When read aloud, they make up the eulogy part of a memorial service. At 250 to 300 words double-spaced per page, it comes to about five-to-seven pages and is read aloud in about seven to 10 minutes.

12. Take each 1,500–1,800 word eulogy and focus on the highlights, significant events, and turning points. Cut the eulogy down to one page of printed magazine-style format.

13. Keep the eulogy typeset so that it all fits on one page of printed material in 12 point font.

14. You can package one-page eulogies for memorial services or include a small photo on the page if space permits.

15. Cut the eulogy down to 50–70 words, average 60 words for an oral presentation using PowerPoint software for a computer-based slide show complete with photos.

16. Put the PowerPoint show on a CD or DVD. Use the shorter eulogy focusing on significant points in the person's life. The purpose of a PowerPoint eulogy is to show the person lived a purposeful life—a design-driven, goal-driven life with purpose and concrete meaning in relation to others.

17. Write biographies, memoirs, and autobiographies by focusing on the highlights of someone's life or your own life story. Turn personal histo-

ries into life stories that you can launch in the media. You need to make a life story salable. It is already valuable.

18. Read autobiographies in print. Compare the autobiographies written by ghostwriters to those written by the authors of autobiographies who write about their own experiences.

19. Read biographies and compare them to autobiographies written by ghost writers and those written as diary novels in first person or as genre novels in first person. Biographies are written in third person.

20. If you write a biography in third person keep objective. If you write an autobiography in first person you can be subjective or objective if you bring in other characters and present all sides of the story equally.

21. If you're writing a biography, whose memories are you using? If you write an autobiography, you can rely on your own memory. Writing in the third person means research verifying facts and fact-checking your resources for credibility. How reliable is the information?

22. Use oral history transcriptions, personal history, videos, audio tapes, and interviews for a biography. You can use the same for an autobiography by checking for all sides of the story with people involved in the life story—either biography or autobiography.

23. With personal histories and oral histories, be sure to obtain letters of permission and to note what is authorized. Celebrities in the public eye are written about with unauthorized or authorized biographies. However, people in private life who are not celebrities may not want their name or photo in anyone's book. Make sure everything you have is in writing in regard to permissions and what information is permitted to be put into your book or article, especially working with people who are not celebrities and those who are.

24. When interviewing, get written approval of what was said on tape. Let the person see the questions beforehand to be able to have time to recall an answer with accuracy regarding facts and dates or times of various events. Give peoples' memories a chance to recall memories before the interview.

25. Write autobiographies in the first person in genre or diary format. You can also dramatize the autobiography in a play or skit first and then flesh

it out into novel format. Another alternative is to focus only on the highlights, events, and turning points in various stages of life.

26. Ghost-written autobiographies usually are written in the first person. A ghost-writer may have a byline such as "***as told to***" or "***with***____(name of ghostwriter)."

27. Condense experience in small chunks or paragraphs. Use the time-capsule approach. Use vignettes. Focus on how people solved problems or obtained results or reached a goal. Find out whether the person wants you to mention a life purpose. Emphasize how the person overcame challenges or obstacles.

28. In an autobiography, instead of dumping your pain on others because it may be therapeutic for you, try to be objective and focus on what you learned from your choices and decisions and how what you learned transformed your life. Be inspirational and nurturing to the reader. Tell how you learned, what you learned, how you rose above your problems, and how you transcended the trouble. Focus on commitment and your relationship to others and what your purpose is in writing the autobiography.

29. Stay objective. Focus on turning points, highlights, and significant events and their relationship to how you learned from your mistakes or choices and rose above the trouble. Decide what your life purpose is and what points you want to emphasize. If you want to hide facts, decide why and what good it will do the reader. Stay away from angry writing and focus instead on depth and analysis.

30. Don't use humor if it puts someone down, including you. Don't put someone down to pick yourself up.

31. Make sure your writing doesn't sound like self-worship or ego soothing. Don't be modest, but don't shock readers either.

32. Before you write your salable autobiography, find out where the market is and who will buy it. If there is no market, use print-on-demand publishing and select a title most likely to be commercial or help market your book. At least you can give copies to friends and family members. Or self-publish with a printer. Another way to go is to self-publish using print-on-demand software yourself. Then distribute via advertising or the Internet and your Web site.

33. You'd be surprised at how many people would be interested in your life story if it were packaged, designed, and promoted. So launch your life story in the media before you publish. Write your life story as a novel or play or both. Every life story has value. I believe all life stories are salable. The hard part is finding the correct niche market for your experiences. So focus on what you are and what you did so people with similar interests, hobbies, or occupations may learn from you. Market to people who are in the same situation as you are.

34. Divide your biography into the 12 stages of life. Then pare down those 12 significant events or turning points and rites of passage into four quarters—age birth to 25 (young adult), age 26–50 (mature adult), age 51–75 (creative adult) and age 76–100 (golden years of self fulfillment).

35. Start with a vignette focusing on each of the most important events and turning points of your life. Do the same in a biography, only writing in third person. For your own life story, write in first person.

36. What's important for the reader to know about your life in relation to social history and the dates in time? For example, what did you do during the various wars?

37. Keep a journal or diary, and record events as they happen. Focus on how you relate to social history. Write in your diary each day. Use the Web and create a diary or Web *blog*.

38. If you keep a daily journal, and make sure it is saved on a computer disk or similar electronic diary, you can put the whole journal together and create a book or play online or have a digital recording of your life. It's your time capsule in virtual reality.

39. A daily journal will keep memories fresh in your mind when you cut down to significant events for a book. You want to recall significant events in detail with resources.

40. If you're young, keep a daily journal on a computer disk and keep transferring it from one technology to the next as technology evolves. Keep a spare saved and up on the Web so you can download it anytime. Use some of the free Web site space available to people online.

41. If you write a book when you're older, at least you'll have all the youthful memories in detail where you can transfer the notes from one com-

puter to another or upload from your disk to a browser for publication with a print-on-demand publisher.

42. Keep writing short vignettes. Include all the details as soon as possible after the event occurs. When you are ready to write a book, you'll be able to look back rationally and from a much more objective and mature perspective on the details. Then you can decide what to put into a salable life story that's about to be published.

43. Don't listen to people who tell you that if you are not famous, your life story is only fit for your own family because no one else will buy it. Fiddle-de-sticks!

44. There are events that happened to you or experiences in your line of work, travel, parenting, research, or lifestyle that people want to read because you have experiences to share.

45. Find a niche market of people with similar interests and market your life story to them.

46. Try out the waters first with a short vignette in magazines. If the magazines buy your vignette, your slice of life story, then you can write a book. Can you imagine if all the travelers and archaeologists, parenting experts and teachers didn't value their life story to the point that they thought it was fit only for relatives (who may be the only ones not interested in reading it because they already know your life story). In fact, your relatives may be angry at you for spilling the details to the public.

47. Instead, focus on that part of your life where you made a choice or decision with which everyone can identify. Inspire and motivate readers. If your experience is universal, we can all identify with it. We all go through the same stages of life.

48. So let us know how you overcame your obstacles, solved problems, and rose above the keen competition.

49. Or if you didn't, let us know how you learned to live with and enjoy your life. Readers want nourishment. If your life isn't about making a difference in the world, then write about how you handled what we all go through.

50. We want to read about the joy of life, and your design-driven life full of purpose, meaning, and inspiration. We want to read about the universal

in you with which we can identify. Most of all readers want information in a life story or personal history from which we can make our own choices. Keep your life story as a novel to 12 to 24 short chapters. Write in short, readable chunks.

## Week Two:

### Use Simplicity and Commitment in Personal History Writing or Time Capsules

Here's useful insight to those who may someday write fiction, or their life stories, true experiences, or other people's life stories as vignettes or books created by linking a dozen or more vignettes together into a publishable book. Look for insight, foresight, and hindsight. Mentoring is about pointing out what pitfalls to avoid. Instead of a formula, aim for simplicity, commitment, and persistence. Use simplicity in your writings.

Simplicity means whatever you write gives you all the answers you were looking for in exotic places, but found it close by. This is the formula for selling anything you write, should you desire to send your writing to publishers. You find simplicity in universal proverbs. Then you expand the proverbs to slice-of-life vignettes. Finally, you link those short vignettes.

Suddenly you have a book-length work of writing that can be divided into short vignettes again to be serialized. With most people's attention span set on seven-minutes per vignette, each vignette can emphasize simplicity, commitment, and universal values. Your conclusion would be to focus on answers that can be found close by.

If you're ever looking for 'formulas' in writing any type of literature, this is it: Simplicity shows how you found the answers you were looking for in exotic places but found close by. In your readings you can see the patterns and universals such as commitment that are valued in the story.

You can choose what the writer emphasizes as important. In your own writing, look around for your favorite proverbs and see how you can expand them in your writing to work with your own stories. Enjoy and find wisdom in creative expression. How do you interpret family history as creative writing, and how to you interpret ancestry-related DNA tests?

## What Makes a Personal History or Life Story Highlight Salable as a Play or Skit?
### Q. What makes a life story saleable?

A. Buzz appeal. High velocity personal memoir. A life story is salable when it has universal appeal and identity. An example is a single parent making great sacrifices to put bread on the table and raise a decent family in hard times. Many people identify with the universal theme of a life story. Buzz appeal draws in the deep interest of the press to publicize and lend credibility to a life story, to put a spin on it in the media, and to sell it to the public because all readers may be able to see themselves in your life story.

### Q. To whom do you sell your life story to?

A. You sell your life story to publishers specializing in life stories. If you look under biographies in a book such as Writer's Guide to Book Editors, Publishers, and Literary Agents, 1999–2000, by Jeff Herman, Prima Publishing, you'll see several pages of publishers of life story, biography, and memoirs or autobiography.

A few include The Anonymous Press, Andrews McMeel Publishing, Applause Theatre Book Publishers, Barricade Books, Inc., Baskerville Publishers, and many more listed in that directory. Also take a look at Writers Market, Writers Digest Books, checkout Memoirs in the index. Publishers include Feminist Press, Hachai, Hollis, Narwhal, Northeastern University Press, Puppy House, Westminster, John Knox, and others.

Check categories such as creative nonfiction, biography, ethnic, historical, multicultural and other categories for lists of publishers in your genre. Don't overlook writing your life story as a play, monologue, or script or for the audio book market.

### Q. How do you present your life story in order to turn it into a saleable book, article, play, or other type of literature so that other people will want to read it?

A. You write a high-velocity powerful personal memoir or autonomedia which emphasizes cultural criticism and theory. Or you write a factual expose, keep a journal on the current cultural pulse, or write a diary about what it feels like to be single and dating in your age group—thirty something, sixty-something, or whatever you choose. You become an investigative biographer. You write a riveting love story, or how to use love to heal. Perhaps you write about breaking through old barriers to create new publishing frontiers.

### Q. How do you write a commercial biography?

A. Make sure someone wants to buy it before you write the whole thing. The details will be forthcoming in the course as it begins. Then contact the press, reporters in the media with credibility who write for a national daily newspaper or reputable magazine. Also contact radio and cable TV stations to do interviews on a selected event in your life story or biography. Pick a niche market where the particular audience has a special interest in that experience.

### Q. The difference between authorized and unauthorized.

A. Authorized means you have permission and approval from the person about whom you're writing.

### Q. Who gets assigned to write biographies of celebrities or other famous people?

A. Usually newspaper columnists who cover the beat or subject area, or you're a known writer who contacts an agent specializing in writing or ghostwriting celebrity biographies. You can enter this profession from many doors. I'll explain in the course.

### Writing Your Ending First Gives You Closure And Clues How To Solve The Problems In Your Life Story. Teaching Life Story Writing On The Internet

When you write a salable life story, it's easier to write your ending first. Eventually, with experience working with a variety of life stories, you can start quality circles or classes in life story writing (writing your salable memoirs, autobiography, biography, corporate history, family history, your diary as a commercial novel or play or true confession, true story, or true crime book or story or script).

Also, you can teach life story writing, interviewing, or videobiography on the Internet for yourself or for an existing school or program. It's relaxing and comforting to sit at home in perfect quiet and type a lecture into a screen browser such as the courses that can be offered through www.blackboard.com and other programs. Or teach online using a live chat screen. Customize your course to the needs of your students.

You may need certification or a graduate degree to teach for a university online, but there's also adult education classes given in nontraditional settings such as churches, libraries, and museums.

Online, you can offer independent classes and go into business for yourself as a personal historian. Another way is to offer time capsules, keepsake albums, gift baskets, greeting cards, life stories on video, DVD, or transcribed from oral history. Work with libraries, museums, or your own independent classes.

You can work at home or be mobile and travel to other people's homes or senior centers and assisted living recreation rooms, community centers, or schools and theaters to work with life stories. Some companies have put life-story recording kiosks in public places such as train stations or airports.

Check out the StoryCorps Web site at http://www.storycorps.net/. Find your own mission or purpose and create your own business recording the life stories of a variety of people in video, sound, text, or multimedia formats. It's all part of the time-capsule generation that emphasizes your life story has value and needs to be preserved as part of history.

The revelation is that your life story isn't only for your family and friends anymore. As part of history, the world can now experience the one universal that connects us—life, and within a life story—insight, foresight, and hindsight.

Diaries of senior citizens are in demand. To sell them, you need buzz appeal, visibility in the press for writing simple stories of how you struggled to put bread on the table and raised a family alone, or what you've learned from your mistakes or experiences, how you solved problems, gave yourself more choices, grew, and came to understand why you were transformed. People are looking for universal experiences to help them make decisions.

Start by finding a newspaper reporter from a publication that is well-respected by the public, and have that person write about your life story experience or what you do with other peoples' life stories as a personal historian. That's the first step to introducing a 'salable' life story.

The technique differs from writing a life story like a first-person diary novel for only your family and/or friends. With a 'salable' life story, you write about the universal experiences that connect all of us. If readers or viewers can identify with what you have to say, your words open doors for them to make decisions and choices by digesting your information.

## The Proliferation of Playwriting Courses Online Targets Writing Your Life Story

The sheer number of classes on the Internet is like an explosion of education. You can now earn a masters degree in the techniques of teaching online from universities such as the California State University at Hayward in their continuing education department. What I see happening is that according to display ads in a variety of magazines of interest to writers, a proliferation of writing courses online has broken out.

How do you develop buzz appeal, pre-sell your book, create press coverage of their writing, all before you send it to a publisher or agent? A few years ago diaries were "in" just like several years before that the books about angels were "in style." What will be next?

Back in the year 2000, what enthralled readers included simple stories on how single parents put bread on the table, reared a family, and learned from their mistakes. What will be big in the future in publishing will be simple tales of what you learned, how you came to understand, and what you'll share with readers because what you learned from my mistakes helped you to grow and become a better person making the world a gentler place. Those books will be about values, virtues, and ethics in simple stories that help people heal. It will be universal stories with which we all can identify and use to solve problems and make decisions.

By the following year books showed readers how to have more choices and find more alternative solutions, more possibilities, and to find more information with which to solve problems and make decisions. A lot of those books will come from salable diaries and life stories as well as corporate histories and executive histories.

What was hot by 2002 was how people escaped domestic violence and made better choices through education and creativity enhancement. By 2003–2004 books focused on creativity enhancement and self-expression. The year 2003 became a utopia for books on creativity enhancement through personal experience and life story. You only have to look at the book lists in the publisher's magazines to see what the fad is for any one year and interview publishing professionals for the trends and directions for the following year.

Write about the human side of careers worked at for years. What did you retire to? How did you survive historic events, rear your family, or solve problems?

The purpose of personal history writing can be, among other goals, to find closure. Those who can't use a hand-operated mouse and need to use a foot pedal mouse, breath straw, or other devices can still operate computers. Others need assistance software to magnify the screen or audio software such as "Jaws," to hear as they type on keyboards.

The idea is to use personal history and life story writing as a healing instrument to make contact with others, find this closure, relieve stress, to talk to parents long gone, to make decisions on how to grow, find understanding, learn from past mistakes, grow, and become a better person in one's own eyes.

Other students take a personal history, oral history, or life story writing classes to pass on to their grandchildren a script, a novel, a story, or a collage of their life experiences, and still others want corporate histories of how they founded their companies and became role models of success for business students to simulate, how they became successful giants for others to follow and benchmark.

Still other students are visionaries who want their life stories to be used to enhance the creativity of readers. Some of my students want to write their life story as a computer or board game on how they solved their own problems that are universal to all of us. And you have students who want careers as personal historians recording, transcribing, and preserving in a variety of formats the personal histories of individuals, families, corporations, art forms, and institutions.

Some are into conservation of videos, photographs, text material, tape recordings, CDs, DVDs, and other multimedia formats. All are involved in making time capsules for future researchers, historians, scholars, librarians, genealogists, and specialists who research personal and oral history or specialized history, such as music and art or rare books and manuscripts.

Others are collectors. Most want a time capsule of a relative, complete with not only a relative's keepsake albums or video diary, but sometimes even a DNA printout for ancestry.

If you look in many publications of interest to writers, you might see online or correspondence courses offered to writers at American College of Journalism, Burlington College, Columbus University, specialists in distance education, or at Gotham Writers' Workshops at www.WritingClasses.com. There's Writers Digest School, and data bases where you can learn about agents at Agent Research & Evaluation, 334 E. 30, NYC, NY 10016 or on the Web at www.agentresearch.com. These are some of the online classes in writing advertised. You'll also see ads for classes in personal story writing in some of these publications.

You can get paid to teach what you love to do so much—share your writing techniques and write. Some writing schools online may put articles up on their trade journal online. And you can always sell articles to paying markets and use the clips with resumes. Thanks to the Internet—even a disabled teacher who isn't able to speak before a class for health reasons or drive to class, can teach and write online.

Personal history writing courses could also aim to show research on how creative writing can heal or have therapeutic qualities in gentle self-expression and quality circles online, and now I've found students who learn how to write a life story as therapy to heal and to find closure, solve problems, and to explore more choices, alternatives, and growth towards a kinder and gentler world.

You can focus strictly on recording, transcribing, and archiving people's or corporation's personal or oral histories and preserving them in a variety of formats as time capsules or target the more creative end of teaching writing personal histories as books, plays, or skits.

In other words, you can be both a personal historian and a writing coach or focus on either career or business—oral and personal historian, or teacher of courses or "quality circles" in writing autobiographies and biographies for commercial markets.

You can start private classes on a mailing list and chat board. A fair price to charge could be about $80 per student for advanced workshops in writing salable material for 4-week courses with a 10-page critique per student. Your aim would be to be an online job coach in a writing or personal history career. Help students find ways to get into print by referring you them to resources. Show how to make writing more commercial. Reveal the techniques of effective story writing in your true story, biography, memoirs, autobiography, diary, journal, novel, story, play, or article.

A lot of biography writing is focused on interviews, whereas writing a diary or monologue focuses on inner reflections and expressions in explaining how you came to understand, learn from your past mistakes or experiences and good choices, and share how you solved problems, grew, and changed or were transformed.

Personal diaries start out with poetic-like descriptions of the senses, with lines such as "Cat shadow plump I arrive, carrying my Siamese kitten like a rifle through Spokane, while the only sensation I feel is my hair stretched like flaxen wires where my new kitten, Patches, hangs on.

A gentle clock, the red beams of light reflected in his blue eyes remind me that my tattered self also must eat. His claws dig into my purse strap like golden flowers curling in unshaven armpits. I inhale his purrs like garlic, warm as the pap mom cat, Rada-Ring flowed into Patches nine weeks ago."

Have an enriching writing experience. I truly believe writing heals in some ways. It's a transformative experience like meditation or having the comforting feeling of watching a waterfall in natural settings or sitting in a garden of hanging green plants. Writing recharges my energy must like petting my kitten, Kokowellen, a Siamese while sitting my orchid garden listening to soothing melodies.

You might want to critique for pay, the pages of other people's writing of personal histories if they want to write for the commercial markets. In that case, critiquing may be done by email and online.

That way they don't send any hard copy to mail back or get lost. You always keep a copy. However, I recommend teaching online a course with the critique, as you'll get far more for your $80 for each ten pages of critiquing as a fair price, plus the tuition of the course as perhaps another $80.

The course provides resources, techniques, and ways to revise your material that helps you gain visibility. It's important to pre-sell your book and gain publicity for your writing before you send it off to a publisher or agent. You'll want to know how not to give too much away, but how to attract positive attention so people will eagerly look forward to hearing more from you.

Keep a separate mailing list for your online students. Make a mailing list. Plays or monologues written from memoirs and diaries or excerpts and highlights of life stories are in right now in the publishing world. It's not a passed fad, yet, like the angel books were a decade ago. If you're writing a diary, you want to write something in your first or second page after the opening that goes like this to be more commercial:

"Eagerness to learn grows on me. I see it reflected in the interviewers who stare at me, their enthusiasm is an approval of my expansive mind. I read so much now, just to look at the pages is to feel nourished. A kind of poetry turns into children's books on DVDs like a stalk that grows no where else is in season.

Creativity, like color, runs off my keyboard into the cooking water of my screen, drenched in pungent brainstorming. Writing online puts me in every farmer's kitchen. My computer has a good scent, and the stories written on its screen are apples bursting on the trees of my fingers. On my Web site, photos hang like lanterns. Teaching online ripens my stories. I analyze what effective storytelling means. Picture in three dimensions, pagodas of the mind."

If you come across writers block, try writing the lyrics to a song as a way to start writing your life story. You don't need to read notes, just fiddle with the words based upon an experience in time. Start by writing the ending first. Perhaps your title on salable diaries could be, "Pretty Little Secret," or "Ending the Silence," or "Results of Promises," or "Guided by a Child's Silence," or "Unraveling a Tale," or "Bravery and Unspeakable Links," or "Unveiled, Unbridled, Unbound." My title was "Insight, Hindsight, Foresight."

### Week Three:
### Opening Your Online Personal History Business
### "Celebration of Life" Plays and Skits Based on Interviewing and Taping:
### How to Motivate People to Interview One Another for Personal History Productions

People are "less camera shy" when two from the same peer group or class pair up and interview each other on video camcorder or on audio tape from a list of questions rehearsed. People also can write the questions they want to be asked and also write out and familiarize themselves with the answers alone and/or with their interviewers from their own peer group.

Some people have their favorite proverbs, or a logo that represents their outlook on life. Others have their own 'crusade' or mission. And some have a slogan that says what they are about in a few words…example, "seeking the joy of life," or "service with a smile."

A play can come from someone's slogan, for example. A slogan, logo, proverb, or motto can form the foundation for a questionnaire on what they want to say in an oral history or personal history video or audio tape on in a multimedia presentation of their life story highlights.

Here are some ways to interview people for personal history time capsules or how to inspire them to interview one another in a group setting or in front of a video camcorder in private with only interviewer and interviewee present.

And then there are those who want to tape themselves alone in their room or office with a camcorder on a tripod and a remote control device or a tape recorder and photographs. When records stop, there are always the DNA-driven genealogy and ancestry printouts.

Some people enjoy writing their life stories more than they like to speak about it. Or they prefer to read from a script as an audio tape. For those whose voices are impaired or for those who prefer to let a synthetic software voice tell their story, I recommend software such as TextAloud.

This software allows anyone to cut and paste their writing from a disk such as a floppy disk, CD, DVD, or hard drive disk to the TextAloud software and select the type of voice to read their writing. With AT&T Natural Voices, you can select a male or female voice.

There are also voices with accents, such as a British accent male voice, and voice software available in a variety of languages to read writing in other languages. TextAloud is made by Nextup.com at the Web site: http://www. nextup.com/. According to their Web site, "TextAloud MP3 is Text-to-Speech software that uses voice synthesis to create spoken audio from text. You can listen on your PC or save text to MP3 or wave files for listening later." I play the MP3 files on my MP3 player.

I save the files to a CD as MP3 files. In this way I can turn my writing into audio books, pamphlets, or articles, poetry, plays, monologues, skits, or any form of writing read aloud by the synthetic software voice software. I save my audio files as MP3 files so I can play my personal history audio in my MP3 player on in my personal computer. MP3 files are condensed and take up a lot less room in your computer or on a Web site or CD and DVD disk than an audio .wav file.

For people who are creating "celebration of life" oral or personal history audio tapes, it works well especially for those who prefer not to read their own writing aloud to a tape recorder. Although most people would like to hear their relatives' voices on tape in audio and video, some people are not able to read their works aloud to a recorder or camcorder.

The synthetic voices will turn any type of writing saved on a disk as a text file into recorded voice—from short poetry to long-length books. The voices are usually recorded with Total Recorder software and saved as an MP3 file so they can be played on MP3 players or on most computers with CD players.

For those taping persons live in video to make time capsules or other keepsake albums in voice and/or video, it's best to let people think what they are going to say by handing them a list of a few questions. If you're working with a group of older adults, let one of the group members interview another group member by asking each question from a list of several questions.

If you give someone a week's notice to come up with an answer to each question from a list of ten questions and give them two minutes to respond to each question by discussing how it relates to events in their lives or their experiences, you have a twenty minute video tape.

If you allow only a minute for each question from a list of thirty questions, you have a thirty-minute tape. Times may not be exact as people tend to elaborate to flesh out a question. Let the interview and interviewee practice before recording. So it's good to pair up two people. One will ask the interview questions, and the other will answer, talking about turning points and significant events in their lives.

They can be asked whether they have a personal proverb or slogan they live by or a motto or personal logo. Tapes can be anywhere from a half hour to an hour for life stories that can be saved as an MP3 file to a CD. Other files such as a Wave file (.wav) take up too much space on a CD. So they could be condensed into an MP3 file and saved that way. TextAloud and Total Recorder are software programs that save audio files. You can also use Music Match to convert .wav files to MP3 files.

I use TextAloud software and Total Recorder. Also I save the files as MP3 files for an audio CD that will also go up on a Web site. I use Windows Media Player to play the video files and save them as a Windows Media file (WMV file) so they can be easily uploaded to a Web site and still play in Windows Media Player that comes with Windows XP software.

When making time capsules in multimedia, I save on a CD and/or a DVD, and upload the file from my hard disk to a Web site. Copies of the CDs can be given to relatives, the interviewee, museums, libraries, and various schools who may be interested in oral history with a theme.

The themes can be celebrations of life, living time capsules, or fit into any group theme under an umbrella title that holds them together. This can be an era, such as living memories of a particular decade, life experiences in oral history of an area in geography, an ethnic group, or any other heading. Or the tapes can be of individuals or family groups.

Not only life stories, but poetry, plays, novels, stories, and any other form of creative nonfiction or fiction writing can be recorded by synthetic voices as audio story or book collections. Some work well as children's stories and other types of writings as life stories or poetry.

Themes can vary from keepsake albums to time capsules to collections of turning points in history from the life stories of individuals. Also, themes can be recorded as "old time radio" programs or as oral military history from the experiences of veterans and notated to the Veterans History Project at the Library of Congress or other groups and museums. Make sure you have signed *release forms* that also release you from liability should any problems arise from putting someone's life story and name on the Web and/or donating it to a library or other public archive.

A good example of a release form is the one posted at the Veteran's History Project Web site where life stories of veterans are donated to the Library of Congress and accessible to the public for educational or scholarly research. Check out the .PDF release forms for both the interviewer and the interviewee at their Web site. The release form for veterans is at: http://www.loc.gov/folklife/vets/vetform-vetrelease.pdf.

◆        ◆        ◆

## Before Video Taping Life Stories of Older Adults: Questions to Ask Interviewing for Writing Plays and Skits from Life Stories for Junior and Senior High-School Students and/or Mature Adults.

STEP 1: Send someone enthusiastic about personal and oral history to senior community centers, lifelong learning programs at universities, nursing homes, or senior apartment complexes activity rooms. You can reach out to a wide variety of older adults in many settings, including at libraries, church groups, hobby and professional or trade associations, unions, retirement resorts, public transportation centers, malls, museums, art galleries, genealogy clubs, and intergenerational social centers.

STEP 2: Have each personal historian or volunteer bring a tape recorder with tape and a note pad. Bring camcorders for recording video to turn into time capsules and CDs or DVDs with life stories, personal history experiences, memoirs, and events highlighting turning points or special times in people's lives.

STEP 3: Assign each personal historian one or two older persons to interview with the following questions.

1.  What were the most significant turning points or events in your life?

2.  How did you survive the Wars?

3.  What were the highlights, turning points, or significant events that you experienced during the economic downturn of 1929–1939? How did you cope or solve your problems?

4.  What did you do to solve your problems during the significant stages of your life at age 10, 20, 30, 40, 50, 60 and 70-plus? Or pick a year that you want to talk about.

5.  What changes in your life do you want to remember and pass on to future generations?

6.  What was the highlight of your life?

7.  How is it best to live your life after 70?

8.   What years do you remember most?

9.   What was your favorite stage of life?

10.   What would you like people to remember about you and the times you lived through?

STEP 3:
Have the student record the older person's answers. Select the most significant events, experiences, or turning points the person chooses to emphasize. Then write the story of that significant event in ten pages or less.

STEP 4: Ask the older person to supply the younger student photos, art work, audio tapes, or video clips. Usually photos, pressed flowers, or art work will be supplied. Have the student or teacher scan the photos onto a disk and return the original photos or art work or music to the owner.

STEP 5: The personal historian, volunteer, student and/or teacher scans the photos and puts them onto a Web site on the Internet at one of the free communities that give away Web site to the public at no cost....some include http://www.tripod.com, http://www.fortunecity.com, http://www.angelfire.com, http://www.geocities.com, and others. Most search engines will give a list of communities at offering free Web sites to the public. Microsoft also offers free family Web sites for family photos and newsletters or information. Ask your Internet service provider whether it offers free Web site space to subscribers. The free Web sites are limited in space.
For larger Web site spaces with room for audio and video material and other keepsake memorabilia, purchase a personal Web site from a Web-hosting company. Shop around for affordable Web site space for a multimedia life story time capsule that would include text, video and/or audio clips, music, art, photos, and any other effects.

1.   Create a Web site with text from the older person's significant life events

2.   Add photos.

3.   Add sound or .wav files with the voice of the older person speaking in small clips or sound bites.

4.   Intersperse text and photos or art work with sound, if available.
     Add video clips, if available and won't take too much bandwidth.

5.  Put Web site on line as TIME CAPSULE of (insert name of person) interviewed and edited by, insert name of student who interviewed older person.

STEP 6: Label each Web site Time Capsule and collect them in a history archives on the lives of older adults at the turn of the millennium. Make sure the older person and all relatives and friends are emailed the Web site link. You have now created a time capsule for future generations.

This can be used as a classroom exercise in elementary and high schools to teach the following:

1.  Making friends with older adults.

2.  Learning to write on intergenerational topics.

3.  Bringing community together of all generations.

4.  Learning about foster grandparents.

5.  History lessons from those who lived through history.

6.  Learning about diversity and how people of diverse origins lived through the 20th century.

7.  Preserving the significant events in the lives of people as time capsules for future generations to know what it was like to live between 1900 and 2000 at any age.

8.  Learning to write skits and plays from the life stories of older adults taken down by young students.

9.  Teaching older adults skills in creative writing at senior centers.

10. Learning what grandma did during World War 2 or the stock market crash of 1929 followed by the economic downturn of 1930–1938.

## What to Ask People about Their Lives before You Write a Play or Skit

Step 1
When you interview, ask for facts and concrete details. Look for statistics, and research whether statistics are deceptive in your case.

Step 2
To write a plan, write one sentence for each topic that moves the story or piece

forward. Then summarize for each topic in a paragraph. Use dialogue at least in every third paragraph.

Step 3
Look for the following facts or headings to organize your plan for a biography or life story.

1.  PROVERB. Ask the people you interview what would be their proverb or slogan if they had to create/invent a slogan that fit themselves or their aspirations: One slogan might be something like the seventies ad for cigarettes, "We've come a long way, baby," to signify ambition. Only look for an original slogan.

2.  PURPOSE. Ask the people you interview or a biography, for what purpose is or was their journey? Is or was it equality in the workplace or something personal and different such as dealing with change—downsizing, working after retirement, or anything else?

3.  IMPRINT. Ask what makes an imprint or impact on people's lives and what impact the people you're interviewing want to make on others?

4.  STATISTICS: How deceptive are they? How can you use them to focus on reality?

5.  How have the people that you're interviewing influenced changes in the way people or corporations function?

6.  To what is the person aspiring?

7.  What kind of communication skills does the person have and how are these skills received? Are the communication skills male or female, thinking or feeling, yin or yang, soft or steeled, and are people around these people negative or positive about those communication skills?

8.  What new styles is the person using? What kind of motivational methods, structure, or leadership? Is the person a follower or leader? How does the person match his or her personality to the character of a corporation or interest?

9.  How does the person handle change?

10. How is the person reinforced?

Once you have titles and summarized paragraphs for each segment of your story, you can more easily flesh out the story by adding dialogue and description to your factual information. Look for differences in style between the people you interview? How does the person want to be remembered?

Is the person a risk taker or cautious for survival? Does the person identify with her job or the people involved in the process of doing the work most creatively or originally?

Does creative expression take precedence over processes of getting work out to the right place at the right time? Does the person want his ashes to spell the words "re-invent yourself" where the sea meets the shore? This is a popular concept appearing in various media.

## Search the Records in the Family History Library of Salt Lake City, Utah

Make use of the database online at the Family History Library of Salt Lake City, Utah. Or visit the branches in many locations. The Family History Library (FHL) is known worldwide as the focal point of family history records preservation.

The FHL collection contains more than 2.2 million rolls of microfilmed genealogical records, 742,000 microfiche, 300,000 books, and 4,500 periodicals that represent data collected from over 105 countries. You don't have to be a member of any particular church or faith to use the library or to go online and search the records.

Family history records owe a lot to the invention of writing. And then there is oral history, but someone needs to transcribe oral history to record and archive them for the future.

Interestingly, isn't it a coincidence that writing is 6,000 years old and DNA that existed 6,000 years ago first reached such crowded conditions in the very cities that had first used writing extensively to measure accounting and trade had very little recourse but to move on to new areas where there were far less people and less use of writing?

A lot of major turning points occurred 6,000 years ago—the switch to a grain-based diet from a meat and root diet, the use of bread and fermented grain beverages, making of oil from plants, and the rise of religions based on building "god houses" in the centers of town in areas known as the "cereal belt" around the world.

Six thousand years ago in India we have the start of the Sanskrit writings, the cultivation of grain. In China, we have the recording of acupuncture points for medicine built on energy meridians that also show up in the blue tattoos of the Ice Man fossil "Otsi" in the Alps—along the same meridians as the Chinese acupuncture points.

At 6,000 years ago the Indo European languages spread out across Europe. Mass migrations expanded by the Danube leaving pottery along the trade routes that correspond to the clines and gradients of gene frequency coming out of the cereal belts.

Then something happened. There was an agricultural frontier cutting off the agriculturists from the hunters. Isn't it a coincidence that the agricultural frontiers or barriers also are genetic barriers at least to some degree?

## Oral History

Here's how to systematically collect, record, and preserve living peoples' testimonies about their own experiences. After you record in audio and/or video the highlights of anyone's experiences, try to verify your findings. See whether you can check any facts in order to find out whether the person being recorded is making up the story or whether it really did happen.

This is going to be difficult unless you have witnesses or other historical records. Once you have verified your findings to the best of your ability, note whether the findings have been verified. Then analyze what you found. Put the oral history recordings in an accurate historical context.

Mark the recordings with the dates and places. Watch where you store your findings so scholars in the future will be able to access the transcript or recording and convert the recording to another, newer technology. For instance, if you have a transcript on paper, have it saved digitally on a disk and somewhere else on tape and perhaps a written transcript on acid-free good paper in case technology moves ahead before the transcript or recording is converted to the new technology.

For example, if you only put your recording on a phonograph record, within a generation or two, there may not be any phonographs around to play the record. The same goes for CDs, DVDs and audio or video tapes.

So make sure you have a readable paper copy to be transcribed or scanned into the new technology as well as the recordings on disk and tape. For example, if you record someone's experiences in a live interview with your video camera, use a cable to save the video in the hard disk of a computer and then burn the file to a CD or DVD.

Keep a copy of audio tape and a copy of regular video tape—all in a safe place such as a time capsule, and make a copy for various archives in libraries and university oral history preservation centers. Be sure scholars in the future can find a way to enjoy the experiences in your time capsule, scrapbook, or other storage device for oral histories.

Use your DNA testing results to add more information to a historical record. As an interviewer with a video camera and/or audio tape recorder, your task is to record as a historical record what the person who you are interviewing recollects.

The events move from the person being interviewed to you, the interviewer, and then into various historical records. In this way you can combine results of DNA testing with actual memories of events. If it's possible, also take notes or have someone take notes in case the tape doesn't pick up sounds clearly.

I had the experience of having a video camera battery go out in spite of all precautions when I was interviewing someone, and only the audio worked. So keep a backup battery on hand whether you use a tape recorder or a video camera. If at all possible, have a partner bring a spare camera and newly recharged battery. A fully charged battery left overnight has a good chance of going out when you need it.

## Writing Skits from Oral and Personal History Transcripts

Emphasize the commitment to family and faith. To create readers' and media attention to an oral history, it should have some redemptive value to a universal audience. That's the most important point. Make your oral history simple and earthy. Write about real people who have values, morals, and a faith in something greater than themselves that is equally valuable to readers or viewers.

Publishers who buy an oral history written as a book on its buzz value are buying simplicity. It is simplicity that sells and nothing else but simplicity. This is true for oral histories, instructional materials, and fiction. It's good storytelling to say it simply.

Simplicity means the oral history or memoirs book or story gives you all the answers you were looking for in your life in exotic places, but found it close by. What's the great proverb that your oral history is telling the world?

Is it to stand on your own two feet and put bread on your own table for your family? That's the moral point, to pull your own weight, and pulling your own weight is a buzz word that sells oral histories and fiction that won't preach, but instead teach and reach through simplicity.

That's the backbone of the oral historian's new media. Buzz means the story is simple to understand. You make the complex easier to grasp. And buzz means you can sell your story or book, script or narrative by focusing on the values of simplicity, morals, faith, and universal values that hold true for everyone.

Doing the best to take care of your family sells and is buzz appeal, hot stuff in the publishing market of today and in the oral history archives. This is true, regardless of genre. Publishers go through fads every two years—angel books, managing techniques books, computer home-based business books, novels about ancient historical characters or tribes, science fiction, children's programming, biography, and oral history transcribed into a book or play.

The genres shift emphasis, but values are consistent in the bestselling books. Perhaps your oral history will be simple enough to become a bestselling book or script. In the new media, simplicity is buzz along with values.

Oral history, like best-selling novels and true stories is built on simplicity, values, morals, and commitment. Include how one person dealt with about trends. Focus your own oral history about life in the lane of your choice. Develop one central issue and divide that issue into a few important questions that highlight or focus on that one central issue.

When you write or speak a personal history either alone or in an interview, you focus on determining the order of your life story. Don't use flashbacks. Focus on the highlights and turning points. Organize what you'll say or write. An autobiography deals in people's relationships. Your autobiography deals as much with what doesn't change—the essentials—as what life changes you and those around you go through.

Your personal history should be more concrete than abstract. You want the majority of people to understand what you mean. Say what you mean, and mean what you say. More people understand concrete details than understand abstract ideas.

**Week Four:**
**How to Gather Personal Histories**
**Use the following sequence when gathering oral/aural histories:**

10. Develop one central issue and divide that issue into a few important questions that highlight or focus on that one central issue.

11. Write out a plan just like a business plan for your oral history project. You may have to use that plan later to ask for a grant for funding, if required. Make a list of all your products that will result from the oral history when it's done.

12. Write out a plan for publicity or public relations and media relations. How are you going to get the message to the public or special audiences?

13. Develop a budget. This is important if you want a grant or to see how much you'll have to spend on creating an oral history project.

14. List the cost of video taping and editing, packaging, publicity, and help with audio or special effects and stock shot photos of required.

15. What kind of equipment will you need? List that and the time slots you give to each part of the project. How much time is available? What are your deadlines?

16. What's your plan for a research? How are you going to approach the people to get the interviews? What questions will you ask?

17. Do the interviews. Arrive prepared with a list of questions. It's okay to ask the people the kind of questions they would like to be asked. Know what dates the interviews will cover in terms of time. Are you covering the economic depression of the thirties? World Wars? Fifties? Sixties? Pick the time parameters.

18. Edit the interviews so you get the highlights of experiences and events, the important parts. Make sure what's important to you also is important to the person you interviewed.

19. Find out what the interviewee wants to emphasize perhaps to highlight events in a life story. Create a video-biography of the highlights of one person's life or an oral history of an event or series of events.

20. Process audio as well as video, and make sure you have written transcripts of anything on audio and/or video in case the technology changes or the tapes go bad.

21. Save the tapes to compact disks, DVDs, a computer hard disk and several other ways to preserve your oral history time capsule. Donate any tapes or CDs to appropriate archives, museums, relatives of the interviewee, and one or more oral history libraries. They are usually found at universities that have an oral history department and library such as UC Berkeley and others.

22. Check the Web for oral history libraries at universities in various states and abroad.

23. Evaluate what you have edited. Make sure the central issue and central questions have been covered in the interview. Find out whether newspapers or magazines want summarized transcripts of the audio and/or video with photos.

24. Contact libraries, archives, university oral history departments and relevant associations and various ethnic genealogy societies that focus on the subject matter of your central topic.

25. Keep organizing what you have until you have long and short versions of your oral history for various archives and publications. Contact magazines and newspapers to see whether editors would assign reporters to do a story on the oral history project.

26. Create a scrapbook with photos and summarized oral histories. Write a synopsis of each oral history on a central topic or issue. Have speakers give public presentations of what you have for each person interviewed and/or for the entire project using highlights of several interviews with the media for publicity. Be sure your project is archived properly and stored in a place devoted to oral history archives and available to researchers and authors.

## Aural/Oral History Techniques

1. Begin with easy to answer questions that don't require you explore and probe deeply in your first question. Focus on one central issue when asking questions. Don't use abstract questions. A plain question would be "What's your purpose?" An abstract question with connotations would be "What's your crusade?" Use questions with denotations instead of connotations. Keep questions short and plain—easy to understand. Examples would be, "What did you want to accomplish? How did you solve those problems? How did you find closure?" Ask the familiar "what, when, who, where, how, and why."

2. First research written or visual resources before you begin to seek an oral history of a central issue, experience, or event.

3. Who is your intended audience?

4. What kind of population niche or sample will you target?

5. What means will you select to choose who you will interview? What group of people will be central to your interview?

6. Write down how you'll explain your project. Have a script ready so you don't digress or forget what to say on your feet.

7. Consult oral history professionals if you need more information. Make sure what you write in your script will be clear to understand by your intended audience.

8. Have all the equipment you need ready and keep a list of what you'll use and the cost. Work up your budget.

9. Choose what kind of recording device is best—video, audio, multimedia, photos, and text transcript. Make sure your video is broadcast quality. I use a Sony Digital eight (high eight) camera.

10. Make sure from cable TV stations or news stations that what type of video and audio you choose ahead of time is broadcast quality.

11. Make sure you have an external microphone and also a second microphone as a second person also tapes the interview in case the quality of your camera breaks down. You can also keep a tape recorder going to capture the audio in case your battery dies.

12. Make sure your battery is fully charged right before the interview. Many batteries die down after a day or two of nonuse.

13. Test all equipment before the interview and before you leave your office or home. I've had batteries go down unexpectedly and happy there was another person ready with another video camera waiting and also an audio tape version going.

14. Make sure the equipment works if it's raining, hot, cold, or other weather variations. Test it before the interview. Practice interviewing someone on your equipment several times to get the hang of it before you show up at the interview.

15. Make up your mind how long the interview will go before a break and use tape of that length, so you have one tape for each segment of the interview. Make several copies of your interview questions.

16. Be sure the interviewee has a copy of the questions long before the interview so the person can practice answering the questions and think of what to say or even take notes. Keep checking your list of what you need to do.

17. Let the interviewee make up his own questions if he wants. Perhaps your questions miss the point. Present your questions first. Then let him embellish the questions or change them as he wants to fit the central issue with his own experiences.

18. Call the person two days and then one day before the interview to make sure the individual will be there on time and understands how to travel to the location. Or if you are going to the person's home, make sure you understand how to get there.

19. Allow yourself one extra hour in case of traffic jams.

20. Choose a quiet place. Turn off cell phones and any ringing noises. Make sure you are away from barking dogs, street noise, and other distractions.

21. Before you interview make sure the person knows he or she is going to be video and audio-taped.

22. If you don't want anyone swearing, make that clear it's for public archives and perhaps broadcast to families.

23. Your interview questions should follow the journalist's information-seeking format of asking, who, what, where, where, how, and why. Oral history is a branch of journalistic research.

24. Let the person talk and don't interrupt. You be the listener and think of oral history as aural history from your perspective.

25. Make sure only one person speaks without being interrupted before someone else takes his turn to speak.

26. Understand silent pauses are for thinking of what to say.

27. Ask one question and let the person gather his thoughts.

28. Finish all your research on one question before jumping to the next question. Keep it organized by not jumping back to the first question after the second is done. Stay in a linear format.

29. Follow up what you can about any one question, finish with it, and move on to the next question without circling back. Focus on listening instead of asking rapid fire questions as they would confuse the speaker.

30. Ask questions that allow the speaker to begin to give a story, anecdote, life experience, or opinion along with facts. Don't ask questions that can be answered only be yes or no. This is not a courtroom. Let the speaker elaborate with facts and feelings or thoughts.

31. Late in the interview, start to ask questions that explore and probe for deeper answers.

32. Wrap up with how the person solved the problem, achieved results, reached a conclusion, or developed an attitude, or found the answer. Keep the wrap-up on a light, uplifting note.

33. Don't leave the individual hanging in emotion after any intensity of. Respect the feelings and opinions of the person. He or she may see the situation from a different point of view than someone else. So respect the person's right to feel as he does. Respect his need to recollect his own experiences.

34. Interview for only one hour at a time. If you have only one chance, interview for an hour. Take a few minutes break. Then interview for the second hour. Don't interview more than two hours at any one meeting.

35. Use prompts such as paintings, photos, music, video, diaries, vintage clothing, crafts, antiques, or memorabilia when appropriate. Carry the photos in labeled files or envelopes to show at appropriate times in order to prime the memory of the interviewee. For example, you may show a childhood photo and ask "What was it like in that orphanage where these pictures were taken?" Or travel photos might suggest a trip to America as a child, or whatever the photo suggests. For example, "Do you remember when this ice cream parlor inside the ABC movie house stood at the corner of X and Y Street? Did you go there as a teenager? What was your funniest memory of this movie theater or the ice cream store inside back in the fifties?"

36. As soon as the interview is over, label all the tapes and put the numbers in order.

37. A signed release form is required before you can broadcast anything. So have the interviewee sign a release form before the interview.

38. Make sure the interviewee gets a copy of the tape and a transcript of what he or she said on tape. If the person insists on making corrections,

send the paper transcript of the tape for correction to the interviewee. Edit the tape as best you can or have it edited professionally.

39. Make sure you comply with all the corrections the interviewee wants changed. He or she may have given inaccurate facts that need to be corrected on the paper transcript.

40. Have the tape edited with the corrections, even if you have to make a tape at the end of the interviewee putting in the corrections that couldn't be edited out or changed.

41. As a last resort, have the interviewee redo the part of the tape that needs correction and have it edited in the tape at the correct place marked on the tape. Keep the paper transcript accurate and up to date, signed with a release form by the interviewee.

42. Oral historians write a journal of field notes about each interview. Make sure these get saved and archived so they can be read with the transcript.

43. Have the field notes go into a computer where someone can read them along with the transcript of the oral history tape or CD.

44. Thank the interviewee in writing for taking the time to do an interview for broadcast and transcript.

45. Put a label on everything you do from the interview to the field notes. Make a file and sub file folders and have everything stored in a computer, in archived storage, and in paper transcript.

46. Make copies and digital copies of all photos and put into the records in a computer. Return originals to owners.

47. Make sure you keep your fingerprints off the photos by wearing white cotton gloves. Use cardboard when sending the photos back and pack securely. Also photocopy the photos and scan the photos into your computer. Treat photos as antique art history in preservation.

48. Make copies for yourself of all photos, tapes, and transcripts. Use your duplicates, and store the original as the master tape in a place that won't be used often, such as a time capsule or safe, or return to a library or museum where the original belongs.

49. Return all original photos to the owners. An oral history archive library or museum also is suitable for original tapes. Use copies only to work from, copy, or distribute.

50. Index your tapes and transcripts. To use oral history library and museum terminology, recordings and transcripts are given "accession numbers."

51. Phone a librarian in an oral history library of a university for directions on how to assign accession numbers to your tapes and transcripts if the materials are going to be stored at that particular library. Store copies in separate places in case of loss or damage.

52. If you don't know where the materials will be stored, use generic accession numbers to label your tapes and transcripts. Always keep copies available for yourself in case you have to duplicate the tapes to send to an institution, museum, or library, or to a broadcast company.

53. Make synopses available to public broadcasting radio and TV stations.

54. Check your facts.

55. Are you missing anything you want to include?

56. Is there some place you want to send these tapes and transcripts such as an ethnic museum, radio show, or TV satellite station specializing in the topics on the tapes, such as public TV stations? Would it be suitable for a world music station? A documentary station?

57. If you need more interviews, arrange them if possible.

58. Give the interviewee a copy of the finished product with the corrections. Make sure the interviewee signs a release form that he or she is satisfied with the corrections and is releasing the tape to you and your project.

59. Store the tapes and transcripts in a library or museum or at a university or other public place where it will be maintained and preserved for many generations and restored when necessary.

60. You can also send copies to a film repository or film library that takes video tapes, an archive for radio or audio tapes for radio broadcast or cable TV.

61. Copies may be sent to various archives for storage that lasts for many generations. Always ask whether there are facilities for restoring the tape.

A museum would most likely have these provisions as would a large library that has an oral history library project or section.

62. Make sure the master copy is well protected and set up for long-term storage in a place where it will be protected and preserved.

63. If the oral history is about events in history, various network news TV stations might be interested. Film stock companies may be interested in copies of old photos.

64. Find out from the subject matter what type of archives, repository, or storage museums and libraries would be interested in receiving copies of the oral history tapes and transcripts.

65. Print media libraries would be interested in the hard paper copy transcripts and photos as would various ethnic associations and historical preservation societies. Find out whether the materials will go to microfiche, film, or be digitized and put on CDs and DVDs, or on the World Wide Web. If you want to create a time capsule for the Web, you can ask the interviewee whether he or she wants the materials or selected materials to be put online or on CD as multimedia or other. Then you would get a signed release from the interviewee authorizing you to put the materials or excerpts online. Also find out in whose name the materials are copyrighted and whether you have print and electronic rights to the material or do the owners-authors-interviewees—or you, the videographer-producer? Get it all in writing, signed by those who have given you any interviews, even if you have to call your local intellectual property rights attorney.

## Week Five:
## Document Recovery for Personal History Time Capsules & Memorabilia

How do you rescue and recover memories from mold using conservation techniques? You transport horizontally and store vertically. Store documents and photos in plastic holders, between sheets of waxed paper, or interleave with acid-free paper. Books are stored spine down. Archive DVDs and CDs in plastic holders and store in plastic crates. To conserve time capsules, according to the American Institute for Conservation of Historic and Artistic Works (AIC), in Washington, DC, neutralize that acid-wracked paper.

## Diaries, Bibles, and Old Family Cookbooks

Here's how to "mend conditions" and restore diaries. First make a book jacket for a diary. Put a title and label on the dust jacket with the name of the diary's author and any dates, city, state, or country.

Use acid-free paper for the jacket. Diaries and book jackets are works of art. If torn, mend the diary. Apply a protective plastic wrapper to your valuable dust jacket or give diaries dust jackets in good condition.

Be cautious using bleach, because chlorine fumes will fade the ink and soak through the opposite page to fade that writing. After testing the bleach, if the diary is dingy and dirty, bleach it white on the edges only using diluted bleach that won't fade old ink. Test the bleach first on similar surfaces, such as a blank page in the book.

Repair old diaries, and turn them into heirlooms for families and valuable collectibles. The current price for repairing handwritten diaries and books is about $50 and up per book or bound diary. Better yet, publish diaries as print-on-demand PDF files and print them out as paperback books with covers for families.

Some diaries served as handwritten cookbooks containing recipes created by a particular family cook. For more repair tips on bound diaries-as-cook-books, I recommend the book titled, *How to Wrap a Book*, Fannie Merit Farmer, Boston Cooking School.

How do you repair an old diary or family recipe book to make it more valuable to heirs? You'll often find a bound diary that's torn in the seams. According to Barbara Gelink, of the 1990s Collector's Old Cookbooks Club, San Diego, to repair a book, you take a bottle of Book Saver Glue (or any other book-repairing or wood glue), and spread the glue along the binder.

Run the glue along the seam and edges. Use wax paper to keep the glue from getting where it shouldn't. Put a heavy glass bottle on the inside page to hold it down while the glue dries.

Use either the *finest* grade sand paper or nail polish remover to unglue tape, tags, or stains from a *glossy* cover. Sit away from heat, light, and sparks. Carefully dampen a terry cloth with nail polish remover, lighter, or cleaning fluid and circle gently until the tag and stain are gone. On a *plastic* book cover, use the finest grade of sandpaper.

Memorabilia such as diaries, genealogy materials, books, photos, ivory, sports trophies, cards, discarded library and school books, or fabrics that end up at estate sales or thrift shops may have adhesive price tags.

To bleach the "discarded book stamp" that libraries and schools often use, or any other rubber stamp mark, price, date, or seals on the pages or edges, use regular bleach, like Clorox. It turns the rubber stamp mark white. The household bleach also turns the edges and pages of the book white as new.

To preserve a valuable, tattered dust jacket with tears along the edges, provide extra firmness. Put a protective plastic wrapper on top of the book jacket cover of a diary, especially if it's handwritten.

To collect diaries or family photos, look in garage sales, flea markets, and antique shops. Attend auctions and book fairs. Two recommended auction houses for rare cookbooks include Pacific Book Auction Galleries, 139 Townsend, #305, San Francisco, CA 94107, or Sotheby's, New York, 1334 York Ave., New York, NY 10021. Pacific Book Auction Galleries sometimes puts cookbook collections up for an auction.

Look for old high-school graduation class year books to collect from various high schools or middle schools found in garage and estate sales. Restore them and find out whether there's an alumni association whose members want that book stored where all can access it, such as in a public or school library offering interstate library loans.

Can the diary, recipe book, or school yearbook be restored and digitized on DVDs with permission from those who copyrighted it? If you're into keepsake album making with family history photos, diaries, or recipes, look for cookbooks printed by high school parent-teacher associations. Some old ones may be valuable, but even the one put out by the depression era San Diego High School Parent Teacher Association for the class of 1933–34 is only worth $10.

You can start a family history business specializing in restoring diaries, domestic history journals, school yearbooks, and certain types of personal, rare, or cook books. For example, *Cornucopia*, run by Carol A. Greenberg, has old and rare books emphasizing cooking, food literature, domestic history, household management, herbs, kitchen gardens, hotels, restaurants, etiquette, manners, pastimes, amusements, and needlework.

They search for out-of-print books, and are interested in material from the 19th century through 1940. Write to: Little Treasures at PO Box 742, Woodbury, NY 11797. Greenberg is always grateful for quotations on old, rare, and unusual materials in fine condition.

You could start a collector's old diaries and photos club. Marge Rice is a pioneer genealogist who created a hobby of returning heirloom photos to their families of origin. See the related article at: http://www.ancestry.com/library/view/ancmag/7643.asp. Or digitize photos for the Web. See the instructional site on digitizing photos for the Web at: http://www.firstmonday.dk/issues/issue8_1/garner/.

Some bound handwritten diaries were purchased as blank or lined notebooks. People who collect autographs may also be interested in diaries of authors. For example, the published diary novel titled *One Day Some Schlemiel Will Marry Me* is a diary that ended up as a published first person life story novel. Other diaries end up as cookbooks.

Are diaries worth as much as rare cookbooks? How much are the thousands of rare cookbooks worth today? A helpful guide is the Price Guide to Cookbooks & Recipe Leaflets, 1990, by Linda J. Dickinson, published by Collector Books, at PO Box 3009, Paducah, KY 42002-3009.

See Bibliography of American Cookery Books, 1742–1860. It's based on Waldo Lincoln's American Cookery Books 1742–1860, by Eleanor Lowenstein. Over 800 books and pamphlets are listed. Order from Oak Knoll Books & Press, 414 Delaware St., Newcastle, Delaware 19720.

Louis & Clark Booksellers specialize in rare and out-of-print cookery, gastronomy, wine and beverages, baking, restaurants, domestic history, etiquette, and travel books. They're at 2402 Van Hise Avenue, Madison, WI 53705. Cook books are much more in demand than diaries, unless the author has celebrity status.

Make copies of diaries. Work with the photocopies when you decipher the writing. Store your old diaries in a dry, cool place. Lining the storage place with plastic that's sealed will keep out vermin, moisture, and bugs. Without moisture, you can keep out the mildew and mold. Store duplicates away from originals.

Was something placed in a diary on a certain page, such as a dried rose, letter, farmer's wheat stain, or a special book mark? What meaning did it have? Look for clues for a time frame. Date the diary. List the date it was begun and when it was ended if you can. List the geographic location of the events in the diary and the writer's travels.

Of what kind of materials is the diary made? Is it improvised, created at low cost by the author? Or is it fancy and belonging to someone of wealth? What is the layout like? Does it show the education of the writer or anything personal? Was it a farmer's almanac, captain's log or sailor's calendar, personal journal or if recent, a Web log (blog)?

What was the writing tool, a quill or a pencil? What's the handwriting like? What century or years? Is it full of details, maps, corsages, and pictures? What is its central message? Do you see patterns or mainly listed facts?

Transcribe the diary with your computer. Read it into a camcorder or on audio tape. It's now oral history. What historical events influenced the writing of the diary? What's the social history? What language is it in or dialect? Are there vital records such as wills or deeds to real estate mentioned in the diary? You've now mended, restored, and conserved a life story and a pattern on the quilt of humanity.

## Acid Paper:

Here's how to prevent acidic paper damage in your paper memorabilia or on your items stored against paper. According to author, Betty Walsh, Conservator, BC Archives, Canada and the Walsh's information at: http://palimpsest. stanford.edu/waac/wn/wn10/wn10-2/wn10-202.html, use acid-free paper around photos. To store paper that has a high acid content, put the papers in folders and storage boxes with an alkaline reserve to prevent acid migration. Interleave your papers with sheets of alkaline-buffered paper.

The buffered paper protects your item from acids that move from areas of high to areas of low concentration. Buffers neutralize acids in paper. A buffer is an alkaline chemical such as calcium carbonate. So you have the choice to use the buffered or non-buffered paper depending on whether your photos are stored against other acid-free materials or printed on acid-free paper.

## Photos:

Interweave photos with waxed paper or polyester web covered blotters. Store photos away from overhead water pipes in a cool, dry area with stable humidity and temperatures, not in attics or basements. Keep photos out of direct sunlight and fluorescent lights when on display. Color slides have their own storage requirements.

Keep photos from touching rubber bands, cellophane tape, rubber cement, or paper clips. Poor quality photo paper and paper used in most envelopes and album sleeves also cause photos to deteriorate. Instead, store photos in chemically stable plastic made of polyester, polypropylene, triacetate, or polyethylene. Don't use PCV or vinyl sleeves. Plastic enclosures preserve photos best and keep out the fingerprints and scratches.

Albumen prints are interleaved between groups of photographs. Matte and glossy collodion prints should not be touched by bare hands. Store the same as albumen prints—interleaved between groups of photos. Silver gelatin printing and developing photo papers are packed in plastic bags inside plastic boxes. Carbon prints and Woodbury prints are packed horizontally. Photomechanical prints are interleaved every two inches and packed in boxes. Transport color photos horizontally—face up.

Chromogenic prints and negatives are packed in plastic bags inside boxes. If you're dealing with cased photos, pack the ambrotypes and pannotypes horizontally in padded containers. Cover the glass of Daguerreotype photos and pack horizontally in padded containers.

Pollutants from the air trapped inside holders and folders destroy photos and paper. Use buffered enclosures for black and white prints and negatives. Use non-buffered paper enclosures to store color prints and color print negatives or cyanotypes and albumen prints.

Store your tintypes horizontally. If you have collodion glass plate negatives, use supports for the glass and binders, and pack horizontally in padded containers. The surface texture of photos stored in plastic can deteriorate. It's called ferrotyping. So don't store negatives in plastic. If you store your photos in paper enclosures, be aware that paper is porous. Instead of plastic or paper storage, put photos in ***glass plate negative sleeves in acid-free non-buffered enclosures***.

Then store vertically between pieces of foam board. Where do you find glass plate negative sleeves that can be stored in acid-free non-buffered enclosures? Buy storage materials from companies catering to conservationists, such as *Light Impressions* ®. They're the leading resource for archival supplies. Also look in local craft stores.

Talk to your state archives conservation specialist. Some documents require the work of a trained conservationist. Before you sterilize mold away with bleach, ask your state archives conservationist whether the bleach will ruin your diary or heirloom.

### Photo Albums:

Don't make or buy photo albums with "peel-back" plastic over sticky cardboard pieces because they are chemically unstable and could damage anything stored there. Instead, use photo-packet pages made from chemically stable plastic made of polyester, polypropylene, triacetate, or polyethylene. An excellent album would contain archival-quality pages using polyester mounting corners. Acid-free paper mounting corners are next best.

### Vellum or Parchment Documents:

Interleave between folders, and pack oversize materials flat. If you have prints and drawings made from chemically stable media, then interleave between folders and pack in cartons. Oversize prints and drawings should be packed in bread trays, or map drawers, placed on poly-covered plywood. Be careful the mildew from plywood doesn't paste onto the back of your print. Look at the poly-covering on the wood.

Take off the frames of your drawings or prints if you can. Books with leather and vellum bindings need to be packed spine down in crates one layer deep. Books and pamphlets should be separated with freezer paper and always packed spine down in crates one layer deep.

Bread trays work well to store parchment and vellum manuscripts that are interleaved between folders. Anything oversize gets packed flat. Posters need to be packed in containers lined with garbage bags because they are *coated* papers. Watercolors and hand-colored prints or inks should be interleaved between folders and packed in crates. Paintings need to be stored *face up* without touching the paint layer. Carry them horizontally.

## Computer Tapes and Disks, Audio and Video Tapes:

Store those 'dinosaur' computer tapes in plastic bags packed vertically with plenty of room. Store in plastic crates away from light, heat, or cold. Never touch the magnetic media. If you have an open reel tape, pick up by the hub or reel. Floppy disks should be packed vertically in plastic bags and stored in plastic crates.

With DVDs and CDs, pack vertically in plastic crates and store in plastic drawers or cardboard cartons. Careful—don't touch or scratch the recordable surface. Handle the CD or DVD by the edge. Place audio and video tapes vertically in plastic holders and store them in plastic crates.

Disks made of shellac or acetate and vinyl disks are held by their edges and packed vertically in ethafoam-padded crates. Make sure nothing heavy is placed on CDs, DVDs, tapes, or other disks. You can find ethafoam in most craft stores, or order from a company specializing in storage and presentation tools such as Light Impressions.®

◆    ◆    ◆

**Resources:**
American Institute for Conservation
1717 K Street, NW, Suite 200
Washington, DC 20006
email: info@aic-faic.org
website: http://aic.stanford.edu

Light Impressions (Archival Supplies)
PO Box 22708
Rochester, NY 14692-2708
http://www.lightimpressionsdirect.com

**Bibliography:**
**WAAC Newsletter**
http://palimpsest.stanford.edu/aic'disaster
WAAC Newsletter, Vol. 19, No 2 (May, 1997) articles and charts online by
Betty Walsh, Conservator, BC Archives, Canada and the Walsh's information at:
http://palimpsest.stanford.edu/waac/wn/wn10/wn10-2/wn10-202.html. The site
contains material from the WAAC Newsletter, Volume 10, Number 2, May
1988, pp.2-5.
Curatorial Care of Works of Art on Paper, New York: Intermuseum Conservation Association, 1987.
Library Materials Preservation Manual: Practical Methods for Preserving Books,
Pamphlets, and Other Printed Materials, Heidi Kyle. 1984
Archives & Manuscripts: Conservation—A Manual on Physical Care and Management, Mary Lynn Ritzenthaler, Society of American Archivists: Chicago,
1993.

◆     ◆     ◆

## Personal Histories as Points of View within Social Histories

Autobiographies, biographies, personal histories, plays, and monologues present a
point of view. Are all sides given equal emphasis? Will the audience choose favorite characters? Cameras give fragments, points of view, and bits and pieces. Viewers will see what the videographer or photographer intends to be seen. The
interviewee will also be trying to put his point of view across and tell the story
from his perspective.

Will the photographer or videographer be in agreement with the interviewee?
Or if you are recording for print transcript, will your point of view agree with the
interviewee's perspective and experience if your basic 'premise,' where you two
are coming from, are not in agreement? Think this over as you write your list of
questions. Do both of you agree on your central issue on which you'll focus for
the interview?

How are you going to turn spoken words into text for your paper hard copy transcript? Will you transcribe verbatim, correct the grammar, or quote as you hear the spoken words? Oral historians really need to transcribe the exact spoken word. You can leave out the 'ahs' and 'oms' or loud pauses, as the interviewee thinks what to say next. You don't want to sound like a court reporter, but you do want to have an accurate record transcribed of what was spoken.

You're also not editing for a movie, unless you have permission to turn the oral history into a TV broadcast, where a lot gets cut out of the interview for time constraints. For that, you'd need written permission so words won't be taken out of context and strung together in the editing room to say something different from what the interviewee intended to say.

Someone talking could put in wrong names, forget what they wanted to say, or repeat themselves. They could mumble, ramble, or do almost anything. So you would have to sit down and weed out redundancy when you can or decide on presenting exactly what you've heard as transcript.

When someone reads the transcript in text, they won't have what you had in front of you, and they didn't see and hear the live presentation or the videotape. It's possible to misinterpret gestures or how something is spoken, the mood or tone, when reading a text transcript. Examine all your sources. Use an ice-breaker to get someone talking.

If a woman is talking about female-interest issues, she may feel more comfortable talking to another woman. Find out whether the interviewee is more comfortable speaking to someone of his or her own age. Some older persons feel they can relate better to someone close to their own age than someone in high school, but it varies. Sometimes older people can speak more freely to a teenager.

The interviewee must be able to feel comfortable with the interviewer and know he or she will not be judged. Sometimes it helps if the interviewer is the same ethnic group or there is someone present of the same group or if new to the language, a translator is present.

Read some books on oral history field techniques. Read the National Genealogical Society Quarterly (NGSQ). Also look at The American Genealogist (TAG), The Genealogist, and The New England Historical and Genealogical Register (The Register). If you don't know the maiden name of say, your grandmother's mother, and no relative knows either because it wasn't on her death certificate, try to reconstruct the lives of the males who had ever met the woman whose maiden name is unknown.

Maybe she did business with someone before marriage or went to school or court. Someone may have recorded the person's maiden name before her marriage. Try medical records if any were kept. There was no way to find my mother's grandmother's maiden name until I started searching to see whether she had any brothers in this country. She had to have come as a passenger on a ship around 1880 as she bought a farm. Did her husband come with her?

Was the farm in his name? How many brothers did she have in this country with her maiden surname? If the brothers were not in this country, what countries did they come from and what cities did they live in before they bought the farm in Albany? If I could find out what my great grandmother's maiden name was through any brothers living at the time, I could contact their descendants perhaps and see whether any male or female lines are still in this country or where else on the globe.

Perhaps a list of midwives in the village at the time is recorded in a church or training school for midwives. Fix the person in time and place. Find out whom she might have done business with and whether any records of that business exist. What businesses did she patronize? Look for divorce or court records, change of name records, and other legal documents.

Look at local sources. Did anyone save records from bills of sale for weddings, purchases of homes, furniture, debutante parties, infant supplies, or even medical records? Look at nurses' licenses, midwives' registers, employment contracts, and teachers' contracts, alumni associations for various schools, passports, passenger lists, alien registration cards, naturalization records, immigrant aid societies, city directories, and cross-references.

Try religious and women's clubs, lineage and village societies, girl scouts and similar groups, orphanages, sanatoriums, hospitals, police records. Years ago there was even a Eugenics Record Office. What about the women's prisons? The first one opened in 1839—Mount Pleasant Female Prison, NY.

Try voters' lists. If your relative is from another country, try records in those villages or cities abroad. Who kept the person's diaries? Have you checked the Orphan Train records? Try ethnic and religious societies and genealogy associations for that country. Most ethnic genealogy societies have a special interest group for even the smallest villages in various countries.

You can start one and put up a Web site for people who also come from there in past centuries. Check alimony, divorce, and court records, widow's pensions of veterans, adoptions, orphanages, foster homes, medical records, birth, marriage, and death certificates, social security, immigration, pet license owners' files, prisons, alumni groups from schools, passenger lists, military, and other legal records.

When all historical records are being tied together, you can add the DNA testing to link all those cousins. Check military pensions on microfilms in the

National Archives. See the bibliography section of this book for further resources on highly recommended books and articles on oral history field techniques and similar historical subjects.

# 30

## *Preparing Personal History Time Capsules for a Journey*

Be personal in a personal history life story. The more personal you are, the more eternal is your life story. More people will view or read it again and again far into the future. You can emphasize your life's journey and look at the world through your own eyes. To make the structure salable, 'meander' your life as you would travel on a journey. Perhaps you're a winding river meandering around obstacles and competitors. At each stop, you learn your own capabilities and your own place in the world.

The more you meander, the more you take away the urgency from your story that sets up tension in the audience and keeps them on the edge of their seat. Don't let the meandering overpower your sense of urgency. Don't dwell on your reaction. Focus on your action to people and situations. Stay active in your own personal history. In other words, don't repeat how you reacted, but show how you acted.

Before you sit down to write your autobiography, think of yourself in terms of going on a journey inside the privacy of your purse or wallet. May your purse is the only place where you really do have any privacy. Come up for air when you have hit bottom. Bob up to the sunshine, completely changed or at least matured.

If you have really grown, you will not be blinded by the light, in the figurative sense, as the song goes. Instead, the light gives you insight. So now you have vision along with some hindsight. The next step is learning how to promote and market your salable personal history or life story.

A biography reports the selected events of another person's life—usually 12 major events in the six various significant events also known as "turning points" and also known as "transition points" of life that would include the highlights of significant events for each of the six stages of growth: 1) infanthood, 2) childhood, 3) teen years 4) young adulthood 5)middle life 6)maturity.

## Selling Life Stories

Launch your salable life story in the major national press and in various newspapers and magazines of niche markets related to the events in your life, such as weekly newspapers catering to a group: senior citizens, your ethnic group, your local area, or your occupation or area of interest. Your personal history time capsule may be saved to disk and also uploaded to the Web. What about looking for movie deals and book publishers?

If you don't have the money to produce your autobiography as a video biography, or even a film or commercial movie, or publish it for far less cost as a print-on-demand published book, you may wish to find a co-production partner to finance the production of your life story as a cinematic film or made-for-TV video.

At the same time you could contact literary agents and publishers, but one front-page article in a national newspaper or daily newspaper can do wonders to move your life story in front of the gaze of publishers and producers. While you're waiting for a reporter to pay attention to the news angle you have selected for your life story, I highly recommend Michael Wiese's book <u>Film and Video Marketing</u> because it lists some co-production partners as the following:

Private Investors/Consortiums
Foreign Governments (blocked funds)
Financiers
Corporations
Theatrical Distributors
International Theatrical Distributors
International Sales Agents
Home Video
International Home Video
Pay TV
Syndicators
Record Companies
Music Publishers
Book Publishers
Toy Companies
Licensing and Merchandising Firms
Sponsors (products, services)
Public Relations Firms
Marketing Companies/Consultants
Film Bookers

You can also contact actors, directors, producers, feature distributors, home video distributors, entertainment lawyers, brokers, accountants, animation houses, production houses, video post production houses, labs, film facilities, and agents with your script and ask the owners whether they'd be interested in bartering budget items, deferring, or investing in your script.

Private investors could also be professional investors, venture capitalists, and even doctors and dentists who may wish to finance a movie if the potential interests them. You can sell points in your film to investors who finance it as a group of investors, each buying a small percentage of the film for an investment fee.

Or you can approach film investment corporations that specialize in investing in and producing films as partners. They are publicized or listed in the entertainment trade magazines going to producers and workers in the entertainment and film or video industry.

You market your script not only to agents and producers, but to feature distributors, film financiers and co-production partners. This is the first step in finding a way to take your autobiography from script to screen. Learn who distributes what before you approach anyone.

If you want to approach video instead of film, you might wish to know that children's video programming is the fastest-growing genre in original programming. Children's titles account for 10%-15% of the overall home video revenues. According to one of Michael Wiese's books written in the nineties, *Home Video: Producing For The Home Market*, "With retail prices falling and alternative retail outlets expanding, children's programming will soon become one of the most profitable segments of the video market." He was right.

What has happened in the new millennium is that children's program is doing wonderfully. Why? Children's video is repeatable. Children watch the same tape 30 to 50 times. Children's video sells for comparatively lower prices than feature films.

Children's video also rents well. Children's tapes sell it toy stores, book stores, children's stores, and in stores like Woolworth's and Child World. Manufacturers sell tapes at Toy Fair and the American Booksellers Association conventions.

For these reasons, you may wish to write your autobiography as a script for children's video or as a children's book. Video is a burgeoning industry.

According to the market research firm, Fairfield Group, in 1985, the prerecorded video business earned $ 3.3 billion in sales and rentals. This nearly equaled the record and theatrical box office revenues for the same year. The world VCR population is about 100 million. Today we have the DVD and the Internet streaming video.

Back in 1985, the U.S. and Japan accounted for half of the VCRs, followed by the United Kingdom, (9 million) West Germany (nearly 7 million), and Canada, Australia, Turkey, and France (about 3 million each). Spain reported 2 million VCRs. By 1991, the number of VCR ownership increased as prices slowly came down.

Today, in the 21$^{st}$ century, the prerecorded video business has quickly moved to DVD disks, downloadable at a price Internet-based movies, and video tapes are on the way to being a memory of the eighties and early nineties. In the next decade, another media format will be in fashion to replace videos on DVDs and streaming Internet video. The idea is to keep transferring the story from one form of technology to another so that videos made today will be able to be viewed by people in the next century.

The European VCR markets grew faster than in the U.S. during the eighties and nineties just as the DVD markets grew in the early 21$^{st}$ century because there were fewer entertainment alternatives—fewer TV stations, restricted viewing hours, fewer pay TV services, and fewer movie theatres.

You should not overlook the foreign producers for your script. Include Canadian cable TV, foreign agents, and foreign feature film and video producers among your contacts. Most university libraries open to the public for research include directories listing foreign producers. Photocopy their addresses and send them a query letter and one-page synopsis of your script. Don't overlook the producers from non-English speaking countries. Your script can be translated or dubbed.

You might attend film market type conventions and conferences. They draw producers from a variety of countries. In 1989 at the former Cinetex Film Market in Las Vegas, producers from Canada, Italy, Israel, Spain, and other foreign countries sat next to script writers. All of them were receptive to receiving scripts. They handed one another their business cards. You can learn a lot at summer film markets and film festivals about what kind of scripts are in demand.

Keep a list of which film markets will meet. In the U.S. there are 3 to 5 film markets a year and many more film festivals. Seek out the foreign and local producers with track records and see whether they'd be interested in your script if you have a life story in the form of a script, treatment, or story. Perhaps your theme has some relation to a producer's country or ethnic group. Lots of films are made in Asia, in the Middle East (Israel, Egypt and Tunisia), in Latin America, and Europe or Canada.

Seek out the Australian producers also and New Zealand or India. If you have a low-budget film or home video script set in Korea, Philippines, Japan, or Taiwan, or a specialty film such as Karate or something that appeals to the Indian film market, contact those producers and script agents in those countries. Find out the budget limitations that producers have in the different countries.

Social issues documentaries based on your autobiography are another market for home video. Vestron and other home video distributors use hard-hitting documentaries. Collecting documentary video tapes is like collecting copies of National Geographic magzine. You never throw them out. Tapes are also sold by direct mail. Companies producing and distributing documentaries include MCA, MGM/UA, Vestron, Victory, CBS/Fox, Warner, Media, Karl, Monterey, Thorn/EMI, Embassy, and USA, to name a few.

If you write your autobiography or another's biography as a romance, you might wish to write a script for the video romance series market. Romance video has its roots in the paperback novel. However, the biggest publishers of romance novels have little recognition in retail video stores.

Among consumers, yes; wholesalers and retailers, no. Bookstores, yes. The problem is with pricing. To sell romance videos in bookstores, the tapes would have to be sold at less than $29. In video stores, they can be positioned the same as $59 feature films on video.

Production costs to make high quality romance videos are high. Top stars, top writers, hit book titles, exotic locations, music and special effects are required. Huge volumes of tapes must be sold to break even. Then producers have to search for pay TV, broadcast, or foreign partners. The budget for a one-hour video tape of a thin romance story comes to $500,000.

It's far better to make a low-budget feature film. Romance as a genre has never previously appealed to the video retail buyer. In contrast, a romance paperback sells for a few dollars. Now the question remains: Would women buy a romance-genre video DVD priced at $9.95?

Romance novels successfully have been adapted to audio tape for listening at far less than the cost of video. There is a market for audio scripts of short romance novels and novellas. What is becoming popular today are videos and 'movies' downloadable from the Internet that you can watch on your computer screen or save to a DVD since DVD burners became affordable and popular. Try adapting highlights of your romance or life story novel to a play, skit, or monologue.

The only way romance videos would work is by putting together a multi-partnered structure that combines pay TV, home video, book publishing, and domestic and foreign TV. In the eighties, was anyone doing romance video tapes?

Yes. Prism Video produced six feature-length romance films, acquired from Comworld. In 1985 the tapes sold for $11.95.

Comworld had limited TV syndication exposure and was one of the first to come out with romance videos. Karl/Lorimar came out with eight romance films from L/A House Productions on a budget of $400,000 each. They were also priced at $11.95 in 1985. To break even, a company has to sell about 60,000 units per title.

Twenty years later, think about adapting to a play the romance DVD video and the downloadable Internet video. What's available to adapt as educational material? Write for various age groups on niche subjects that would appeal to teachers. Follow their rules on what is appropriate for their classrooms. The market also is open for stage and radio/Internet broadcast skits and plays geared to older adults as performers and audiences.

Other media are like open doors to finding a way to put your life story on a disk. Any interview, script, or story can go from print-on-demand published novel or true story book to radio script or stage play. A video can move from a digital high 8 camcorder with a Firewire 1394 cable attached to a personal computer rapidly into the hard disk drive via Windows XP Movie Maker software. Or you can purchase the latest camcorders that record directly onto a mini-disk that looks similar to a small CD or DVD and which can be played directly on your CD or DVD player or saved and played in your computer.

From there it can be saved as a WMV file (a Windows Media file). Then the file can be recorded on a DVD, if long, or a CD if under one hour. Poems can be written, read, and 'burned' to a compact disk (CD) and then mailed out as greeting cards, love letters, or personal histories. Short videos can be emailed.

Romance or life story highlights novels and scripts on audio tape cost less to produce. This market occasionally advertises for romantic novel manuscripts, scripts, and stories in a variety of writer's magazines.

Check out the needs of various magazines for journalists and writers online. If you read a lot of romance genre novels or write in this style, you may want to write your autobiography in this genre, but you'd have to market to publishers who use this genre or biographies in other genres such as factual biography.

If your autobiography is set on events which occurred in your childhood, you might prefer to concentrate on writing appropriate for children's video programming. It's a lot easier to sell to the producers who are basking in the current explosion of children's video programming. Perhaps it's your mission to use the video format to teach children.

## Will the script of your life story do the following?

teach,
mentor,
motivate,
inspire,
or inform viewers who can be:
children,
teenagers,
parents
or midlifers on their quests for self-identify:
or in their search for facts:
to use as guidelines in making their own decisions:
about life's journeys and writing an introspective journal?

Can your diary be dynamic, dramatic, and empowering to others who may be going through similar stages of life? Are your characters charismatic and memorable, likable and strong?

A life story or autobiography when videotaped or filed as a feature-length movie can spring out of a diary or an inner personal journal (which dialogues with the people who impact your life and observes selected, important events).

# APPENDIX A

## *Genealogy Associations on the Web*

Ancestry.com: http://www.ancestry.com/main.htm?lfl=m

BMD Certificates, London, England, UK: http://www.bmd-certificates.co.uk

Cyndi's List of Genealogy on the Internet: http://www.cyndislist.com/

Cyndi's List is a categorized & cross-referenced index to genealogical resources on the Internet with thousands of links.

DistantCousin.com (Uniting Cousins Worldwide) http://distantcousin.com/Links/surname.html

Ellis Island Online: http://www.ellisisland.org/

Family History Library: http://www.familysearch.org/Eng/default.asp

http://www.familysearch.org/Eng/Search/frameset_search.asp

(The Church of Jesus Christ of Latter Day Saints) International Genealogical Index

Female Ancestors: http://www.cyndislist.com/female.htm

Genealogist's Index to the Web: http://www.genealogytoday.com/GIWWW/?

Genealogy Web: http://www.genealogyweb.com/

Genealogy Authors and Speakers: http://feefhs.org/frg/frg-a&l.html

Genealogy Today: http://www.genealogytoday.com/

My Genealogy.com: http://www.genealogy.com/cgi-bin/my_main.cgi

Scriver, Dr. Charles: The Canadian Medical Hall of Fame http://www.virtualmuseum.ca/Exhibitions/Medicentre/en/scri_print.htm

Surname Sites: http://www.cyndislist.com/surn-gen.htm

National Genealogical Society: http://www.ngsgenealogy.org/index.htm

United States List of Local by State Genealogical Societies: http://www.daddezio.com/society/hill/index.html

United States Vital Records List: http://www.daddezio.com/records/room/index.html or http://www.cyndislist.com/usvital.htm

Ancestry.com: http://www.ancestry.com/main.htm?lfl=m

Cyndi's List of Genealogy on the Internet: http://www.cyndislist.com/

Cyndi's List is a categorized & cross-referenced index to genealogical resources on the Internet with thousands of links.

DistantCousin.com (Uniting Cousins Worldwide) http://distantcousin.com/Links/surname.html

Ellis Island Online: http://www.ellisisland.org/

Family History Library: http://www.familysearch.org/Eng/default.asp

http://www.familysearch.org/Eng/Search/frameset_search.asp

(The Church of Jesus Christ of Latter Day Saints) International Genealogical Index

Female Ancestors: http://www.cyndislist.com/female.htm

Genealogist's Index to the Web: http://www.genealogytoday.com/GIWWW/?

Genealogy Web: http://www.genealogyweb.com/

Genealogy Authors and Speakers: http://feefhs.org/frg/frg-a&l.html

Genealogy Today: http://www.genealogytoday.com/

My Genealogy.com: http://www.genealogy.com/cgi-bin/my_main.cgi

Scriver, Dr. Charles: The Canadian Medical Hall of Fame http://www.virtualmuseum.ca/Exhibitions/Medicentre/en/scri_print.htm

Surname Sites: http://www.cyndislist.com/surn-gen.htm

National Genealogical Society: http://www.ngsgenealogy.org/index.htm

United States List of Local by State Genealogical Societies: http://www.daddezio.com/society/hill/index.html

United States Vital Records List: http://www.daddezio.com/records/room/index.html or http://www.cyndislist.com/usvital.htm

# APPENDIX B

## *Multi-Ethnic Genealogy Web Sites on the Web*

(Usually, there are several genealogy sites on the Web for each ethnic group.)

**Acadian/Cajun: & French Canadian:** http://www.acadian.org/tidbits.html

**Afghanistan Genealogy:** http://www.kindredtrails.com/afghanistan.html

**African-American:** http://www.cyndislist.com/african.htm

**African Royalty Genealogy:** http://www.uq.net.au/~zzhsoszy/

**Albanian Research List:** http://feefhs.org/al/alrl.html

**Armenian Genealogical Society:** http://feefhs.org/am/frg-amgs.html

**Asia and the Pacific:** http://www.cyndislist.com/asia.htm

**Austria-Hungary Empire:** http://feefhs.org/ah/indexah.html

**Baltic-Russian Information Center:** http://feefhs.org/blitz/frgblitz.html

**Belarusian—Association of the Belarusian Nobility:** http://feefhs.org/by/frg-zbs.html

**Blitz** (Jewish Genealogy from St. Petersburg, Russia and also Blitz USA from California): http://feefhs.org/blitz/frgblitz.html

**Bukovina Genealogy:** http://feefhs.org/bukovina/bukovina.html

**Carpatho-Rusyn Knowledge Base:** http://feefhs.org/rusyn/frg-crkb.html

**Chinese Genealogy:** http://www.chineseroots.com.

**Croatia Genealogy Cross Index:** http://feefhs.org/cro/indexcro.html

**Czechoslovak Genealogical Society Int'l, Inc.:** http://feefhs.org/czs/cgsi/frg-cgsi.html

**Eastern Europe:** http://www.cyndislist.com/easteuro.htm

**Eastern European Genealogical Society, Inc.:** http://feefhs.org/ca/frg-eegs.html

**Eastern Europe Ethnic, Religious, and National Index with Home Pages. Includes the FEEFHS Resource Guide that lists organizations associated with FEEFHS from 14 Countries. It also includes Finnish and Armenian genealogy resources:** http://feefhs.org/ethnic.html

**Ethnic, Religious, and National Index 14 countries:** http://feefhs.org/ethnic.html

**(Finland) Genealogical Society of Finland:** http://www.genealogia.fi/indexe.htm

**Finnish Genealogy Group:** http://feefhs.org/misc/frgfinmn.html

**Galicia Jewish SIG:** http://feefhs.org/jsig/frg-gsig.html

**German Genealogical Digest:** http://feefhs.org/pub/frg-ggdp.html

**Greek Genealogy Sources on the Internet:** http://www-personal.umich.edu/~cgaunt/greece.html

**Genealogy Societies Online List:** http://www.daddezio.com/catalog/grkndx04.html

**German Research Association:** http://feefhs.org/gra/frg-gra.html

**Greek Genealogy (Hellenes-Diaspora Greek Genealogy):** http://www.geocities.com/SouthBeach/Cove/4537/

**Greek Genealogy Home Page:** http://www.daddezio.com/grekgen.html

**Greek Genealogy Articles:** http://www.daddezio.com/catalog/grkndx01.html

**India Genealogy:** http://genforum.genealogy.com/india/

**India Family Histories:** http://www.mycinnamontoast.com/perl/results.cgi?region=79&sort=n

**India-Anglo-Indian/Europeans in India genealogy:** http://members.ozemail.com.au/~clday/

**Irish Travelers:** http://www.pitt.edu/~alkst3/Traveller.html

**Japanese Genealogy:** http://www.rootsweb.com/~jpnwgw/

**Jewish Genealogy:** http://www.jewishgen.org/infofiles/

**Latvian Jewish Genealogy Page:** http://feefhs.org/jsig/frg-lsig.html

**Lebanese Genealogy:** http://www.rootsweb.com/~lbnwgw/

**Lithuanian American Genealogy Society:** http://feefhs.org/frg-lags.html

**Melungeon:** http://www.geocities.com/Paris/5121/melungeon.htm

**Mennonite Heritage Center:** http://feefhs.org/men/frg-mhc.html

**Middle East Genealogy:** http://www.rootsweb.com/~mdeastgw/index.html

**Middle East Genealogy by country:** http://www.rootsweb.com/~mdeastgw/index.html#country

**Native American:** http://www.cyndislist.com/native.htm

**Polish Genealogical Society of America:** http://feefhs.org/pol/frg-pgsa.html

**Quebec and Francophone:** http://www.francogene.com/quebec/amerin.html

**Romanian American Heritage Center:** http://feefhs.org/ro/frg-rahc.html

**Slovak World:** http://feefhs.org/slovak/frg-sw.html

**Slavs, South: Cultural Society:** http://feefhs.org/frg-csss.html

**Syrian and Lebanese Genealogy:** http://www.genealogytoday.com/family/syrian/

**Syria Genealogy:** http://www.rootsweb.com/~syrwgw/

**Tibetan Genealogy:** http://www.distantcousin.com/Links/Ethnic/China/Tibetan.html

**Turkish Genealogy Discussion Group:** http://www.turkey.com/forums/forumdisplay.php3?forumid=18

**Ukrainian Genealogical and Historical Society of Canada:** http://feefhs.org/ca/frgughsc.html

**Unique Peoples:** http://www.cyndislist.com/peoples.htm **Note: The Unique People's list includes: Black Dutch, Doukhobors, Gypsy, Romani, Romany & Travellers, Melungeons, Metis, Miscellaneous, and Wends/Sorbs**

# Appendix C

## *Bibliographies*

**Bibliography 1.**
**Genealogy:**

A Bintel Brief: Sixty Years of Letters From the Lower East Side to the Jewish Daily Forward. Metzker, Isaac, ed Doubleday and Co. 1971. Garden City, NY

Climbing Your Family Tree: Online and Offline Genealogy for Kids IRA Wolfman, Tim Robinson (Illustrator), Alex Haley (Introduction) / Paperback / Workman Publishing Company, Inc. / October 2001

Complete Beginner's Guide to Genealogy, the Internet, and Your Genealogy Computer Program Karen Clifford / Paperback / Genealogical Publishing Company, Incorporated / February 2001

Complete Idiot's Guide(R) to Online Geneology Rhonda McClure / Paperback / Pearson Education / January 2002

Creating Your Family Heritage Scrapbook: From Ancestors to Grandchildren, Your Complete Resource & Idea Book for Creating a Treasured Heirloom. Nerius, Maria Given, Bill Gardner ISBN: 0761530142 Published by Prima Publishing, Aug 2001

Cyndi's List: A Comprehensive List of 70,000 Genealogy Sites on the Internet (Vol. 1 & 2) Cyndi Howells / Paperback / Genealogical Publishing Company, Incorporated / June 2001.

Discovering Your Female Ancestors: Special strategies for uncovering your hard-to-find information about your female lineage. Carmack, Sharon DeBartolo. Conference Lecture on Audio Tape: Carmack, Sharon DeBartolo.

Folklife and Fieldwork: A Layman's Introduction to Field Techniques. Bartis, Peter. Washington, DC: Library of Congress, 1990.

Genealogy Online for Dummies Matthew L. Helm, April Leigh Helm, April Leigh Helm, Matthew L. Helm / Paperback / Wiley, John & Sons, Incorporated / February 2001

Genealogy Online Elizabeth Powell Crowe / Paperback / McGraw-Hill Companies, November 2001

History From Below: How to Uncover and Tell the Story of Your Community, Association, or Union. Brecher, Jeremy. New Haven: Advocate Press/Commonwork Pamphlets, 1988.

My Family Tree Workbook: Genealogy for Beginners Rosemary A. Chorzempa / Paperback / Dover Publications, Incorporated /

National Genealogical Society Quarterly 79, no. 3 (September 19991): 183–93

"Numbering Your Genealogy: Sound and Simple Systems." Curran, Joan Ferris.

Oral History and the Law. Neuenschwander, John. Pamphlet Series #1. Albuquerque: Oral History Association, 1993.

Oral History for the Local Historical Society. Baum, Willa K. Nashville: American Association for State and Local History, 1987.

Scrapbook Storytelling: Save Family Stories & Memories with Photos, Journaling & Your Own Creativity Slan, Joanna Campbell, Published by EFG, Incorporated, ISBN: 0963022288 May 1999

"The Silent Woman: Bringing a Name to Life." NE-59. Boston, MA: New England Historic Genealogical Society Sesquicentennial Conference, 1995.

The Source: A Guidebook of American Genealogy Alice Eichholz, Loretto Dennis Szucs (Editor), Sandra Hargreaves Luebking (Editor), Sandra Hargreaves Luebking (Editor) / Hardcover / MyFamily.com, Incorporated / February 1997

To Our Children's Children: Journal of Family Members, Bob Greene, D. G. Fulford 240pp. ISBN: 038549064X Publisher: Doubleday & Company, Incorporated: October 1998.

<u>Transcribing and Editing Oral History</u>. Nashville: American Association for State and Local History, 1991.

<u>Using Oral History in Community History Projects</u>. Buckendorf, Madeline, and Laurie Mercier. Pamphlet Series #4. Albuqueque: Oral History Association, 1992.

<u>Unpuzzling Your Past: The Best-Selling Basic Guide to Genealogy (Expanded, Updated and Revised)</u> Emily Anne Croom, Emily Croom / Paperback / F & W Publications, Incorporated / August 2001

<u>Writing a Woman's Life</u>. Heilbrun, Carolyn G. New York: W.W. Norton, 1988

<u>Your Guide to the Family History Library: How to Access the World's Largest Genealogy Resource</u> Paula Stuart Warren, James W. Warren / Paperback / F & W Publications, Incorporated / August 2001

<u>Your Story: A Guided Interview Through Your Personal and Family History</u>, 2nd ed., 64pp.ISBN: 0966604105 Publisher: Stack Resources, LLC

◆    ◆    ◆

## Bibliography 2.
## Genealogy in the Former Ottoman Empire

See: <u>McGowan, Bruce William, 1933-</u> Defter-i mufassal-i liva-i Sirem: an Ottoman revenue survey dating from the reign of Selim II. / Bruce William McGowan.

Ann Arbor, Mich.: University Microfilms, 1967.

See: Bogaziçi University Library Web sites:

<u>http://seyhan.library.boun.edu.tr/search/wN{232}ufus+Defter/</u>
<u>wN{232}ufus+Defter/1,29,29,B/frameset&FF=wN{232}ufus+Defter&9,9</u>,

or <u>http://seyhan.library.boun.edu.tr/search/dTaxation+--+Turkey.</u>
<u>/dtaxation+turkey/-5,-1,0,B/exact&FF=dtaxation+turkey&1,57</u>,

Jurisdictions and localities in Bulgaria:

Michev N. and P. Koledarov. Rechnik na selishchata i selishchnite imena v Bulgariia, 1878–1987 (Dictionary of villages and village names in Bulgaria, 1878–1987), Sofia: Nauka i izkustvo, 1989 (FHL book 949.77 E5m).

See: <u>McGowan, Bruce William, 1933-</u> Defter-i mufassal-i liva-i Sirem: an Ottoman revenue survey dating from the reign of Selim II. / Bruce William McGowan.

Ann Arbor, Mich.: University Microfilms, 1967.

Web sites Research and Genealogy in the Former Ottoman Empire

See: Bogaziçi University Library Web sites:

<u>http://seyhan.library.boun.edu.tr/search/wN{232}ufus+Defter/
wN{232}ufus+Defter/1,29,29,B/frameset&FF=wN{232}ufus+Defter&9,9</u>,

or <u>http://seyhan.library.boun.edu.tr/search/dTaxation+--+Turkey.
/dtaxation+turkey/-5,-1,0,B/exact&FF=dtaxation+turkey&1,57</u>,

◆     ◆     ◆

**Bibliography 3.**
**DNA Testing and Genetics**

<u>A Biologist's Guide to Analysis of DNA Microarray Data</u> Steen Knudsen / Hardcover / Wiley, John & Sons, Incorporated / April 2002

<u>Advances and Opportunities in DNA Testing and Gene Probes</u> Business Communications Company Incorporated (Editor) / Hardcover / Business Communications / September 1996

<u>African Exodus, The Origins of Modern Humanity</u> Stringer, Christopher and Robin McKie. Henry Holt And Company 1997

<u>An A to Z of DNA Science: What Scientists Mean when They Talk about Genes and Genomes</u> Jeffre L. Witherly, Galen P. Perry, Darryl L. Leja / Paperback / Cold Spring Harbor Laboratory Press / September 2002

An Introduction to Forensic DNA Analysis Norah Rudin, Keith Inman / Hardcover / CRC Press / December 2001

Archaeogenetics: DNA and the population prehistory of Europe, Ed. Colin Renfrew & Katie Boyle. McDonald Institute Monographs. Cambridge, UK, Distributed by Oxbow Books UK. In USA: The David Brown Book Company, Oakville, CT. 2000

Cartoon Guide to Genetics Gonick, Larry, With Mark Wheelis: Paperback / HarperInformation / July 1991

DNA Detectives, The—Working Against Time, novel, Hart, Anne. Mystery and Suspense Press, iuniverse.com paperback 248 pages at http://www.iuniverse.com or 1-877-823-9235.

DNA for Family Historians (ISBN 0-9539171-0-X). Savin, Alan of Maidenhead, England, is author of the 32-page book. See the Web site: http://www.savin.org/dna/dna-book.html

DNA Microarrays and Gene Expression Pierre Baldi, G. Wesley Hatfield, G. Wesley Hatfield / Hardcover / Cambridge University Press / August 2002

Microarrays for an Integrative Genomics Isaac S. Kohane, Alvin Kho, Atul J. Butte / Hardcover / MIT Press / August 2002

Does It Run in the Family?: A Consumers Guide to DNA Testing for Genetic Disorders Doris Teichler Zallen, Doris Teichler-Zallen, Doris Teichler Zallen / Hardcover / Rutgers University Press / May 1997

Double Helix, The: A Personal Account of the Discovery of the Structure of DNA James D. Watson / Paperback / Simon & Schuster Trade Paperbacks / June 2001

Genes, Peoples, and Languages Luigi Luca Cavalli-Sforza, Mark Seielstad (Translator).

Genetic Witness: Forensic Uses of DNA Tests DIANE Publishing Company (Editor) / Paperback / DIANE Publishing Company / April 1993

History and Geography of Human Genes, The [ABRIDGED] L. Luca Cavalli-Sforza, Paolo Menozzi (Contributor), Alberto Piazza (Contributor).

How to DNA Test Our Family Relationships Terry Carmichael, Alexander Ivanof Kuklin, Ed Grotjan / Paperback / Acen Press / November 2000

Introduction to Genetic Analysis Anthony J. Griffiths, Suzuki, Lewontin, Gelbart, David T. Suzuki, Richard C. Lewontin, Willi Gelbart, Miller, Jeffrey H. Miller / Hardcover / W. H. Freeman Company / February 2000

Jefferson's Children: The Story of One American Family Shannon Lanier, Jane Feldman, Lucian K. Truscott (Introduction) / Hardcover / Random House Books for Young Readers / September 2000

Medical Genetics Lynn B. B. Jorde, Michael J. Bamshad, Raymond L. White, Michael J. Bamshad, John C. Carey, John C. Carey, Raymond L. White, John C. Carey / Paperback / Mosby-Year Book, Inc. / July 2000

Molecule Hunt, The: Archaeology and the Search for Ancient DNA Martin Jones / Hardcover / Arcade / April 2002

More Chemistry and Crime: From Marsh Arsenic Test to DNA Profile Richard Saferstein, Samuel M. Gerber (Editor) / Hardcover / American Chemical Society / August 1998

1996, Quest For Perfection—The Drive to Breed Better Human Beings, Maranto, Gina. Scribner, 1996

Our Molecular Future: How Nanotechnology, Robotics, Genetics, and Artificial Intelligence Will Transform Our World Mulhall, Douglas./ Hardcover / Prometheus Books / March 2002

Paternity—Disputed, Typing, PCR and DNA Tests: Index of New Information Dexter Z. Franklin / Hardcover / Abbe Pub Assn of Washington Dc / January 1998

Paternity in Primates: Tests and Theories R. D. Martin (Editor), A. F. Dickson (Editor), E. J. Wickings (Editor) / Hardcover / Karger, S Publishers / December 1991

Queen Victoria's Gene: Hemophilia and the Royal Family (Pbk) D. M. Potts, W. T. Potts / Paperback / Sutton Publishing, Limited / June 1999

Redesigning Humans: Our Inevitable Genetic Future Stock, Gregory. / Hardcover / Houghton Mifflin Company / April 2002

Rosalind Franklin: The Dark Lady of DNA, Brenda Maddox / Hardcover / HarperCollins Publishers / October 2002

Schaum's Outline Of Genetics Susan Elrod, William D. Stansfield / Paperback / McGraw-Hill Companies, The / December 2001

Seven Daughters of Eve, The: The Science That Reveals Our Genetic Ancestry. Sykes, Bryan. ISBN: 0393323145 Publisher: Norton, W. W. & Company, Inc. May 2002

Stedman's OB-GYN & Genetics Words Ellen Atwood (Editor), Stedmans / Paperback / Lippincott Williams & Wilkins / December 2000

◆　　　◆　　　◆

## Middle East Genealogy Books

Before Taliban: Genealogies of the Afghan Jihad
by David B. Edwards (Paperback—April 2002)

Nationalism and the Genealogical Imagination: Oral History and Textual Authority in Tribal Jordan (Comparative Studies on Muslim Societies; 23)
by Andrew Shryock (Paperback—February 1997)

Old Bohemian and Moravian Jewish Cemeteries
by Arno Parik, et al

Al-Sabah: Genealogy and History of Kuwait's Ruling Family, 1752–1986 (Middle East Cultures Series, No 13)
by Alan Rush

Genealogies of Conflict: Class, Identity, and State in Palestine/Israel and South Africa
by Ran Greenstein

History of Seyd Said, Sultan of Muscat
by Shaik Mansur, Robin Bidewell (Introduction) (Hardcover—1984)

Amarna Personal Names (American Schools of Oriental Research Dissertation, Vol 9)
by Richard S. Hess (Hardcover—October 1996)

Soberanos de leyenda
by Antonio García Jiménez

◆     ◆     ◆

## Iran Genealogy-Related Books

Another Sea, Another Shore: Stories of Iranian Migration
by Shouleh Vatanabadi, et all (2003)

Funny in Farsi: A Memoir of Growing Up Iranian in America
by Firoozeh Dumas (2003)

Wedding Song: Memoirs of an Iranian Jewish Woman
by Farideh Goldin (2003)

Exiled Memories: Stories of the Iranian Diaspora
by Zohreh Sullivan (2001)

Journey from the Land of No: A Girlhood Caught in Revolutionary Iran
by Roya Hakakian (2004)

Inside Iran: Women's Lives
by Jane Mary Howard (2002)

# Index

978-0-595-41316-4
0-595-41316-1